THE ROYAL COMMISSION ON CRIMINAL JUSTICE

Criminal Justice Systems in
Other Jurisdictions

Edited by

Nigel Osner, Anne Quinn & Giles Crown

LONDON: HMSO

© Crown Copyright 1993
Applications for reproductions should be made to HMSO
First published 1993

ISBN 0 11 341082 4

Mention of a particular jurisdiction in this report is not to be taken as reflecting the views of the Royal Commission on that jurisdiction or any of its features. The intention is merely to provide a factual summary of the answers to the Royal Commission's questionnaire on the jurisdiction concerned.

CONTENTS

		Page
PART 1:	Introduction	1
PART 2:	Australia	3
	A. Australian Commonwealth Law	15
	B. New South Wales	16
	C. Northern Territory	23
	D. Queensland	27
	E. South Australia	34
	F. Victoria	38
	G. Western Australia	45
PART 3:	Belgium	51
PART 4:	Canada	59
PART 5:	Denmark	75
PART 6:	France	83
PART 7:	Germany	93
PART 8:	The Republic of Ireland	105
PART 9:	Israel	115
PART 10:	Italy	133
PART 11:	The Netherlands	147
PART 12:	New Zealand	157
PART 13:	Spain	173
PART 14:	Sweden	185
PART 15:	The United States of America	193

ANNEX 1: Information about Criminal Justice Procedures – The Questionnaire   221

ANNEX 2: List of the individuals and organisations who either provided information on the criminal justice systems in other jurisdictions or assisted in the distribution of the Commission's other jurisdictions questionnaire.   227

PART 1
INTRODUCTION

1.1   The Royal Commission on Criminal Justice sought information on criminal justice systems in a number of other jurisdictions in order to see whether there were lessons to be learned from them which might be applied to the criminal justice system in England and Wales. In particular, it examined the Scottish system in some depth, and made two visits to Scotland.[1] With regard to other systems, the Commission felt that the best way to obtain the information which it was seeking was to set out specific questions in a questionnaire, a copy of which is at Annex 1. The Commission received a large number of replies and it is grateful to everyone who sent in answers to the questionnaire and provided any supplementary information. Annex 2 lists all the individuals and organisations who either provided information in response to the questionnaire or who assisted in its distribution.

1.2   This volume contains a number of reports on foreign jurisdictions. Some systems have been omitted because the material available to the Commission, while of value to its deliberations, was not sufficiently detailed to enable a sufficiently full report to be written. The Commission is aware that some of what is set out is either readily or more fully available elsewhere, but it felt that it was worth publishing it even so, in order to offer in one volume a series of reports to facilitate comparison.

1.3   The Commission wishes to stress that these reports have been completed very largely on the information submitted in reply to the questionnaire, although further information was sought in some cases. In addition several of the reports have benefited from advice from people with expert knowledge of the system concerned and from the comments of a number of visitors from abroad who met either members of the Commission or the Secretariat. (Any errors which remain are, however, the editors' own).

1.4   The Commission would like to thank the Ministry of Justice in Canada for reviewing the Canadian report. It would like to thank the New

---

[1] No attempt is made here to describe the Scottish system. A useful account can be found in 'The Legal System in Scotland', HMSO 1981 chapters 4 and 5, though this is out of print and overdue for revision. More detailed accounts can be found in the standard textbooks e.g., D M Walker, 'The Scottish Legal System', Edinburgh 1992.

Zealand Law Commission for reviewing the New Zealand report. Similarly it would like to thank the Honourable Mr Justice Mackenzie of the Supreme Court of Queensland for reviewing the Queensland report and Professor Ennio Amodio of Milan University for reviewing the Italian report. It is also grateful to Mr Kenneth Caruso, a partner in Shearman and Sterling, New York, and formerly a Federal Prosecutor, for acting as a consultant on the United States system and for the amount of time he devoted to the development of the report on that system. Finally, the Commission would like to thank Professor Leonard Leigh for his assistance in reviewing the Commission's work on foreign jurisdictions, and for advising on what might usefully be included in this publication. We stress that none of the above, nor any of the people and organisations listed in Annex 2, are responsible for any errors or inaccuracies which inevitably a compilation of this nature is likely to contain.

1.5 The reports have been prepared by Nigel Osner, Anne Quinn and Giles Crown, all members of the Commission's Secretariat. The Commission is most grateful to them for undertaking this task.

Part 2
Australia

2.1 Australia is a federation consisting of six states and two self-governing territories, each with its own criminal laws, laws of evidence and criminal procedure. In addition, there is a federal (Commonwealth) criminal law system in relation to certain offences operating throughout the country. Answers to the Commission's questionnaire on other jurisdictions were received from five of the states, Victoria, New South Wales, South Australia, Western Australia and Queensland and one of the territories, the Northern Territory. Information about the investigation and prosecution of Commonwealth offences was also received. The criminal justice system of each of these jurisdictions is considered separately below. The following general section gives a brief overview of the information obtained on these seven jurisdictions and a summary of some of the recent relevant decisions of the High Court of Australia, for, although each state has its own Court of Appeal, a defendant can appeal from the State Court of Appeal with leave to the High Court of Australia. A decision of the High Court is binding on all the states and territories of Australia regardless of the origin of the appeal, unless there is conflicting state legislation on the matter. Reference is also made to the proposals contained in the Australian Law Reform Commission's report on evidence.

Police investigations

2.2 Prior to 1986 many states had, and some still have, a provision whereby the police must bring a person whom they have taken into custody before a court as "soon as practicable" or "forthwith". In *Williams*[1] the High Court of Australia held that the time limited by such phrases could not be extended to allow the police to detain a suspect for questioning. The facts of *Williams* were as follows. Williams was arrested at about 6am one morning, having been seen in the act of committing a burglary. He was suspected of committing other crimes and after his arrest he was interviewed in relation to the burglary and a number of other offences for approximately seven hours, in the course of which he made confessions to the offences. He was not taken before a magistrate until the following morning – some twenty six hours after his arrest. The trial judge found that it would have been practicable to take Williams before a Magistrates' Court within approximately six hours of his arrest. In the exercise of his discretion,

---

[1] (1986) 161 CLR 278.

the trial judge refused to admit the confessions in evidence on the ground that they had been obtained during a period of unlawful detention.

2.3   On appeal the Court of Criminal Appeal of Tasmania examined the provisions of section 34A(1) of the Tasmanian Justices Act 1959, which required a person taken into custody to be taken before a justice "as soon as practicable", and concluded that the phrase encompassed the time taken to establish whether charges should be laid and if so what charges. The majority of the High Court took a different view. The Court stated:

> "If a person cannot be taken into custody for the purpose of interrogation, he cannot be kept in custody for that purpose and the time limited by the words 'as soon as practicable' cannot be extended to provide time for interrogation. Therefore, it is unlawful for a police officer having the custody of an arrested person to delay taking him before a justice in order to provide an opportunity to investigate the person's complicity in a criminal offence, whether the offence under investigation is the offence for which he was arrested or another offence. ...
>
> The jealous protection of personal liberty accorded by the common law of Australia requires police so to conduct their investigation as not to infringe the arrested person's right to seek to regain his personal liberty as soon as practicable. Practicability is not assessed by reference to exigencies of the criminal investigation: the right to personal liberty is not left over after the police investigation is finished."

2.4   The High Court in *Williams* recognised that its ruling did nothing to assist the police in the investigation of criminal offences, but held that if the balance between the personal liberty of the subject and the exigencies of criminal investigation was to be changed, that was a matter not for the courts but for the legislature. The Court added:

> "If the legislature thinks it right to enhance the armoury of law enforcement, at least the legislature is able – as the courts are not – to prescribe some safeguards which might ameliorate the risk of unconscionable pressure being applied to persons under interrogation while they are kept in custody."

2.5   The decision in *Williams*, that the police have no power to detain a suspect for questioning, still applies in Queensland, New South Wales and Western Australia. Queensland and New South Wales are at the present considering proposals to change this. In South Australia, legislation provides that the police may detain a suspect for questioning about a serious offence for a period of four hours, with a possible extension on application to a stipendiary magistrate for a further four hours. In calculating the four hours, account must not be taken of delays occasioned by the time spent waiting for a lawyer or any other requested person to arrive. In Victoria, legislation provides that police may hold a suspect for questioning for "a reasonable time". What constitutes a reasonable time depends upon the circumstances of each case and is to be determined by reference to criteria specified in the statute. Similarly, in the Northern Territory legislation provides that a person may be detained for a "reasonable period" to enable the person to be questioned or investigations to be carried out. Again, what constitutes a "reasonable period" is to be determined by reference to criteria specified in the statute. The Crimes (Investigation of Commonwealth Offences) Amendment Act 1991 provides that the maximum time the police can hold a suspect for questioning is four hours (two hours in the case of a person under the age of eighteen or an Aboriginal person or a Torres Strait Islander). However, in calculating the period of detention certain times are to be disregarded, for example, time taken travelling to the police station. Furthermore, the police may apply to a magistrate for an extension of the period, but the period cannot exceed eight hours.

2.6   In Victoria, South Australia and under Commonwealth law, the police must inform a suspect of his right to silence and his right to legal advice before questioning him. In Queensland, Western Australia, New South Wales and the Northern Territory, the police must inform a suspect of his right to silence when they decide to charge him. In these jurisdictions, apart from the Northern Territory, the police are under no duty to inform the suspect of the right to consult a lawyer.

Evidence

(i) Confessions

2.7   In Victoria and under Commonwealth law[2], there are provisions restricting the admissibility of confessions that have not been tape recorded, but only where the confession is made to an investigating official. However, in both jurisdictions, there is not an absolute prohibition. In Victoria, the court may admit an untaped confession if the prosecution satisfy the court that the circumstances are exceptional and justify the reception of the evidence. Under Commonwealth law, the court may admit an untaped confession if the court is satisfied that, in the special circumstances of the case, admission of the evidence would not be contrary to the interests of justice. The New South Wales Evidence Bill 1990 contains similar restrictions on the admissibility of untaped confessions[3]. The

---

[2] For further details of the Victorian legisaltion see paragraphs 2.214–2.220 below and for the Commonwealth legislation see paragraphs 2.51–2.52 below.
[3] See paragraph 2.60 below.

Australian Law Reform Commission, in its report on evidence, proposed that evidence of an admission made to an investigating official should be inadmissible, unless it had been made or confirmed on tape or made in the presence of a legal practitioner or other person chosen by the suspect or "it was not reasonably practicable to make such a recording or have such a person present".

2.8 In the other jurisdictions, the High Court decision in *McKinney and Judge*[4] applies. In this case, a majority of the High Court declared the following general rule of practice:

> "The jury should be informed that it is comparatively more difficult for an accused person, held in police custody without access to legal advice or other means of corroboration, to have evidence available to support a challenge to police evidence of confessional statements than it is for such evidence to be fabricated, and accordingly it is necessary that they be instructed that they should give careful consideration as to the dangers involved in convicting an accused person in circumstances where the only (or substantially only) basis for finding that guilt has been established beyond reasonable doubt is a confessional statement allegedly made whilst in police custody, the making of which is not corroborated. Within the context of this warning it will ordinarily be necessary to emphasise the need for careful scrutiny of the evidence and to direct attention to the fact that police witnesses are often practised witnesses and it is not an easy matter to determine whether a practised witness is telling the truth. And of course the trial judge's duty to ensure that the defence case is fairly and adequately put will require that attention will be drawn to those matters which bring the reliability of the confession into question. Equally, in the context of and as part of the warning it will be proper for the trial judge to remind the jury with appropriate comment that persons who make confessions sometimes repudiate them."

2.9 The "making of the confession" could be corroborated, the court held, by a lawyer or independent person, audio or video recording and "usually" by the suspect signing the record of the interview, but not always. The court did not give any guidance for deciding when "the only (or substantially the only)" basis for guilt was the confession.

2.10 The Law Reform Commission of New South Wales has proposed statutory provisions excluding admissions influenced by violence or oppression and a discretion to exclude admissions on the basis of unfairness[5]. The Australian Law Reform Commission made proposals, in its

---

[4] (1991) 65 ALJR 241.
[5] See paragraph 2.63 below.

report on evidence, for the exclusion of admissions influenced by violence, oppressive, inhuman or degrading conduct, whether towards the person who made the admission or towards some other person, or by threat of conduct of that kind. The Commission also proposed that evidence of an admission should not be admissible unless the circumstances in which the admission was made were such as to make it unlikely that the truth of the admission was adversely affected. In deciding this, the court should take into account the condition or characteristics of the person who made the confession, including age, personality, education, and mental or physical disability and in addition the nature of the questions and the manner in which they were put.

(ii) Identification evidence

2.11 At present, in all the jurisdictions, there is no requirement that identification evidence must be corroborated. However, the judge must give a warning about the dangers of identification evidence. The Australian Law Reform Commission proposed in its report on evidence that a judge should warn the jury that it should not convict on the basis of identification evidence, unless there were special circumstances that tended to support the identification, such as the defendant being known to the person who made the identification or the identification being made on the basis of a characteristic that was unusual, or there was substantial evidence, apart from the identification evidence, that tended to prove the guilt of the defendant.

(iii) The accused's silence

2.12 In 1991, in *Petty and Maiden*[6], the High Court of Australia laid down the following propositions:

> (1) a person who believes on reasonable grounds that he or she is suspected of having been party to an offence is entitled to remain silent when questioned or asked to supply information by any person in authority;

> (2) silence about an offence on the part of a person liable to be suspected of being criminally involved in its commission cannot constitute misprision of felony;

> (3) an incident of that right to silence [i.e. silence when questioned about an offence] is that no adverse inference can be drawn against an accused person by reason of his or her failure to provide such information [i.e. information about the offence];

---

[6] (1991) 65 ALJR 625.

(4) the right to remain silent applies to the conduct of a committal proceeding and silence maintained provides no basis for any inference against an accused;

(5) previous silence about a defence (or explanation) raised at the trial does *not* provide a basis for inferring that the defence or explanation is a new invention or is rendered suspect or unacceptable or otherwise less credible;

(6) a jury should not be directed that an accused is under some duty to disclose a defence or explanation before the trial so that the Crown may properly investigate it.

(iv) Improperly or illegally obtained evidence

2.13 At present, in all of the jurisdictions, the court has a discretion at common law to exclude illegally or improperly obtained evidence. In *R. v. Ireland*[7], Barwick CJ stated:

> "On the one hand there is the public need to bring to conviction those who commit criminal offences. On the other hand there is the public interest in the protection of the individual from unlawful and unfair treatment. Convictions obtained by the aid of unlawful or unfair acts may be obtained at too high a price. Hence the judicial discretion."

2.14 In *Bunning v Cross*[8], the High Court of Australia set out the following criteria as being relevant to the decision to exclude improperly obtained evidence:

> Intent: if the impropriety were due to a mistake and made in good faith then this factor weighs in favour of including the evidence; however a deliberate or reckless disregard of the accused's rights has the opposite effect.

> Cogency of the evidence: cogent evidence should be readily admitted when there has been an error by the police committed in good faith, and if the illegality in question has not affected the cogency of the evidence. When there has been deliberate or reckless impropriety by the police, the cogency of the evidence should not make the evidence more readily admissible, but an exception is where the evidence is vital and of a perishable or evanescent nature. If there is equally cogent and legally obtained evidence available, there is less need to admit the illegally obtained evidence.

---

[7] (1970) 126 CLR 321.
[8] (1978) 141 CLR 54.

Ease of compliance with the law: sometimes the ease with which the law could have been complied with may be a factor tending against admission, but this will not always be so.

Gravity of the offence: evidence should be more readily admitted in the trials of more serious offences; the comparative seriousness of the offence and the unlawful conduct of the law enforcement authority should be examined.

Nature of the irregularity: if there is legislation which deliberately limits the police power to obtain the evidence in question, then evidence obtained in breach of the legislation should be more readily excluded.

2.15 The Australian Law Reform Commission, in its report on evidence, proposed that improperly obtained evidence should be inadmissible unless the desirability of admitting the evidence outweighed the undesirability of admitting the evidence.

The Commission listed the following matters which the court should take into account when making this decision:

(a) the probative value of the evidence;

(b) the importance of the evidence in the proceedings;

(c) the nature of the relevant offence, cause of action or defence and the nature of the subject matter of the proceedings;

(d) the gravity of the impropriety or the contravention;

(e) whether the impropriety or contravention was deliberate or reckless;

(f) whether the impropriety or contravention was contrary to or inconsistent with a right recognised by the International Covenant on Civil and Political Rights;

(g) whether any other proceedings (whether or not in court) have been or are likely to be taken in relation to the impropriety or contravention;

(h) the difficulty, if any, of obtaining the evidence without impropriety or contravention of the law.

2.16 The Commission also proposed a general discretion to exclude evidence where the probative value of the evidence is substantially outweighed by the danger of unfair prejudice, confusion, or the danger that the evidence might mislead or cause an undue waste of time; and a discretion to exclude evidence where the probative value of the evidence is outweighed by the danger of unfair prejudice to the defendant.

2.17 The Law Reform Commission of New South Wales has made a similar recommendation with regard to improperly obtained evidence[9].

(v) Warnings for unreliable witnesses

2.18 The Australian Law Reform Commission has proposed a scheme whereby the judge on the request of one the parties must, unless there are good reasons for not doing so, warn the jury that evidence falling within certain specified categories is unreliable, explain why it is unreliable, and warn of the need for caution in determining whether to accept the evidence and the weight to be given to it. In giving the warning, the judge is not bound by any particular form of words. The categories of evidence for which this scheme is to apply include hearsay, admissions, evidence the reliability of which may be effected by age or ill health, the evidence of a prosecution witness who has been concerned in the events giving rise to the proceedings and the evidence of a victim in a sexual offence.

Prosecution

2.19 In general, the police prosecute in summary cases and Crown Prosecutors prosecute in judge and jury trials. Crown Prosecutors do not normally direct or supervise police investigations but may occasionally do so in complex or controversial cases.

Disclosure

2.20 The law and practice governing defence access to prosecution evidence varies between jurisdictions, but, with the exception of the Northern Territory, in the main is the same as in England and Wales. In the Northern Territory, the defence has no right to the depositions of the prosecution witnesses at committal, although they are usually provided in practice.

2.21 In general, the defence need only disclose evidence of an alibi. However, in the Northern Territory, as a matter of practice, the defence supply the prosecution with a copy of the depositions of the witnesses upon which they intend to rely. In Western Australia, in practice, medical evidence as to unsoundness of mind and automatism is also disclosed in advance so as to save unnecessary adjournments of the trial. There are also pre-arraignment hearings where the defence may reveal certain evidence, but there is no statutory requirement to do so.

---

[9] See paragraph 2.67 below.

Expert evidence

2.22   The information received from the jurisdictions suggests that there is no adequate system for ensuring the defence have assistance from scientific experts. Some funding is given through legal aid, but this is considered inadequate. However, information from the Attorney General's Department of Australia states that a national forensic science institute has recently been established for the purposes of providing an independent forensic science service.

2.23   At present, experts employed by the state in Victoria and South Australia can work for the defence. In the Northern Territory, although experts employed by the state have not in practice ever worked for the defence, it is thought that subject to the consent of the Commissioner of Police there would be no objection to them so doing. In New South Wales and Queensland, experts employed by the state cannot work for the defence. In Western Australia, experts employed by the state cannot work for the defence, but will answer questions put to them by the defence.

2.24   In none of the jurisdictions is there a system attempting to get defence and prosecution experts to agree their evidence pre-trial.

2.25   Only in South Australia has the court the power to commission an expert of its own and this power is rarely used in practice. This is because, according to one witness, "judges have an ingrained fear that they are descending into the arena if they do so".

Juries

2.26   In all jurisdictions juries deliberate alone.

2.27   In no jurisdiction are steps taken to ensure that juries reflect a racial balance in appropriate cases.

Trial

2.28   The judge does have the power to call witnesses in exceptional circumstances, but it is rarely used. The High Court in *R. v. Apostilides*[10] laid down the following general propositions:

   (1) in a criminal trial, the Crown Prosecutor alone bears the responsibility of deciding whether a person will be called as a witness for the Crown;

   (2) the judge may, but is not obliged to, question the Prosecutor to ascertain the reasons that led the Prosecutor to decline to call a particular person. He is not called upon to adjudicate the sufficiency of those reasons;

---

[10] (1984) 154 CLR 563.

(3) while at the close of the Crown case the judge may properly invite the Prosecutor to reconsider such a decision and to have regard to the implications as appear to the judge at that stage of the proceedings, he cannot direct the Prosecutor to call a particular witness;

(4) when charging the jury, the judge may make such comment as he thinks appropriate about the effect that the Prosecutor's failure to call a particular witness would appear to have had on the course of the trial;

(5) save in the most exceptional circumstances, the judge should not himself call a person to give evidence;

(6) a decision of a Prosecutor not to call a particular witness will only constitute a ground for setting aside a conviction, if, when viewed against the conduct of the trial as a whole, it is seen to give rise to a miscarriage of justice.

2.29   In all of the jurisdictions, the Prosecutor is allowed to make an opening speech.

2.30   The judge's powers when summing up are the same as in England and Wales.

Previous convictions

2.31   In Victoria and Western Australia, judges do have the accused's prior convictions before them during the trial, but in the other states they do not.

2.32   The rules governing the admissibility of previous convictions are similar to those in England and Wales.

Appeal

2.33   In all the jurisdictions, as in England and Wales, leave is required unless the appeal is on a point of law.

2.34   The Appeal Court can increase a sentence for an unmeritorious appeal in the Northern Territory. In Western Australia, where there is an appeal against conviction or an application is made to appeal against a sentence, the prisoner will generally be treated as a remand prisoner pending the outcome of the appeal. Under section 20 of the Criminal Code, the Court of Appeal may order that the time which the prisoner has been so treated may count towards the service of the sentence. The Court will refuse to make an order where the appeal is hopeless. Similarly, in New South Wales, the Court must make an order if the time spent awaiting appeal is to count towards the sentence. By failing to make the order in unmeritorious cases, the Court can in theory discourage hopeless appeals. However, in practice orders are almost always made. In South Australia, if an appeal is frivolous, the Court can direct that the sentence should not run pending the determination of the appeal.

2.35   As regards "fresh evidence", in *Gallagher*[11] the High Court held:

> "The authorities disclose three main considerations which will guide a Court of Criminal Appeal in deciding whether a miscarriage of justice has occurred because evidence now available was not led at the trial. The first of these, that the conviction will not usually be set aside if the evidence now relied on could with reasonable diligence have been produced by the accused at the trial, is satisfied in the present case, and need not be discussed, although it should be noted that this is not a universal and inflexible requirement: the strength of the fresh evidence may in some cases be such as to justify interference with the verdict, even though that evidence might have been discovered before the trial. Two other matters that should be taken into consideration are whether the evidence is apparently credible (or at least capable of belief) and whether, if believed, the evidence might reasonably have led the jury to return a different verdict."

2.36   In the information received it was stated that in Queensland and the Northern Territory the Court of Appeal will not consider as "fresh evidence" evidence which was available at the trial but not called by the defence. In South Australia, the Court could consider such evidence but rarely did. In New South Wales, the Court normally did not consider such evidence, but could if a reasonable explanation were given. In Victoria, it was stated that under section 574A of the Crimes Act, the Court of Criminal Appeal may allow the admission of new evidence upon appeal if it thinks it necessary or expedient in the interests of justice to do so. It does not matter that the new evidence is not "fresh evidence" in the sense that the latter means evidence that could not reasonably have been available to the accused at the trial.

2.37   In Queensland, appeals are allowed on the ground that the case was mishandled by the lawyers, but the conduct of the lawyer must be "gross". In the Northern Territory, appeals on this ground are allowed. In New South Wales and Western Australia, such an appeal would be allowed only

---

[11] (1986) 20 A Crim R.

where the mishandling resulted in a miscarriage of justice. In Victoria, this is not a ground of appeal, but the Court has the power to interfere to protect an accused from his or her own counsel's mismanagement of the case. In South Australia, it was thought that the Court could allow such an appeal but the witnesses were not aware of any instances in that state.

2.38   In all of the jurisdictions retrials are common. No witness said that this caused problems, although one witness wrote: "A retrial mostly helps the Crown because the accused's defence is known and he will be taxed at the later trial with any variations in his testimony from that given at the earlier trial but neither of these considerations deters courts in practice from ordering retrials".

2.39   In all the jurisdictions, the statutory formula that the Appeal Court must consider when deciding whether to quash a conviction is:

> "The Court on any such ground against conviction shall allow the appeal if it is of opinion that it is unreasonable, or cannot be supported having regard to the evidence, or that the judgment of the court of trial should be set aside on the ground of the wrong decision of any question of law, or that on any ground whatsoever there was a miscarriage of justice, and in any other case shall dismiss the appeal:

> Provided that the Court may, notwithstanding that it is of the opinion that the point or points raised by the appeal might be decided in favour of the appellant, dismiss the appeal if it considers that no substantial miscarriage of justice has actually occurred."

2.40   In all the jurisdictions except the Northern Territory, a defendant may not appeal more than once. In the Northern Territory, there are no rules restricting the number of appeals.

2.41   In all jurisdictions, there is a procedure whereby a member of the Executive can refer cases back to the Court of Appeal. In these cases, except in the Northern Territory, the Court of Appeal applies the normal rules. In the Northern Territory, the Court of Appeal is not bound by the normal rules of evidence and can, for example, receive in evidence the report of a commission or inquiry.

2.42   In no jurisdiction is there a "Court of Last Resort" or equivalent. However, Royal Commissions and judges are sometimes appointed to investigate alleged miscarriages of justice, as for example in the Chamberlain case.

Training

2.43   There is no formal training of judges in any of the jurisdictions.

2.44   Police training in all of the jurisdictions usually does cover the problems of false confessions, unreliable eye-witness evidence and bias.

A. AUSTRALIAN COMMONWEALTH LAW

2.45   Unless a Commonwealth law provides otherwise, offences against laws of the Commonwealth are dealt with in the courts of the state or territory in which the offence occurred, under the practices and procedures of that state or territory.

Police investigations

2.46   The investigation of offences against Commonwealth laws is governed by the Crimes (Investigation of Commonwealth Offences) Amendment Act 1991 (the "Act"). That Act is based on the recommendations of a report prepared by the Review of Commonwealth Law Committee. The Act also applies to the investigation of Australian Capital Territory offences punishable by more than twelve months imprisonment.

2.47   Section 23C of the Act provides that the maximum time the police can hold a suspect for questioning is four hours (two hours in the case of a person under the age of eighteen or an Aboriginal person or a Torres Strait Islander). However, in calculating the period of detention, certain times are to be disregarded, for example, time taken travelling to the police station, time taken for a lawyer or friend or relative to arrive, time taken to receive medical treatment or recover from intoxication. If a person is under arrest for a serious offence, an investigating official may apply to a magistrate for an extension of the period, but the period cannot exceed eight hours.

2.48   Section 23F provides that an investigating official must, before starting to question the person, caution the person that he or she does not have to say or do anything, but that anything the person does say or do may be used in evidence.

2.49   Section 23G provides that an investigating officer must, before starting to question the person, inform the person that (a) he or she may communicate with a friend or relative and (b) that he or she may communicate with a legal practitioner and arrange for a legal practitioner to be present during the questioning.

2.50   Section 23F and G make no distinction between serious and non-serious offences.

Evidence

2.51   Under section 23V of the Crimes (Investigation of Commonwealth Offences) Amendment Act 1991, a confession made to an investigating official in circumstances where it is reasonably practicable to tape record the confession is inadmissible unless tape recorded. In cases where it is not practicable to tape record at the time the confession was made, a confession is inadmissible unless the following procedure has been complied with. At the time of the interview or as soon as practicable afterwards, a record of the interview must be made in writing. As soon as practicable after the record has been made, it must be read to the suspect who must then be given an opportunity to point out any errors or omissions. A tape recording must be made of the reading and the suspect's comments.

2.52 A court may still admit a confession, even if the requirements of section 23V have not been complied with if, having regard to the non-compliance, the court is satisfied that, in the special circumstances of the case, "admission of the evidence would not be contrary to the interests of justice".

Prosecution

2.53 Offences against Commonwealth laws are prosecuted by the Commonwealth Director of Public Prosecutions, including summary prosecutions instituted by the Australian Federal Police. The office of the Director has no role in directing or supervising police investigations, although the Australian Federal Police and other Commonwealth agencies carrying out investigations of suspected Commonwealth offences seek advice from the DPP.

B. NEW SOUTH WALES

Police investigations

2.54 The police have no power to hold a suspect for questioning. They must bring the arrested person before a justice (or court) as quickly as possible. The High Court decision in *Williams* applies[12].

2.55 The Judges' Rules do not apply in New South Wales. The New South Wales Police Commissioner's Instructions currently direct police officers to inform a suspect of his right of silence when they decide to charge him.

2.56 There is no duty to inform a suspect of his right to legal advice. A suspect has a right to legal advice, but must claim it. Failure to enable him to claim it may affect the discretionary admission of evidence at the trial. No distinction is drawn in regard to the right to consult a lawyer between serious cases and less serious cases.

---

[12] See paragraphs 2.2–2.4 above.

2.57 The Law Reform Commission of New South Wales, in a report *Police Powers of Detention and Arrest After Detention*, proposes a complete statutory scheme to govern police powers and the rights of suspects. With regard to detention for questioning, the Commission recommends that a suspect may be detained for such time as is "reasonable" in the circumstances, but for no longer than four hours. There is provision for extension up to eight hours by application to a judicial officer. What is a "reasonable" time must be determined by reference to all of the relevant circumstances, including such factors as the complexity of the matters under investigation; whether a person has indicated a willingness to make a statement and answer questions; and whether appropriate facilities are available to conduct an interview. Furthermore certain periods are not to be counted as part of the four hours, for example the time taken to travel to the police station; and the time spent waiting for a lawyer to arrive. No distinction is made between serious and less serious cases.

2.58 The Commission also recommends that on arrest a suspect must be informed of his right to silence and his right to communicate with a friend or relative and a lawyer. The suspect must be informed of these rights again before any questioning.

Evidence

(i) Confessions

2.59 At present, to be admissible confessions must be voluntary (section 410, Crimes Act (NSW)). There is no requirement that a confession must be tape recorded or corroborated. However, the judge must warn the jury about convicting where the case against the accused is based wholly or substantially on a confession the making of which has not been reliably corroborated. (*McKinney and Judge*[13]).

2.60 The Attorney General of New South Wales intends to re-introduce the Evidence Bill 1991 into the New South Wales Parliament in March 1993. Clause 70 of the Bill provides that an admission made to a investigating officer is not admissible unless:

(a) there is available to the court a sound recording made by a police officer at the police station of the interview in the course of which the admission was made; or

(b) if the prosecution establishes that there was a reasonable excuse as to why a sound recording referred to in paragraph (a) could not be made, there is available to the court a sound recording of

---
[13] See paragraph 2.8 above.

an interview with the person who made the admission about the making and terms of the admission in the course of which the person states that he or she made an admission in those terms; or

(c) if the prosecution establishes that there was a reasonable excuse as to why the sound recording referred to in paragraph (a) and (b) could not be made, there is available to the court a sound recording made as soon as practicable after the interview in the course of which the admission was made in which a police officer (who was present at the interview) states that the admission was made and describes the terms of the admission; or

(d) the prosecution establishes that there was a reasonable excuse as to why the sound recordings referred to in paragraphs (a), (b) and (c) could not be made.

2.61 Under section 71 of the Bill, a confession made to an investigating official is not admissible unless the suspect was cautioned before the confession was made or the prosecution establish that there was a reasonable excuse for the investigating official failing to caution the suspect.

2.62 The above provision of the Bill are similar, but not identical, to the proposals made by the Law Reform Commission of New South Wales in its report, *Police Powers of Detention and Investigation After Arrest*. The Commission proposed that a confession should be inadmissible, unless there was a tape recording of the interview in which the confession was made or there was a tape recording of the defendant freely and expressly adopting an admission which has been read back to him or the admission was made in the presence of an independent person.

2.63 The Commission also proposed a statutory provision excluding admissions influenced by violent or oppressive, inhuman or degrading conduct, whether towards the person who made the confession or towards some other person, or by a threat of conduct of that kind. It also proposed that the court should have a discretion to exclude evidence of a confession if it believes that it would be unfair to the defendant to use the evidence.

2.64 At present, special rules apply to admissions made by children. An admission made by a child is admissible only if:

(a) there was present at the place where, and throughout the period of time during which, it was made or given

(i) a person responsible for the child; or

(ii) an adult (other than a member of the police force) who was present with the consent of the person responsible for the child; or

(iii) in the case of a child who is above the age of sixteen years an adult (other than a member of the police force) who was present with the consent of the child; or

(iv) a barrister or solicitor of the child's own choosing; or

(b) the person acting judicially in those proceedings

(i) is satisfied that there was proper and sufficient reason for the absence of such an adult from the place where, or throughout the period during which, the statement, confession, admission or information was made or given; and

(ii) considers that, in the particular circumstances of the case, the statement should be admitted in evidence in those proceedings.

(ii) Identification evidence

2.65   There is no requirement of corroboration for identification evidence. However, a warning must be given about the dangers of relying on identification evidence.

(iii) The accused's silence

2.66   Adverse inferences cannot be drawn from an accused's silence.

(iv) Illegally or improperly obtained evidence

2.67   Illegally or improperly obtained evidence can be excluded at the discretion of the court. The Law Reform Commission has proposed that such evidence should be presumed inadmissible unless the desirability of admitting the evidence substantially outweighs the undesirability of excluding the evidence. The following factors are to be taken into account when making this decision:

(a) the probative value of the evidence;

(b) the importance of the evidence in the proceedings;

(c) the nature of the relevant offence or defence;

(d) the gravity of the contravention;

(e) whether the conduct concerned was deliberate or reckless;

(f) whether the impropriety or contravention was contrary to or inconsistent with codes of practice regulating the police treatment of persons in custody, or any other applicable human rights legislation;

(g) whether any other proceedings (whether or not in court) have been or are likely to be taken in relation to the impropriety or contravention;

(h) whether the evidence could have been obtained in some other proper way.

2.68 The Commission has also proposed that the court should have a general discretion to exclude evidence where the probative value of the evidence is outweighed by the danger of unfair prejudice to the defendant.

Prosecution

2.69 Only in exceptional circumstances will the Director of Public Prosecutions direct an investigation.

Disclosure

2.70 The statements of prosecution witnesses are disclosed at committal. The prosecution are under an obligation to disclose material evidence, including that unhelpful to the prosecution. However, there is no system in place to ensure that the obligation is carried out, or indeed the prosecution receives all material evidence from investigators.

2.80 The defence need disclose only evidence of alibis in advance of the trial.

Expert evidence

2.81 There are no methods or systems to ensure that the defence have adequate assistance from forensic or scientific evidence. State-employed experts are not able to work for the defence.

2.82 There is no system for attempting to get prosecution and defence experts to agree their evidence before the trial.

2.83 There is no system whereby the court can commission its own expert.

Juries

2.84 Juries deliberate alone.

2.85 No steps are taken to ensure the jury reflects a racial balance in cases where that seems appropriate.

Trial

2.86 The District Court in its criminal jurisdiction can deal with all matters except murder and treason. Trials are given a fixed date. Listing for the courts in the state is the responsibility of the Criminal Listing Director. He is assisted by four Deputy Directors. The Director and Deputies conduct "call-overs" of matters to be listed. The call-over is used to monitor the matters going before the Court. By obtaining information at a call-over, from the parties regarding the readiness of the matters to proceed and any expected problems, the Director attempts to minimise the amount of court sitting time lost. Trials are fixed for a hearing at a call-over, and are then relisted, for a further call-over six weeks prior to the hearing date, to confirm inter alia the availability of the parties and the estimated duration of the trial. Cases are listed on the basis of five trials each week per judge or Court. One category A and two category B trials are listed each Monday and one category B trial each Wednesday.

2.87 The Supreme Court acts as a court of first instance in cases of murder and treason. Call-overs are conducted monthly by a Listing Judge who consults the Judges' Roster and then lists the trial for hearing commencing on a specified date, with the number of trials listed according to the number of available judges. Any applications for adjournments must be argued before the Listing Judge. Few are allowed.

2.88 The court does have the power to call witnesses of its own motion but rarely, if ever, uses it.

2.89 The prosecutor is required to open the case.

2.90 The judge's powers when summing up are the same as in England and Wales.

Previous convictions

2.91 The judge does not have the accused's prior convictions before him during the trial.

2.92 The law governing the admissibility of previous convictions is the same as in England and Wales.

Appeal

2.93 Appeals are of right on a question of law. They are by leave if on a question of fact, or of mixed law and fact.

2.94   The Court must make an order if the time spent waiting for an appeal is to count towards the sentence. By failing to make the order in unmeritorious cases, the Court can in theory discourage hopeless appeals. However, in practice orders are almost always made.

2.95   Evidence which was available at the trial but which was not called by the defence is not normally considered fresh evidence for the purposes of the appeal. However, where there is a reasonable explanation, the evidence may be accepted.

2.96   The Court of Appeal would allow an appeal on the ground that the case has been mishandled by the lawyers, but only where the mishandling produced a miscarriage of justice.

2.97   The statutory formula that the Appeal Court must consider when deciding whether to quash a conviction is:

> "The Court on any such ground against conviction shall allow the appeal if it is of opinion that it is unreasonable, or cannot be supported having regard to the evidence, or that the judgment of the court of trial should be set aside on the ground of the wrong decision of any question of law, or that on any ground whatsoever there was a miscarriage of justice, and in any other case shall dismiss the appeal.
>
> Provided that the Court may, notwithstanding that it is of the opinion that the point or points raised by the appeal might be decided in favour of the appellant, dismiss the appeal if it considers that no substantial miscarriage of justice has actually occurred."

2.98   Retrials are ordered unless there is no case in law or fact, or the circumstances are exceptional. One witness wrote "No serious problems in the vast majority of cases."

2.99   Only one appeal is permitted.

2.100   The Minister of Justice can refer cases back to the Court of Appeal, in which case the normal rules apply.

2.101   There is no "Court of Last Resort".

Training

2.102   There is no formal training of judges.

2.103   Police officers training covers the problems of false confessions, unreliable eye-witness evidence, bias in police officers etc.

C. THE NORTHERN TERRITORY

Police investigations

2.104   Section 137(1) of the Police Administration Act provides that a person should be brought before a justice or a court of competent jurisdiction as soon as practicable after being taken into lawful custody. However, a person may be detained for a "reasonable period" to enable the person to be questioned (section 137(2)(a)) or investigations to be carried out (section 137(2)(b)). In determining what is a "reasonable period" for the purposes of section 137, factors to be considered are set out in section 138. These include the time taken for the interview of the suspect or any witnesses, the number and complexity of the matters to be investigated, the time taken for completing forensic investigations or conducting an identification parade and the time taken to contact and await the arrival of a legal adviser. In *R. v. Heles and Kamm*[14] the Supreme Court of the Northern Territory stated that in deciding what is a reasonable period the trial judge should "keep in the forefront of his mind the jealousy with which the courts and the law regard the liberty of the subject."

2.105   Northern Territory Police General Orders QI (18) provide that, before questioning a person whom he has decided to charge, the police officer should inform the person that he or she is not obliged to answer any questions, unless he or she wishes to do so, but whatever he or she does say may be given in evidence against him or her.

2.106   Northern Territory Police General Orders QI (26) provide that a person held in custody shall be given the opportunity to have a lawyer informed of his or her detention. No distinction is drawn between serious and less serious cases.

Evidence

2.107   The judge must warn the jury about the dangers of convicting the accused where the only (or substantially the only) evidence against the accused is a confession the making of which is not corroborated[15].

2.108   Neither a judge, magistrate or prosecutor may draw any adverse inference from the accused's silence at the police station.

2.109   The judge must warn the jury about the dangers of relying on identification evidence.

2.110   The court has a discretion at common law to exclude illegally or improperly obtained evidence.

---

[14] unreported; numbers 151 and 152 of 1989.
[15] *McKinney and Judge* (1991) 65 ALJR 241. See paragraph 2.8 above.

Prosecution

2.111   As part of the pre-trial process prosecutors may give directions to the police.

Disclosure

2.112   Unlike in some other states, the defence have no right to the depositions of prosecution witnesses at a committal. However, as a matter of practice, the prosecutor will normally give the defence a copy of the depositions some time before the committal, but this does not always occur. At trial, the defence will always be in possession of the transcript of the proceedings at the committal, which contains the oral evidence of the Crown witnesses. If the Crown is leading additional witnesses at the trial, the practice is for the prosecutor to give depositions of these witnesses to the defence before the trial.

2.113   The defence have no right to see relevant material in the possession of the prosecution which the prosecution do not intend to use. However, the prosecutor is under a duty to call all relevant witnesses and not to conceal relevant evidence or information. If the prosecutor fails to comply with these obligations, the verdict may be held to be unsafe and unsound.

2.114   There is no comprehensive system to ensure that police or forensic scientists produce all relevant material to the prosecutor. However, the witness who provided the information stated, "Once the prosecutor has seen the exhibit lists and work sheets for the relevant police officers involved in the investigation, usually that provides all the relevant information."

2.115   The defence need only disclose evidence of alibi in advance of the trial. However, as a matter of practice the defence will normally supply the prosecution with a copy of the depositions of the witnesses upon whom they intend to rely.

Expert evidence

2.116   No special rules exist to ensure that in the gravest cases scientific evidence taken at the scene of the crime or from suspects themselves will be collected properly.

2.117   Usually the defence engage their own forensic or scientific experts. The witness who provided the information, although not aware of any cases where the defence has had assistance from experts employed by the state, did not think that there would be any objection to this, subject to obtaining the consent of the Commissioner of Police.

2.118 There is no actual system for attempting to get the defence and the prosecution experts to agree their evidence before the trial, but any party is free to admit any fact alleged by the other party in advance of the trial.

2.119 There is no system for the court to commission expert evidence of its own.

Pre-trial

2.120 There is no procedure enabling the prosecution to examine the accused in front of a judge or other judicial officer.

Statistics for detention pre-trial

2.121 As at 23 January 1992, there were thirty two males in prison who had not yet been convicted. There were no prisoners who had been convicted but not yet sentenced. As at 6 August 1992, the total population of the Northern Territory of Australia was 175,253.

Juries

2.122 Juries deliberate alone.

2.123 No steps are taken to ensure that the jury reflects a racial balance in cases where that might seem to be appropriate.

Trial

2.124 The judge has the power to call witnesses, but the power is only exercisable in exceptional circumstances and is rarely used.

2.125 The prosecutor is allowed to make an opening speech.

2.126 Section 364 of the Criminal Code provides that the judge must in his summing up instruct the jury as to the law applicable to the case and "make such observations upon the evidence as the court thinks fit to make." Personal comments regarding the facts by a judge are permitted provided the judge makes it clear to the jury that questions of fact are ultimately for them.

Previous convictions

2.127 The trial judge does not have before him or her the accused's prior convictions during the trial.

2.128 The rules regarding the admissibility of previous convictions are the same as in England and Wales.

Appeal

2.129   Leave is required for an appeal.

2.130   The Appeal Court does have the power to discourage hopeless appeals by adding on time to the sentence for unmeritorious appeals.

2.131   The Appeal Court would not consider that evidence which was available at the trial but which was not called by the defence was "fresh evidence".

2.132   The Appeal Court does allow appeals on the ground that the case was mishandled by the lawyers.

2.133   Retrials are common.

2.134   Section 411(3) of the Criminal Code provides

(i)   "the verdict of the jury should be set aside on the ground that it was unreasonable or cannot be supported having regard to the evidence, or

(ii)   the judgment of the court of trial should be set aside on the ground of a wrong decision on any question of law or that on any ground there was a miscarriage of justice and in any other case dismiss the appeal."

2.135   There are no rules restricting the number of appeals.

2.136   The Attorney General can refer a case back to the Appeal Court. In such cases, under section 433(A)(5), the Appeal Court is not bound by the rules of evidence. The Court may inform itself in such a manner as it thinks fit. A discretion exists as to what the Court can receive in evidence and includes:

(i)   a transcript taken and exhibits produced in a proceeding before a court or a commission of inquiry;

(ii)   a report of a commission of inquiry.

2.137   There is no "Court of Last Resort" or equivalent.

Training

2.138   At their initial training and subsequent training, police officers are trained to deal with the problems of false confessions, unreliable eye-witness evidence and bias.

2.139 For lawyers, these matters are dealt with in continuing legal education seminars.

D. QUEENSLAND

Police investigations

2.140 At present, the law governing police powers in Queensland is to be found in the common law and in a number of separate pieces of legislation. In an issues paper, *Police Powers in Queensland*, prepared jointly by the Office of the Minister for Police and Emergency Services and the Criminal Justice Commission (see paragraphs 2.178–2.179 below) consideration is given to the reform of law governing police powers and its codification in a single piece of legislation. The paper, however, makes no specific recommendations for reform, but simply raises issues for discussion.

2.141 At present, the police may not hold a suspect for questioning without his consent prior to charge. After arrest, the police are under an obligation to take the suspect before a justice "forthwith" or "as soon as practicable". The ruling in *Williams v the Queen* is therefore still applicable in Queensland[16].

2.142 The police have a duty to inform suspects of their right to silence, but do not have a duty to inform them that they may obtain legal advice. The duty to warn is outlined in Rule 2 of the Judges' Rules of 1912 and arises whenever a police officer has made up his or her mind to charge a person with a crime. Rule 3 is also applicable. It provides that persons in custody should not be questioned without the caution first being administered. The term "in custody" is not confined to a person who has been arrested, but includes any person who, although not arrested, is given reason to think that he or she is not free to leave.

Evidence

(i) Confessions

2.143 There are no rules restricting the admissibility of confessions that have not been tape-recorded or repeated in front of a judge or magistrate. However, by an administrative arrangement which has not been statutorily incorporated to date, Queensland police are required under the General Instructions of the Queensland Police Service to tape-record and video confessions at the police station. There is no requirement on the police to attempt to get the suspect to confirm on tape an admission alleged by the police to have been made prior to the formal tape recording at the police station, although in practice a prudent officer would attempt to do this.

---

[16] See paragraph 2.2–2.4 above.

2.144   There is no requirement that confessions must be corroborated. However, where the case against the accused is wholly or substantially based upon a confession and the making of the confession is not corroborated, the judge must warn the jury of the dangers of convicting the accused in those circumstances[17].

(ii) Identification evidence

2.145   There is no rule requiring the corroboration of identification evidence. However, as in England, the trial judge has to give a warning as to the dangers inherent in identification evidence, the strength of which will vary according to the circumstances of the case.

(iii) The accused's silence

2.146   Silence by the accused at the police station is treated in the same way as it is in England and Wales. It cannot be the subject of adverse comment at the trial.

(iv) Illegally or improperly obtained evidence

2.147   The court has a discretion to exclude illegally or improperly obtained evidence.

Prosecution

2.148   At present, in Queensland almost all summary hearings are conducted by police prosecutors, who are police officers not necessarily holding any legal qualifications but more often having received some limited training in prosecution and court practice. Occasionally (but not very often) the Director of Prosecutions will conduct summary trials or committals where the case is a controversial one. All proceedings in judge and jury trials before the District Courts and the Supreme Court are conducted by Crown Prosecutors, who are qualified lawyers most often employed within the office of the Director of Prosecutions. In the most serious cases, however, the Director of Prosecutions will brief barristers at the private Bar, but he or she never involves private solicitors in the preparation of cases for the prosecution.

2.149   Police prosecutors rarely have a role in directing or supervising police investigations. Occasionally the Director of Prosecutions does involve himself or herself in directing and supervising police investigations, mainly in controversial cases or serious matters such as murder cases which have attracted a degree of notoriety.

---

[17] *McKinney and Judge* (1991) 65 ALJR 241. See paragraph 2.8 above.

Disclosure

2.150 As a result of a directive issued by the Director of Prosecutions in 1988, police officers should supply the defence with statements intended to be relied upon by the prosecution in committal hearings at least seven days before the committal. One witness said that this directive has largely been ignored by the police because there are no enforcement or punitive powers exercisable against the police. Another said that it could not be met because of the workload of the police.

2.151 In indictable matters after a person has been committed for trial, the prosecution should make available any further statements at a "reasonable" time before trial. One witness wrote: "Too often they are produced on the eve of the court hearing." In relation to summary hearings, there is no time limit by which the Police Prosecutors are required to supply particulars to the defence. One witness wrote: "This has been a sore point for some years with defence lawyers."

2.152 Crown Prosecutors are under an ethical obligation to reveal to the defence all evidence which they do not intend to call as part of their own case but which may be relevant to the defence. However, the defence have no absolute right to see such evidence. One witness said that as a matter of practice the prosecution do not make such evidence available even if specifically requested to do so. Furthermore, there is no mechanism in existence which is designed to deal with the danger that all relevant material might not have been revealed to the prosecution by the police or forensic scientists. However, some investigators provide all of the material collected during the investigation, a great deal of which is not used at committal, leaving it to the discretion of the prosecutor to decide what part of the unused material should be disclosed to the defence. This, it is said, places a very large burden on the prosecutor.

2.153 The defence are under no general obligation to disclose their evidence. The defence must, however, give advance disclosure of alibi evidence. The defence also disclose medical evidence before the trial in cases referred to the mental health tribunal which decides whether a suspect is fit to stand trial.

Expert evidence

2.154 There are no methods for ensuring that the defence have adequate assistance from forensic or scientific experts. Forensic experts in the employment of the police or State Government are not able to work for the defence. The defence have to obtain their own scientific/forensic experts.

2.155   There is no system for getting the prosecution and defence to agree expert evidence in advance of the trial. In practice, however, because of the size of the jurisdiction, prosecution experts are known to defence counsel and informal talks will take place.

2.156   There is no system for the court to commission its own expert.

Pre-trial Procedures

2.157   In June 1992, the Criminal Code Review Committee made a recommendation that, if the trial judge thought fit, any of the following steps could be taken before the jury was sworn:

- (a) "The trial judge may determine, and hear such evidence as is necessary to determine, the admissibility of any matter in evidence in the trial;

- (b) counsel for any party to the trial may announce his or her intention to include any matter in, or to exclude any matter from, the evidence to be adduced for that party in the trial;

- (c) any party to the trial may object to any matter being admitted in evidence in the trial;

- (d) counsel for any party to the trial may agree upon a condition subject to which a matter is adduced in evidence at the trial;

- (e) the trial judge may determine any question of law arising, or which it is anticipated will arise, in the trial;

- (f) a party to the trial may admit a fact for purposes of the trial; and

- (g) the Court may take or allow to be taken any other step which, in its opinion, may properly be taken before the jury is sworn or before any evidence is tendered in the trial."

2.158   The Litigation Reform Commission are at present considering this recommendation along with other issues relating to the pre-trial stage.

Juries

2.159   Juries deliberate alone.

2.160   No attempt is made to ensure that juries reflect a racial balance in cases where that might seem appropriate. In June 1992, however, the

Criminal Code Review Committee recommended that the judge should have the power to discharge a jury that has been selected, if, in his or her opinion, the exercise of the rights of peremptory challenges has resulted in a jury whose composition is such that the trial might be or might appear to be unfair.

Trial

2.161   The trial judge technically has the power to call witnesses but in practice never does.

2.162   Opening speeches by the prosecution are permitted. One witness said that he "would consider it a grave dereliction of duty if a prosecutor did not open his case to the jury."

2.163   The judge's powers when summing up are the same as in England and Wales.

Previous convictions

2.164   The trial judge does not have before him the accused's prior convictions during the trial.

2.165   The rules relating to the admissibility of prior convictions are the same as in England and Wales.

Appeals

2.166   In the year 1990, guilty verdicts were returned in 463 cases. 46 defendants appealed against conviction alone. 16 were successful in getting their convictions quashed. 54 appealed against both conviction and sentence. Only 1 succeeded in having his appeal against conviction quashed.

2.167   Under section 668D of the Criminal Code, a person convicted on indictment may appeal to the Court of Appeal:

   (a)   against his conviction on any ground which involves a question of law alone; and

   (b)   with the leave of the Court, or upon the certificate of the judge of the court of trial that it is a fit case for appeal, against his conviction on any ground of appeal which involves a question of fact alone, or a question of mixed law and fact, or any other ground which appears to the Court to be sufficient ground of appeal; and

   (c)   with leave of the Court, against the sentence passed on conviction.

In practice, however, all conviction appeals are dealt with as though they are appealable as of right.

2.168   The appeal court cannot increase a sentence for unmeritorious appeals.

2.169   The appeal court does not consider that evidence which was available at the trial but not called by the defence is "fresh evidence".

2.170   The statutory formula that the appeal court must consider when deciding whether to quash a conviction is:

> "The Court on any such ground against conviction shall allow the appeal if it is of opinion that it is unreasonable, or cannot be supported having regard to the evidence, or that the judgment of the court of trial should be set aside on the ground of the wrong decision of any question of law, or that on any ground whatsoever there was a miscarriage of justice, and in any other case shall dismiss the appeal:
>
> Provided that the Court may, notwithstanding that it is of the opinion that the point or points raised by the appeal might be decided in favour of the appellant, dismiss the appeal if it considers that no substantial miscarriage of justice has actually occurred."

2.171   Appeals are allowed on the ground that the case was mishandled by the lawyers, but a successful appeal on this ground would be rare. The conduct of the lawyer would have to be gross.

2.172   It is common for a retrial to be ordered following the quashing of a conviction. The power to grant a retrial is a discretionary one and in deciding whether to exercise it the court that quashed the conviction must decide whether the interests of justice require a retrial. In so deciding, the court should first consider whether the admissible evidence given at the original trial was sufficiently cogent to justify a conviction, for it is said that if it were not, it would be wrong by making an order for a new trial to give the prosecution an opportunity to supplement a defective case. The court must also take into account that it might be unjust to the accused to make him stand trial again, remembering that the public interest in the proper administration of justice must be considered. No serious problems arise from the making of an order for a retrial.

2.173   A defendant can appeal only once to the Court of Appeal. An appeal can however be made with special leave on a question of law from the State Court of Appeal to the Australian High Court.

2.174   The Attorney General and the Director of Prosecutions have the power to refer "the whole case to the Court (of Criminal Appeal) and the case shall be heard and determined by the Court as in the case of an appeal by a person convicted." In such cases, no special rules are applied by the Court of Appeal.

2.175 There is no "Court of Last Resort".

Training

2.176 There is no formal training of judges.

The Fitzgerald Inquiry and the Criminal Justice Commission

2.177 Between 26 May and 29 June 1989 an inquiry (the "Fitzgerald" inquiry) was conducted in Queensland, initially into certain police practices and eventually into a much wider range of justice related issues. One consequence of the inquiry has been that the former Commissioner of Queensland Police Force was convicted of official corruption and sentenced to fourteen years imprisonment. A number of other senior police officers, former members of the legislative assembly and business persons have also been convicted of a range of criminal offences. The former Premier of Queensland also stood trial for alleged perjury, committed at the Fitzgerald hearings. After five days of deliberation a verdict was not forthcoming and the jury was discharged. There is to be no retrial.

2.178 The most significant consequence of the Fitzgerald inquiry was the creation of the Criminal Justice Commission. The aims and objectives of the Commission are as follows:

> "to conduct research into, and enhance public, parliamentary and forensic awareness of the issues confronting the administration of criminal justice in Queensland;
>
> to expose corruption and official misconduct through hearings and reports to Parliament;
>
> to provide evidence which leads to appropriate action being taken against persons engaged in corruption or misconduct (including official misconduct) before the courts, misconduct tribunals or other disciplinary proceedings;
>
> to provide evidence which leads to the prosecution of persons engaged in major or organised crime which cannot be effectively investigated by the Police Service or the agencies of the State;
>
> to reduce the incidence of misconduct, official misconduct and corruption in the Police Service and other units of public administration;

to upgrade the ability of the Police Service to tackle major and organised crime; and

to provide comprehensive and accurate intelligence briefings to law enforcement agencies, Parliament and the community on the state of major and organised crime."

2.179   The Commission currently consists of a number of organisational units, one of which is the Official Misconduct Division, which investigates official misconduct including misconduct by the police. The division has very wide powers of investigation. For example, it has the power to compel a person to furnish a statement of information or to give evidence before the Commission. Generally, however, the Commission has no role in the prosecution of the criminal offences investigated by the Commission beyond the preparation of a brief of evidence which then is handed over to the Director of Prosecutions.

E. SOUTH AUSTRALIA

Police investigations

2.180   Prior to 1985, the police had no power to detain a person for the purposes of interrogation, and a person arrested without a warrant had to be delivered forthwith into the custody of the officer in charge of the nearest police station and either released on bail or taken before a judge as soon as was possible.

2.181   Since 1985, where a person is arrested without warrant for a serious offence, the police may hold him or her for four hours. On application to a stipendiary magistrate the police may be granted an extension of this time up to a further four hours. In calculating the four hours, account must not be taken of any delays occasioned by the time spent waiting for the arrival of a solicitor or other person. A serious offence is an indictable offence punishable by imprisonment for two years or more. If the offence is not serious, there is no power to detain the suspect for questioning.

2.182   Before any questioning a suspect must be informed of his or her right to silence and his or her right to legal advice.

Evidence

2.183   There are no rules restricting the admissibility of confessions that have not been tape-recorded. However, a programme has commenced in South Australia to equip all metropolitan charging stations and the six major stations in the country region with video/audio units.

2.184   There is no requirement that confessions must be corroborated. However, the judge must warn the jury about the dangers of convicting where the only (or substantially the only) evidence against the accused is a confession, the making of which is not corroborated[18].

2.185   There is no rule requiring identification evidence to be corroborated. However, the judge must warn the jury in the strongest terms about the dangers of identification evidence.

2.186   Adverse inferences cannot be drawn from silence.

2.187   The court has a discretion to exclude illegally or improperly obtained evidence.

Prosecution

2.188   The police have their own prosecution branch who prosecute in summary cases and who sometimes, but by no means always, take part in the investigation process.

2.189   Crown prosecutors prosecute in judge and jury trials. It is rare for Crown prosecutors to take any part in directing investigations, except in cases of white collar crime.

Disclosure

2.190   Disclosure by the prosecution is normally done at the committal hearing, or often before it. If further witnesses are called at the trial, their proofs must be supplied to the defence. The prosecution must call all relevant witnesses, and if a failure causes a miscarriage of justice, the conviction may be quashed.[19]

2.191   The defence need only disclose evidence of alibis.

Expert evidence

2.192   Police instructions govern the collection of scientific evidence at the scene of the crime and from suspects.

2.193   There is no adequate system for ensuring that the defence have assistance from scientific experts. Some funding is given by legal aid for this purpose, but it is frequently inadequate. If the defendant cannot get legal aid, he can use the experts at the State Forensic Centre. However, this is

---

[18] *McKinney and Judge* (1991) 65 ALJR 241. See paragraph 2.8 above.
[19] see *Re Van Beelan* (1974) 9 SASR 163.

seen as unsatisfactory. There have been problems with defence access to forensic evidence in the past. In one particular murder case, *R. v. Splatt [1977]*, there was an almost total reliance on forensic evidence. A Royal Commission, established in 1982 to inquire into the conviction, determined that the additional scientific evidence presented to the Commission cast doubt on the jury's verdict as a whole. Accordingly, it determined that it would be unjust and dangerous to allow the verdict of guilty to stand and recommended that Mr Splatt be released.

2.194 The court has the power to commission expert evidence, but one witness wrote, "the power is rarely used in practice. Judges have an ingrained fear that they are descending into the arena if they do so."

Pre-trial procedures

2.195 One judge of the Court of Appeal and one judge of the District Court hold pre-trial conferences each month. That judge does not preside at the trial. One witness wrote, "it works well in excluding extraneous and peripheral material."

Statistics for detention in custody

2.196 In 1989, 1,309 out of 3,913 new prison admissions were on remand. The population of South Australia is approximately 1.5 million.

Juries

2.197 Juries deliberate alone.

2.198 No steps are taken at present to ensure that juries reflect a racial balance in cases where that seems appropriate. One witness wrote, "as South Australia is likely to have war crimes trials next year, some thought is being given to this but nothing so far has been done."

Trial

2.199 Judges do have the power to call witnesses, but it is rarely used in practice.

2.200 The prosecutor is allowed to make an opening speech.

2.201 The judge's powers when summing up are the same as in England and Wales.

Previous convictions

2.202 The judge does not have the accused's prior convictions before him or her during the trial.

2.203   The rules relating to the admissibility of previous convictions are virtually identical to those in England and Wales.

Appeals

2.204   Appeals are of right on a question of law, and by leave on a mixed question of law and fact. Leave is usually given if there is any reasonably arguable point. A judge can also grant a certificate to appeal but this is less frequently done.

2.205   If an appeal is frivolous, the court can direct that the sentence should not run pending the determination of the appeal.

2.206   The Appeal Court can consider evidence that was available at the trial but which was not called by the defence as "fresh evidence", but rarely does.

2.207   The Appeal Court can allow an appeal on the ground that the case had been mishandled by the lawyers, but those who had submitted evidence to the Commission were not aware of any instances of that happening in South Australia.

2.208   Retrials are common. A retrial is ordered unless it is obvious from the hearing that a retrial has no, or very little, hope of success. It is also possible to refuse a retrial because a retrial would be oppressive, but this is rarely done. One witness cited a case where a school teacher charged with molestation of a pupil was retried three times, but he says that this is rare. The same witness wrote, "a retrial mostly helps the Crown because the accused's defence is known and he will be taxed at the later trial with any variations in his testimony from that given at the earlier trial but neither of these considerations deters Courts in practice from ordering retrials."

2.209   Section 353 of the Criminal Law Consolidation Act provides that the Full Court "shall allow an appeal against conviction on the ground that it is unreasonable or cannot be supported having regard to the evidence, or ... on the ground of a wrong decision on any question of law, or that on any ground there was a miscarriage of justice". A witness wrote, "although section 353 does not say so in so many words, the Court assumes power to quash a conviction as unsafe or unsatisfactory in addition to the grounds listed in the section."

2.210   There can be only one appeal.

2.211   The Governor in Council can refer a case back to the Full Court for reconsideration after the dismissal of an appeal. However, this power is rarely used. If the Governor does refer a case back, the same rules apply as on an appeal by the defendant.

F. VICTORIA
Police investigations

2.212   The police may hold a suspect for questioning prior to charge for a "reasonable time". What constitutes a reasonable time depends upon the circumstances of each case and is to be determined by reference to criteria specified in section 464 of the Crimes Act 1958, as amended in 1988. These include the complexity of the matter; travelling time to the police station; the time taken to communicate with a friend or relative; the time taken for a solicitor to arrive; periods of rest.

2.213   The history leading up to the amendments of the Crimes Act in 1988 is of some interest. In 1983 a number of Victorian judges exercised their discretion to exclude confessions illegally or unfairly obtained, on the basis that the confessions took place after arrest and before the arrestee was taken before a justice, while section 460 of the Crimes Act required the arrested person to be taken before the court as soon as practicable. Accordingly, the courts found the confession evidence to have been obtained during a period of unlawful detention. This led the Attorney General to request that the Director of Public Prosecutions, Mr John Phillips QC, set up a committee to look at section 460 of the Crimes Act. This committee recommended that section 460 be amended so as to allow a suspect to be detained for questioning for six hours before being brought before a magistrate. This was done in 1984. The operation of the amended section was monitored carefully. The police found it unsatisfactory and requested an extension from six hours to twenty four hours. As a consequence the Attorney General then requested that the new Director of Public Prosecutions, Mr John Coldrey QC, examine the section again. The committee looked at the statistics, which indicated that 99.5% of all consensual interrogations and investigations were completed within six hours of the suspect being taken into custody. They accepted the police submission that the complex cases (often of the most public concern) were the ones most likely to fall outside the six hour limit. In the committee's opinion it was in the community's interest to enable the police legitimately to obtain evidence that would assist in the conviction of the guilty and they recommended the removal of specific time restraints and the substitution of the concept of reasonableness.

2.214   Under section 464C of the Crimes Act the police must inform a person in custody prior to any question or investigation that they may communicate with or attempt to communicate with a legal practitioner. Unless the police officer believes on reasonable grounds that the communication would result in the escape of an accomplice, the fabrication or destruction of evidence, or the questioning or investigation is so urgent having regard to the safety of other people that it should not be delayed, the police must defer the questioning and investigation for a time that is reasonable in the circumstances to enable the person to make, or attempt to make the communication. This is so regardless of whether the suspect is inside or outside the police station and regardless of the seriousness of the offence.

2.215   Persons should be informed of their right to silence prior to being asked any questions.

Evidence

(i) Confessions

2.216   In proceedings for an indictable offence, the Crimes Act 1958, as amended in 1988, lays down rules restricting the admissibility of confessions that have not been tape recorded. Section 464H provides:

(1) "Subject to sub-section (2), evidence of a confession or admission made to an investigating official by a person who –

    (a) was suspected; or

    (b) ought reasonably to have been suspected –

of having committed an offence is inadmissible as evidence against the person in proceedings for an indictable offence unless –

    (c) if the confession or admission was made before the commencement of questioning, the confession or admission was tape-recorded, or the substance of the confession or admission was confirmed by the person questioned and the confirmation was tape-recorded; or

    (d) if the confession or admission was made during questioning at the place where facilities were available to conduct an interview, the questioning and anything said by the person was tape-recorded; or

    (e) if the confession or admission was made during questioning at a place where facilities were not available to conduct an interview, the questioning and anything said by the person questioned was tape-recorded, or the substance of the confession or admission was confirmed by the person questioned and the confirmation was tape-recorded.

(2) A court may admit evidence of a confession or admission otherwise inadmissible by reason of sub-section (1) if the person seeking to adduce the evidence satisfies the court on the balance of probabilities that the circumstances –

(a) are exceptional; and

(b) justify the reception of the evidence."

2.217 Section 464H was one provision to emerge from the deliberations of the Coldrey Committee Report. The committee noted that "It would not be useful or possible to list the circumstances which might be taken into account under the exceptions provisions. However, one example would be the availability of an independent witness to the making of the statement and to whom the legislation did not apply. It would be for the Judges to decide whether in their judgement the circumstances were exceptional."

2.218 As regards how the section has been working in practice, there is a widely held view that section 464H has resulted in a material reduction in the number of disputed confessions, although there is no hard evidence on this point. One issue currently being addressed by the courts is the question of when an interrupted interview is really two interviews, with the effect that section 464H applies separately to both interviews. In *Pollard*[20] the Full Court of the Supreme Court of Victoria, held that the questioning of a suspect, which took place in two locations, only the latter location being equipped with tape facilities, may only be rendered inadmissible under the section if as a matter of fact the interview could be considered indivisible and consequently all of it should have been recorded. The Court decided that there was no reason to so find on the facts of this case. The case is presently on appeal to the Australian High Court.

2.219 The police are concerned that the courts are also rendering inadmissible confessions where there is additional conversational material which is not tape recorded, along with the formal record of interview. In a County Court decision, *R v Andersen and Andersen*[21], Judge Bland stated:

"The clear and unambiguous meaning of s.464H(1)(d) is that if a confession or admission is made during questioning at a place where

---

[20] 56 A Crim R 171.
[21] Unreported, 21 January, 1991.

tape recording facilities are available to conduct an interview, all of the questioning must be tape-recorded if any confession or admission said to have been made during the whole of that questioning is to be admitted into evidence."

2.220 A further practical issue is what should be the approach of investigators when commencing an investigation where there is the possibility, however slight, that the evidence of indictable matters might emerge. Section 464H only applies to indictable matters but what starts out as a summary investigation may reveal graver matters.

2.221 There have been very few cases in which the courts have admitted an untaped confession under section 464H(2). In *R v Faure*[22], the judge dismissed the prosecution's argument that confessions allegedly made during a telephone conversation were made in exceptional circumstances, since the conversations had been instigated by the accused and had occurred unexpectedly, making a tape recording impossible. The judge said that generally "the type of circumstances which may be regarded as exceptional could, it seems to me, include those where an unrecorded admission or confession may be attested to by an independent third party or, where a recording has proved impossible or has failed through technical difficulties, there exists an independent acknowledgement or adoption of any admissions or confessions in documentary form, or where both the Crown and the accused consent to material being placed before the Court, or where cross-examination by counsel for an accused person upon aspects of the prima facie excluded material makes the admission of it appropriate in the interests of balance. However, it is neither sensible nor profitable to seek to set out all the situations which require consideration."

2.222 The police view is that section 464H has solved old problems but created some new ones. Police officers are now less open to defence attack on the substance of their evidence and more likely to be questioned about the procedures followed in obtaining evidence. There is a perception that the law now discriminates between the obtaining of confessions and admissions by police officers and by other persons in the community, implying that police officers constitute unreliable witnesses as a class.

2.223 There is no requirement that confessions must be corroborated.

(ii) Identification evidence

2.224 There is no requirement that identification evidence has to be corroborated, although the judge should warn the jury about the dangers

---

[22] Unreported, 7 September, 1992.

of relying on identification evidence. However, no court has been prepared to hold that "the warning is mandatory in the sense that absence to adequately warn is ipso facto an error of law entitling a successful appeal".

(iii) *The accused's silence*

2.225   Neither the judge nor the prosecution may suggest at the trial that silence is evidence of guilt.

(iv) *Improperly obtained evidence*

2.226   The admissibility of illegally or improperly obtained evidence is in the discretion of the court.

Prosecution

2.227   The police charge the suspect and collect the evidence related to the case. The Director of Public Prosecutions has no powers of investigation, but may request the Chief Commissioner of police in writing for the assistance of the police in conducting necessary investigations in relation to any criminal proceedings under consideration by the office. The Director of Public Prosecutions also has the power to discontinue cases started by the police or to alter the charges laid.

2.228   The Director of Public Prosecutions is responsible for preparing, instituting and conducting criminal prosecutions and appeals on behalf of the Crown in the High Court of Australia, the Victorian Supreme Court, and the County Court. In certain situations the Director of Public Prosecutions may also get involved in proceedings before magistrates or coroners. The Director of Public Prosecutions is authorised to furnish general guidelines to Crown prosecutors, members of the police force and other persons with respect to the prosecution of offences.

Disclosure

2.229   If the case is subject to a committal by a magistrate, the prosecution is required to give all witness statements to the defence prior to the commencement of the committal. Any further evidence to be relied upon by the Crown at the trial must be provided to the defence at the time it becomes available. The general principle is that the accused should be given a fair trial and be aware of the details of the case which he or she is required to answer.

2.230   The prosecution is under a duty to reveal to the defence all relevant material, including that which it does not intend to use at the trial.

2.231   The defence need only disclose alibi evidence.

Expert evidence

2.232 There are no rules or procedures to ensure that scientific evidence taken from the scene of the crime or the suspect will be collected properly, apart from internal police procedures.

2.233 There is a power to take samples of blood, semen, fingernails, hair etc from the accused either with his consent or after obtaining a court order. These have to be examined in accordance with regulations laid down in the Crimes Act. Failure to comply with these regulations would result in the judge having to exercise his or her discretion whether in all the circumstances it would be fair to admit the evidence.

2.234 The defence must employ its own expert. In serious crimes the accused has legal aid and, while the facilities and finances are not as adequate as those available to the prosecution, in a serious case, where required, efforts would be made to have adequate forensic examinations available for the defence.

2.235 In Victoria, the body which handles most of the forensic science work for the prosecution is the State Forensic Laboratory. The Charter of this organisation permits it to undertake work on behalf of the defence, upon payment of the necessary fees. In practice, it is unusual for experts in this organisation to act both for the prosecution and the defence in any given case. The experts from this organisation are generally used by the defence in cases where they have not been involved in the collection and analysis of the evidence for the prosecution. There also exists the Department of Forensic Medicine, which took over the role of police surgeons, but has itself a much wider role. It provides forensic medical services not only to the Victoria Police, but to any persons concerned with the administration of justice and any person charged with a criminal offence or involved in a judicial inquiry. The Department aims to assist the administration of justice professionally and impartially. It promotes and conducts education and research programmes in clinical forensic medicine.

2.236 There are no formal systems for attempting to enable prosecution and defence experts to agree on their evidence before the trial.

2.237 There is no system for the court to commission an expert.

Statistics for detention in custody pre-trial

2.238 On 30 June 1990 the number of people in custody but not yet convicted in Victoria was 348, with the total in Australia being 1,781. On the same day the number of people awaiting sentence was 13, the total in

Australia being 114. The population of Victoria is approximately 4.3 million.

Juries

2.239   Juries deliberate alone.

2.240   No steps are taken to ensure racial balance in cases where that seems appropriate.

Trial

2.241   The judge does have the power to call witnesses. However, it is very seldom if ever used.

2.242   The prosecutor starts with an opening speech, in which he states often in detail the evidence which he intends to call.

2.243   The rules governing how a judge can sum up are the same as those in England and Wales.

Previous convictions

2.244   The judge does have the accused's prior convictions before him or her during the trial.

2.245   The rules governing the admissibility of prior convictions are in substance the same as those in England and Wales.

Appeal

2.246   In 1990 approximately 40% of defendants appealed against conviction in the higher courts. Approximately one third of these appeals were successful.

2.247   A person may appeal against conviction as of right on a question of law alone; on the certificate of the trial judge on any question which involves a question of fact or mixed fact and law; with leave of the Court of Criminal Appeal on any ground involving a question of fact alone or mixed law and fact or any other ground which the court considers would justify the adoption of this course (s.359A Crimes Act). However, one witness wrote that "the application for leave is treated as the hearing of the appeal so that in fact every person who wants to appeal can do so".

2.248   It is not a ground of appeal that the case was mishandled by the lawyers, but the Court may interfere in order to protect an accused from his or her own counsel, and from the result of bad management or misconduct in his or her case at the trial.[23]

2.249 Under section 574A of the Crimes Act, the Court of Criminal Appeal may allow the admission of new evidence upon appeal if it thinks it necessary or expedient in the interests of justice to do so. It does not matter that the new evidence is not "fresh evidence", in the sense that the latter means evidence that could not reasonably have been available to the accused at the trial.

2.250 It is common to order a retrial. The substitution of a verdict of acquittal is fairly rare. One witness wrote: "It is something we have learnt to live with, it is just regarded as normal and we find no difficulties with it".

2.251 The Court should allow an appeal if it thinks the verdict of the jury was "unreasonable and not supported by the evidence"; that there was a wrong decision of law; or there was a "miscarriage of justice".

2.252 A person can appeal to the Court of Appeal once and in rare cases a person may be granted special leave to appeal to the High Court.

2.253 There is a procedure for cases to be referred back to the Appeal Court by the Executive. In these cases the normal rules apply.

2.254 There is no equivalent of a "Court of Last Resort".

Training

2.255 Judges receive no formal training. Training takes place by means of seminars organised by the judges themselves as well as the Australian Institute of Judicial Administration. This may change, as Victoria has now passed legislation relating to the establishing of a Judicial Studies Board. But at present, if the problems of false confessions and the like have been addressed, it has been on an ad hoc basis.

2.256 Police recruits have twenty two hours of instruction over a nineteen week training course in matters relating to the collection of evidence, including the taking of witness statements and the problems of interviewing, confessional evidence and identification.

G. WESTERN AUSTRALIA

Police investigations

2.257 There is no power to detain a suspect for questioning prior to charge. Once a person is charged, the Bail Act requires that his or her case

---

[23] Re *Knowles* (1984) VR 851.

must be considered for bail as soon as practicable or the person must be brought before a court as soon as practicable. The case of *Williams* therefore still applies[24].

2.258 The requirement to inform the suspect of his or her right to silence is not cast as a duty but is a requirement under the Commissioner's (of Police) Guidelines for questioning suspects. It is delivered as part of the caution which is given when a police officer has decided to charge a suspect with an offence.

2.259 There is no duty to inform a suspect of his or her right to legal advice. Access to a telephone for the purpose of obtaining such advice is provided on request.

Evidence

2.260 There are no statutory rules restricting the admissibility of confessions. A trial judge must warn juries of the dangers of convicting where the only (or substantially the only) evidence against the accused is a confession statement, the making of which has not reliably been corroborated[25].

2.261 A two year trial project on the video recording of police interviews was carried out between May 1989 and April 1991. The findings of this project were considered by a monitoring committee which recommended in its final report that all police interviews in indictable cases should be video recorded. The Committee felt that this would "ensure that confidence in our criminal justice system, and the integrity of that system, is maintained".

2.262 Silence is not evidence of guilt.

2.263 The admissibility of illegally or improperly obtained evidence is in the discretion of the court. Two competing requirements of public policy must be weighed against each other. These are the desirable goals of bringing a wrongdoer to justice and the undesirable effect of approval, or even encouragement, being given by the court to the unlawful conduct of those whose task it is to enforce the law.

Prosecution

2.264 In indictable cases, the police charge offenders but crown law officers decide on the form of the subsequent indictment and prosecute the case. There is no power to direct or supervise inquiries. At summary level, police officers prosecute and crown law officers' involvement is minimal.

---

[24] See paragraph 2.2 above.
[25] *McKinney and Judge* (1991) 65 ALJR 241. See paragraph 2.8 above.

2.265   Under the Director of Public Prosecutions Act 1991, which came into force in February 1992, the Director of Public Prosecutions has the power to take over prosecutions.

Disclosure

2.266   In indictable offences, the defence have access to some prosecution evidence prior to committal proceedings. The prosecution are not required to provide all the evidence against an accused, only sufficient evidence to establish a prima facie case. In practice, the defence are more often than not provided with all the evidence.

2.267   There are no rules requiring the prosecution to permit the defence access to material which the prosecution do not intend to use.

2.268   The only disclosure requirement on the defence is that they must reveal evidence of an alibi in advance of the trial. In practice, medical evidence as to unsoundness of mind and automatism is also disclosed in advance so as to save unnecessary adjournments of the trial. In addition, there are now pre-arraignment hearings where the defence may reveal certain evidence, but there is no statutory requirement to do so.

Expert evidence

2.269   There are no specific rules to ensure that evidence at the scene of the crime is collected properly. Evidence is collected by scenes of crime officers from the police department. Internal training and procedures cover such matters as collection and storage.

2.270   The defence must employ their own experts. Legal aid is available for some defendants. Experts employed by the state cannot work for the defence, but will answer questions put to them by the defence.

2.271   There is no system for getting defence and prosecution experts to agree evidence before the trial.

2.272 There is no system for the court to commission expert evidence.

Pre-trial Procedures

2.273   There is no pre-trial procedure whereby the prosecution can question the accused in front of the judge.

Statistics for detention in custody pre-trial

2.274   Between July 1 1990 – June 30 1991 there were

(a) 1,970 defendants in custody not convicted

(b) 323 convicted awaiting sentence.

Juries

2.275   Juries deliberate alone.

2.276   No steps are taken to ensure racial balance in cases where that might seem appropriate. Amendments to the Juries Act have recently been made which, when they come in to force, will allow the prosecution and the accused the right to challenge peremptorily four jurors.

Trial

2.277   The judge has the power to call witnesses but the power is rarely used.

2.278   The prosecution can make an opening speech.

2.279   The judge's powers when summing up are the same as in England and Wales.

Previous convictions

2.280   The judge does have access to the accused's prior convictions during the trial if he or she wishes to look at them. They are usually supplied by the prosecution with the papers prior to the trial.

2.281   The law governing the admissibility of previous convictions is the same as that in England and Wales.

Appeals

2.282   The relevant provisions on appeals are to be found in the Criminal Code 1913. Under section 688 a person convicted on indictment can appeal to the Court of Appeal on any ground of appeal which involves a question of law alone and, with leave of the Court of Appeal or upon the certificate of the judge who tried him or her on any ground of appeal which involves a question of fact alone or mixed law and fact.

2.283   Where there is an appeal against conviction or an application is made to appeal against a sentence, the prisoner will generally be treated as a remand prisoner pending the outcome of the appeal. Under section 20 of the Criminal Code, the Court of Appeal may order that the time during which the prisoner has been so treated may count towards the service of the sentence. The Court will refuse to make an order where the appeal is hopeless.

2.284 Under section 689 the Court of Appeal should allow the appeal, if they think that the verdict of the jury should be set aside on the ground that it is unreasonable or cannot be supported having regard to the evidence, or there was a wrong decision of a question of law or there was on any ground a miscarriage of justice, with a proviso that the court, not withstanding that the point of the appeal might be decided in favour of the defendant, may dismiss the appeal if they consider that no substantial miscarriage of justice occurred.

2.285 Appeals are allowed on the grounds that the case was mishandled by the lawyers, if there has been a miscarriage of justice.

2.286 The rules as to when the Court of Appeal will consider fresh evidence are to be found in a number of High Court decisions[26].

2.287 The Court of Appeal can either quash the conviction or order a new trial. If they order a retrial, they can fix the time and place.

2.288 There can be only one appeal. However, after a consideration of any petition for the exercise of the Royal Prerogative, the Attorney General can refer a case to the Court of Appeal even if it has already been the subject of an appeal. It will then be decided as an ordinary appeal against a conviction.

2.289 There is no "Court of Last Resort". However, Royal Commissions and judges are sometimes appointed to investigate alleged miscarriages of justice, for example the Chamberlain case.

Training

2.290 Police training generally concentrates on the legal requirements to ensure the admissibility of evidence. The unreliability of some witnesses is a matter that receives mention within this context.

---

[26] For example, in *Gallagher* – see paragraph 2.35 above.

PART 3
BELGIUM

Police investigations

3.1   If the police catch someone in the act of committing a crime, they may hold the suspect for questioning for no more than twenty four hours. This period of time starts from the moment that the suspect is "arrested". The police officer who made the "arrest" must place the suspect immediately at the disposal of a senior police officer who will "arrest him officially". The senior police officer must inform the public prosecutor immediately of his or her decision. As from this moment, the public prosecutor decides on whether the suspect is to be kept in custody or not.

3.2   In a case where there are serious grounds for suspecting that someone has committed a crime, either a public prosecutor or an investigating judge must order his or her arrest. The duration of this arrest is also twenty four hours. Police officers in this case have only the power to take measures to prevent the suspect from running away.

3.3   In both cases, if the suspect has not been set free by the public prosecutor, the suspect must be taken before the investigating judge within twenty four hours. When deciding whether the suspect should be remanded in custody, the investigating judge should consider whether it is absolutely necessary for public safety and should have regard to the severity of the possible punishment.

3.4   Neither the police nor the investigating judge are under any duty to inform the suspect of his or her right to silence.

3.5   During interrogation by the police and the investigating magistrate the suspect has no right to consult a lawyer.

3.6   At the end of questioning by the investigating judge, the suspect must be informed of his or her right to choose a lawyer. If the suspect does not make a choice, the judge must inform the President of the Bar or his or her representative. If the defendant is without means to retain counsel, he or she has the right to free legal assistance. This assistance is usually given by junior members of the Bar, who are then compensated at what is said to be a very low rate by the Government.

Evidence

3.7 The law of evidence in Belgium is an example of a system of "free evidence". The judge is free to appreciate the intrinsic value and procedural significance of the evidence put forward by the prosecutor. However, one limitation on the judge's freedom to assess the evidence is that he or she may only take into account evidence which has been obtained in a lawful way.

3.8 There are no specific rules restricting the admissibility of confessions made to the police during interrogation. Confessions do not have to be corroborated.

3.9 The accused is presumed innocent and cannot be compelled to cooperate in an active way in his or her own condemnation. Silence is not considered evidence of guilt. The prosecution is obliged to prove its case beyond reasonable doubt.

Prosecution/pre-trial procedures

3.10 The pre-trial inquiry can be divided into two parts: the preliminary inquiry carried out by the police under the guidance of the prosecutor, on the one hand, and the judicial inquiry carried out by the investigating judge, usually at the request of the public prosecutor. These inquiries do not take place at the same time. They must take place in succession. Two inquiries do not take place in all cases. In most cases there is only a preliminary inquiry.

3.11 The police perform their investigative duties under the authority of the public prosecutor. As noted above, the police can only arrest a suspect when he or she is caught in the act of committing a crime. In other situations, the public prosecutor – and in the case of a judicial inquiry – the investigating judge direct and supervise the police. They will give very precise instructions to the police as to the tasks to be carried out.

3.12 Once the preliminary inquiry is finished, prosecutors have to decide on one of the following courses of action:

(i) if they are of the opinion that there are good reasons not to prosecute, they can dismiss the case.

(ii) they have the right to settle a case on payment of a sum of money. The sum is fixed by the prosecutor and can vary between 10 francs to the maximum fine that can be imposed for the offence in question. There are conditions on when the prosecutor can make such a settlement:

(a) there must have been complete compensation for the damage that has been caused;

(b) the criminal offence is one which is punishable with a fine and/or maximum five year prison sentence;

(c) the prosecutor is satisfied that, if the case did go to trial, he would recommend only a fine or a fine together with a seizure of goods.

(iii) they can decide that a prosecution should go ahead;

(iv) they can request that the investigating judge make a judicial inquiry. Generally they will only do this in cases that are serious and complicated and where they feel that the powers of the investigating judge are necessary.

3.13 In the case of a judicial inquiry, when the investigating judge comes to the conclusion that the inquiry is complete, he or she returns the dossier to the public prosecutor. If the prosecutor is of the opinion that further inquiries should be carried out, he or she can request that the investigating judge reopen the inquiry. When prosecutors are satisfied that the inquiry is complete, it is they, and not the investigating judge, who then decide whether the case should continue to trial.

3.14 When a prosecutor decides that the case should continue to trial, and the offence is either a contravention or a misdemeanour and there has been no judicial investigation, the case will then proceed directly to the trial court. In the case of serious offences, "crimes", and cases where there has been a judicial investigation, the case must be referred first to the Council Chamber, which is composed of one judge. The Council Chamber decides whether there is enough evidence to justify a prosecution; whether further investigations are necessary and, if the case is ready to go to trial, determines in which court the case is to be tried. The public prosecutor and the civil party have the right to appeal against decisions of the Council Chamber.

3.15 In cases where the Council chamber decides that the offence should be tried by an Assize Court, it refers the case to a special chamber of one of the Courts of Appeal. This Chamber must decide whether the evidence is strong enough to justify the charge. The Chamber must hear the accused. It has the power to order new inquiries. The accused can appeal against the decision of the Chamber to the Court of Cassation.

3.16 Before the trial in an Assize Court, the President of the Court must visit the accused. The President has a duty to interview the accused about the facts concerned, to ask if a defence lawyer has been chosen and, if not, assign one. The President must also inform the accused of the right to appeal against the decision of the Special Chamber.

3.17 No real empirical research has been done about the working relations between public prosecutors, investigating judges and the police. However, some parliamentary reports and research projects illustrate that these relations are not always that good. In some cases they were very poor.

Disclosure

3.18 Where a suspect is in custody, he or she has the right to inspect the dossier in the course of the investigation every time a judge has to decide upon the continuation of the detention. (This is after five days from the interrogation by the investigating judge and then at thirty day intervals.)

3.19 In any case the defence lawyer has the right of full access to the complete dossier after the summons for his or her client to appear in court has been issued. So that the defence can utilise this right, a period of ten days has to be observed between the issue of the summons and the beginning of the trial, or a period of three days if the suspect is detained in custody.

3.20 A basic assumption of Belgian criminal procedure is that every piece of evidence collected is incorporated into the dossier. However, there is no clearly stated right that the defence must have access to relevant but undisclosed material in the possession of the prosecutor. Nevertheless, if defence lawyers have reasonable grounds for supposing that such material is in the hands of the authorities, no rule prohibits them from asking the trial judge to order an inquiry into this question.

3.21 The defence are under no duty to make advance disclosure of the nature of their case.

Expert evidence

3.22 There are no rules to ensure that scientific evidence is collected in a proper way. The criminal justice system is totally dependent on the personal qualities of the police officers and experts concerned and on the practical arrangements within and between the police forces, the prosecutor/investigating judges and experts. Recently, in some notorious cases it was revealed that the collecting of evidence had been very poorly done, and as a result, the government has decided to invest more money in the staff, equipment etc. of police laboratories.

3.23 There is no official assistance to ensure that the defence have adequate assistance from forensic or scientific experts.

3.24   Experts are appointed by the investigating judge. The defence may suggest to the investigating judge that a certain expert be appointed or assist the judge's appointee or that certain investigations be carried out, but the judge is free to refuse. The defence may appoint their own experts.

3.25   There is no system for attempting to get the investigating and defence experts to agree on their evidence. In general the experts of the defence will make their comments to the investigating experts, who are free to take them into account or not. In practice, it is at the time of the trial that the report from the investigating experts will be criticised.

3.26   There is no system for the court to commission expert evidence either instead of, or in addition to, expert evidence commissioned by the investigating judge or the defence.

Detention pre-trial

3.27   The population of Belgium is approximately 10 million. In 1989, 7,997 people were detained in custody awaiting trial.

3.28   One witness estimated that there were at any one time approximately 3,000 people in custody who had been convicted but were awaiting sentence.

Courts/juries

3.29   There are three courts which try cases at first instance. The Police Courts are competent to try petty offences (contraventions). The Correctional Courts are competent to try misdemeanours. The Assize Courts are competent to try very serious offences, political crimes, and crimes and misdemeanours against the press code.

3.30   Juries sit only in the Assize Court. The Assize Courts are temporary courts. They are established on a case by case basis. They consist of a Court of Appeal judge, who is the President of the Court, two judges from the Correctional Court in the city where the tribunal is established, and a jury of twelve lay persons.

3.31   Jurors are drawn from the electoral list by lot. There are no provisions for the court to ensure that the jury is racially balanced. However, the accused can challenge six members of the proposed jury.

Trial

3.32   Before the trial the judge has the opportunity to read the dossier. At the trial the judge is responsible for calling and questioning the accused and the witnesses. The judge can decide which witnesses to call. The prosecutor, the defence and any civil party cannot directly question a witness. They can merely ask the judge if he or she is willing to ask the witnesses the questions they would like to be answered. In practice, witnesses are not called to give evidence at the trial. The court relies on the dossier containing statements taken by the police. However, in serious cases witnesses will be heard again.

3.33   In the Assize Court the prosecution lawyer will, at the opening of the trial, set out why he or she is requesting that the person charged be convicted and refer to the evidence in support. In the lower courts, he or she usually does this at the end of the hearing.

3.34   In the Assize Court, after the end of the trial, the President of the Court formulates the questions which the jury have to answer with "yes" or "no". It is not customary for the judge to sum up the facts for the jury. The judge is not permitted to make personal comments. The jury deliberates alone on the a question of guilt. However, if the accused is found guilty by the jury only by a simple majority, the judges deliberate among themselves on the same questions. If a majority of them do not agree with the majority of jurors, the accused must be acquitted. The jury decides together with the judges upon the penalty to apply when the accused has been pronounced guilty.

Previous convictions

3.35   Judges will have before them the accused's prior convictions. There are no specific rules about the admissibility of previous convictions. The dossier will contain the police record mentioning the previous convictions. The prosecutor may refer to them. It is up to the judge to determine the weight of this evidence.

Appeals

(i) Appeals from the Police and Correctional Courts

3.36   A defendant convicted in the Police Court can appeal to the Correctional Court. A defendant convicted in the Correctional Court can appeal to one of the five Courts of Appeal.

3.37   In 1988, 4,104 cases were brought before the Courts of Appeal. In 1,052 (25.6%) cases, the accused person was acquitted.

3.38   Appeals from both the Police and the Correctional Courts are of right. Leave is not required.

3.39   The appeal courts do not have power to discourage hopeless appeals.

3.40   Evidence which was available at the trial but not used can be invoked by the defence before the appeal courts.

3.41   The appeal courts are free to decide how to deal with the case. They can therefore decide that the appeal will take the form of a retrial (hearing witnesses) but in practice the court will examine the case on the basis of the existing file and the proceedings of the court of first instance.

3.42   There is no statutory formula for the appeal courts to apply before quashing a conviction.

3.43   A person may appeal only once. However, after the appeal courts, there is a special procedure before the Court of Cassation for recourse against a judge in cases of alleged miscarriages of justice. This court does not judge the facts of the case but is only concerned with the lawfulness of the decisions appealed against. If a decision is unlawful, the court can quash the decision and in some cases send the case for a retrial.

3.44   There is no procedure for cases to be referred back to the appeal courts by the Executive.

(ii) *Appeals from the Assize Court*

3.45   There is no appeal on the facts from the Assize Court. However, an appeal can be made on matters of law to the Court of Cassation, as above (paragraph 3.43).

Training

3.46   In the training of judges and police no special attention is given to the problems of false confessions, unreliable eye identification, bias of police officers, prosecutors, experts etc.

Reform

3.47   In 1985, in Belgium there was a number of attacks from left-wing terrorist groups. There was also a large number of armed robberies in supermarkets and banks. These were not cleared up by the police and the judiciary. This led to a great deal of public unrest and debate.

3.48   After two years, Parliament decided to establish a committee of inquiry to examine the way the criminal justice system was organised with a view to the fight against terrorism and banditry. In May 1990, this committee published a report very critical of the judiciary and criminal procedure (notably the pre-trial proceedings). In answer to this report the Government made public in June 1990 the "Whitsun-plan". This policy plan stated that further deliberations were necessary into issues relating to pre-trial proceedings. To this end the Minister of Justice set up, on 23 October 1991, a committee to examine several questions in relation to criminal procedure. The committee is composed of university professors, a public prosecutor, a defence lawyer and an investigating judge.

Part 4
Canada

Introduction

4.1 The Constitution Act 1867 (now included in the Constitution Act 1982) confers jurisdiction on the Parliament of Canada to enact legislation for criminal law and procedure. However, the ten provinces and two territories are delegated power to make their own laws for the administration of justice. They enforce the law, and are responsible for the establishment of law enforcement agencies, courts, and correctional institutions.

4.2 Canadian criminal law is governed by a Criminal Code which includes offences, defences and all procedural matters. Overriding this is the Canadian Charter of Rights and Freedoms (the Charter).

Police investigations

4.3 A person in police custody must be brought before a justice of the peace to be charged without unreasonable delay and in any event within twenty four hours after arrest. If a justice of the peace is not available within that time, then the suspect must be brought before a justice of the peace as soon as possible thereafter. The justice of the peace will then decide if the suspect should remain in custody or be released.

4.4 Suspects cannot be held for questioning unless they have been arrested. They do not need to attend the police premises unless arrested, and they are free to leave if they have voluntarily attended the police station. There is no statutory regime set out in the Criminal Code for the questioning of suspects, although the Law Reform Commission has proposed that the procedure which should be followed is codified.

4.5 The Charter states that "everyone has the right on arrest and detention to retain and instruct counsel without delay and to be informed of that right". Thus, the right to counsel arises on arrest or detention, and not only when the accused has been brought to a police station. The Supreme Court of Canada has held[1] that "detention" includes not only physical compulsion or coercion by the police but also psychological compulsion. However, circumstances may dictate that suspects cannot

---
[1] *R. v. Therens* (1985) 1 S.C.R. 6/3.

exercise their right to counsel until they are at the police station and a telephone is available. If the police do not tell suspects of their right to counsel or do not give them a reasonable opportunity to speak to counsel, any self-incriminatory evidence subsequently obtained will probably not be permitted into evidence (see paragraphs 4.13 below). The Court has also held that the police must advise the suspect of the existence of legal aid[2].

4.6 The Supreme Court of Canada has recently recognised that the right to silence is a basic tenet of the legal system and is protected by the Charter. The police do not have a duty to inform suspects of their right to remain silent. However, the courts are moving in a direction where that may soon be required. If the police do not inform suspects of their right to remain silent, that is a factor the trial judge may consider when determining the voluntariness of the statement.

Evidence

4.7 The fact that a confession has not been videotaped or repeated in front of a judge or magistrate does not in itself render the confession inadmissible, provided that the confession is otherwise admissible according to evidentiary or Charter rules. The Law Reform Commission of Canada has recommended videotaping procedures.

4.8 There is no rule saying that a prosecution cannot be commenced on the basis of an uncorroborated confession. Nor is it likely that such a rule will develop, for in recent years the Supreme Court of Canada has rejected what it refers to as the "ultra-technical approach to corroboration" taken in cases like *Baskerville*. In the absence of any mandatory legislative provision, the Court said that it should be a matter left to the common sense of the judge to determine in the particular circumstances of the case what, if any, warning should be given to the jury about uncorroborated evidence. Nevertheless, as a matter of prosecutorial discretion, it would be rare for the prosecution to commence a case if a confession were the only evidence linking the accused to the crime, for there would be nothing left to fall back on if for any reason the confession were held to be inadmissible, or its weight were rendered nugatory.

4.9 In Canada, the admissibility of confessions is governed by common law voluntariness requirements and Charter guarantees, as fleshed out in constitutional jurisprudence. By reason of the Charter, the use of unfair police practices to obtain a confession can render the confession inadmissible as evidence (e.g. using an undercover police officer placed in an accused's cell to solicit incriminating statements from an accused violates

---

[2] *R. v. Brydges* (1990) 1 S.C.R. 190.

the accused's right to silence[3]). In addition, the Young Offenders Act 1985 sets out a statutory regime for the admissibility of confessions of young suspects in Canada.

4.10   Where the confession is made before a number of officers, the Supreme Court of Canada has held that the statement should not be admitted unless, in the absence of some adequate reason for their absence, those who were present are produced by the prosecution as witnesses. However, recent cases suggest a trend away from this rigid rule.

4.11   In cases involving identification evidence, there is a very strong warning given by the trial judge to the jury about the unreliability of eye witness identification evidence. However, a trier of fact is entitled to convict on the evidence of one eye witness.

4.12   The prosecution is not permitted to lead evidence or cross-examine an accused about the failure of an accused to answer questions, unless the accused's silence or the late raising of a defence becomes a material issue in the case, as it may do in certain circumstances such as alibi defences.

4.13   The Charter (section 24) provides that where a court concludes that evidence was obtained in a manner that infringed or denied any rights or freedoms guaranteed by the Charter, the evidence shall be excluded if it is established that, having regard to all the circumstances, the admission of it in the proceedings would bring the administration of justice into disrepute. Thus, if evidence is obtained that breaches a legal right of the Charter and that also violates the standard set out in section 24, the judge is constitutionally required to exclude the evidence. The seriousness of the violation is relevant on an application to admit the evidence in spite of the Charter breach.

Prosecution

4.14   The relationship between the powers of the prosecution service vis-à-vis the police is a complex one, given the constitutional division of powers that exists in Canada between the federal government and the provinces and territories. There is no single Attorney General, but instead a federal Minister of Justice who is ex officio Attorney General of Canada. In each province there is a provincial Attorney General. Most criminal cases are prosecuted by agents of the provincial Attorneys General. Agents for the Attorney General of Canada prosecute criminal cases in the territories and non Criminal Code offences (e.g. narcotic cases) throughout Canada. Agents of the provincial Attorneys General can also prosecute such cases in

---

[3] *R. v. Hebert* (1990) 2 S.C.R. 151.

their provinces. Responsibility for the police falls under the charge of a different minister – the Solicitor General of Canada, or the Solicitor General of a province.

4.15   As a general rule, the police have the responsibility to investigate the crime and to lay the charge, although the involvement of the prosecutor is required if investigative techniques, such as wiretaps, special search warrants, or restraint orders, are needed. Prosecutors have responsibility for the preparation of a case after a charge has been laid, and have the power to withdraw or stay proceedings. A minority of provinces (e.g. British Columbia) have instituted procedures for the pre-screening of charges by prosecutors. There the prosecutors do not direct the police investigation. However, it is common for the police to consult with the prosecution on serious matters.

Disclosure

4.16   At present there is no statutory formulation in the Criminal Code fully setting out the extent to which the defence is entitled to disclosure of the prosecution's evidence, so that the issue is one that has had to be determined largely by case law.

4.17   The Supreme Court of Canada has interpreted section 7 of the Charter so as generally to require the prosecution to disclose all relevant material to the defence, even if the prosecution does not intend to use it, in order to ensure that an accused may make full answer and defence. The duty includes disclosure of all statements obtained from persons who have provided relevant information to the authorities, whether they aid the prosecution or the defence, and whether or not the prosecution propose to call the person as a witness. There must also be disclosure of the indictment, the accused's statement, and copies of all medical and laboratory reports which relate to the offence. The initial disclosure should occur before the preliminary inquiry and if material comes to light after that, it should be disclosed as it becomes available.

4.18   The prosecution has a discretion not to disclose certain information – for example, information which is privileged or contains the name of an informer. This limitation should be used only when there is a real need to protect the integrity of the prosecution, including the need to prevent the endangerment of the life or safety of witnesses, their intimidation or harassment, or to prevent other interference with the administration of justice. This decision not to disclose is reviewable by the trial judge.

4.19   The prosecution does not have the ability to order the police to deliver up all of the material they have in their possession, except by a court order.

4.20   There is no duty placed on the defence to make advance disclosure to the prosecution of the nature of the defence, although, in cases where the defence is one of alibi, the defence must raise it at an early opportunity or risk unfavourable comment by the judge. Also, the longer the delay in raising the defence the less likely it is that the defence will be believed by the judge or jury.

Expert evidence

4.21   The Criminal Code sets out the statutory scheme by which anything seized should be brought before a justice of the peace or in special circumstances a judge of a superior court of criminal jurisdiction. The court, on determining that the property is required for an investigation or a trial, can order any item to be detained, and order that reasonable care must be taken so that the evidence is preserved until the conclusion of any proceedings. The court is allowed, on the request of the accused or prosecutor, to order the release of an exhibit for scientific tests or examinations. The release is subject to terms that are necessary to safeguard and preserve the exhibit for use at the trial. The Law Reform Commission has proposed a comprehensive scheme for obtaining forensic evidence, and for the collection and safeguarding of evidence that is seized.

4.22   There are standard practices that the police follow to collect forensic evidence. In drinking and driving cases where blood samples are taken, there is legislation which prescribes "approved containers" and the procedure that must be followed by doctors taking the blood and how the blood is to be preserved.

4.23   There are no systems to ensure that the defence have adequate assistance from forensic or scientific experts. They are, however, entitled to have material tested by their own experts. In British Columbia, prosecution forensic experts often conduct tests on behalf of the defence.

4.24   Expert evidence will be one of the issues discussed at a "pre-hearing conference" (see paragraph 4.29 below).

4.25   Counsel for the prosecution and defence may make "Admissions of Fact" which are drafted in writing and are often tendered in trials to dispense with the necessity of calling the expert. This is sometimes done less formally by simply orally admitting the evidence.

4.26   Expert witnesses are usually called by the prosecution and the defence respectively. The judge has the power to call expert witnesses, but the power is rarely used. The Law Commission in a report on evidence in 1975 recommended that this power should be retained and proposed codification of the power. This is set out in section 73 of the report. The section provides that the judge may, if he considers it desirable, appoint an independent expert, who should, if possible, be a person agreed upon by the parties. The judge should give the independent expert instructions regarding his duties, and the expert should inform the judge and parties in writing of his opinion. The expert may be called to testify by the judge or any party, and be subject to examination by any party. The expert would be entitled to reasonable compensation for his work.

Pre-trial procedures

4.27   If the accused testifies at a bail hearing, he or she can be questioned by the prosecutor, although the prosecutor is prohibited from asking questions about the commission of the alleged crime itself.

4.28   There is a preliminary hearing for indictable offences, similar to committal proceedings in England and Wales. However, in all cases, the prosecution calls sufficient witnesses to prove a prima facie case and the defence are entitled to cross-examine these witnesses. The defence are also entitled to call witnesses if they so choose, although this is seldom done in practice. The preliminary hearing can last six–eight months in some cases. The preliminary hearing has become a discovery device and it is not necessarily appropriate in every case.

4.29   A recent amendment to the Criminal Code now creates a formal process called the "pre-hearing conference". Section 625.1 provides:

> (1) "subject to subsection (2), on application by the prosecutor or the accused or on its own motion, the court before which or the judge, provincial court judge or justice before whom, any proceedings are to be held may, with the consent of the prosecutor and the accused, order that a conference between the prosecutor and the accused or counsel for the accused, to be presided over by the court, judge, provincial court judge or justice, be held prior to the proceedings to consider such matters as will promote a fair and expeditious hearing;
>
> (2) in any case to be tried with a jury, a judge of the court before which the accused is to be tried shall, prior to the trial, order that a conference between the prosecutor and the accused or counsel for the accused to be held in accordance with the rules of court made under section 482 to consider such matters as will promote a fair and expeditious trial."

The Ministry of Justice state that they have received no criticisms to date about the section and state that in practice it is working well.

Statistics for detention in custody

Table
Number of Persons Charged for Federal Statute Offences, Number of Admissions and Persons to Provincial Prisons on Remand

Adults

Year	Number of persons charged	Number of remand admissions	Average number of persons in custody
1986	436,003	67,638	3,287
1987	458,952	72,638	3,557
1988	467,172	81,847	3,986
1989	473,401	83,947	4,495
1990	489,679	92,008	4,174

Youths (aged 12 to 17)

Year	Number of persons charged	Average number of persons in custody
1986	113,026	685
1987	111,731	682
1988	114,017	738
1989	120,231	813
1990	130,782	814

4.30 The total population of Canada on January 1, 1990 was 26,440,300.

Juries

4.31 The jury deliberates alone. Jury deliberations are in secret and it is an offence for a juror to disclose the substance of the deliberations. No verdict can be rendered unless it is the result of a unanimous decision of the jury.

4.32 Under present law, there is no requirement that a jury reflect a particular racial balance, although the whole area of the access to justice and more equitable treatment for Aboriginal and multicultural groups is under review (see paragraphs 4.62 – 4.66 below).

4.33 In some judicial districts of Quebec, an accused may move to be tried by a jury composed entirely of jurors who speak the language of the accused, if that language is English or French.

4.34 The defendant has the right to elect to be tried by a judge without a jury in most indictable offences. However, the Attorney General has the power to require a trial by jury. In certain specific offences an election to non-jury trial requires the consent of the Attorney General.

Trial

4.35   While a judge has an undoubted power to call witnesses, the power is one that normally should not have to be exercised. The test applied is whether this course is necessary in the interests of justice. When there is a dispute between the prosecution and the defence over the calling of a witness, the judge may call the witness in order to permit each party to cross-examine him or her.

4.36   The prosecutor is allowed to start the trial with an opening address. In a trial before a jury, prosecutors invariably open to the jury by outlining the evidence that they intend to call. If the matter is before the trial judge alone, the prosecutor may deliver an opening address, but it is not necessary except in a lengthy or complex case.

4.37   In the summing up judges must advise jurors that they are bound to accept directions on the law, but that all issues of fact, including credibility of the witnesses, are theirs, and only theirs, to determine. Judges must explain the relevant law in a manner sufficient to enable the jury to apply it to the particular facts of the case. Judges must assist juries in determination of the facts by reviewing the evidence and by relating the evidence to the issues and to the law. They must explain the respective theories of the prosecution and of the defence. Although judges may express their own opinion on matters of credibility or evidence, they must clearly leave the matter to the jury for its own determination. Any comments from the judge should be indirect and dispassionate.

Previous convictions

4.38   To avoid an apprehension of bias, prior convictions of an accused should be placed before the trial judge only after it is held that they are admissible in evidence. There are some specific statutory provisions dealing with the introduction of prior convictions. If the accused gives evidence, the prosecution may cross-examine the accused on his or her prior criminal record for the sole purpose of attacking the accused's credibility. The trial judge has a discretion whether or not to permit the prosecution to cross-examine on the criminal record and whether or not to permit the prosecution to cross-examine on all of the offences or just those relevant to credibility. If a co-accused testifies, then the prior convictions of the other co-accused cannot be admitted unless he or she testifies as well.

4.39   The Criminal Code allows the introduction of a person's prior conviction for theft or possession of property obtained from crime where, within a five year period of that conviction, there are further criminal proceedings commenced against that person for possession of property obtained from crime, or possession of stolen mail. In this case, the prior conviction may be taken into account for the purpose of proving that the accused knew that the property that formed the subject matter of the later proceedings was unlawfully obtained.

4.40   The Criminal Code states that "where, at a trial, the accused adduces evidence of his good character, the prosecutor may, in answer thereto, before a verdict is returned, adduce evidence of the previous convictions of the accused for any offences, including any previous conviction by reason of which a greater punishment may be imposed".

4.41   Prior convictions are admissible where there is a striking similarity between the facts of cases (similar fact evidence rule).

Appeals

Appeals against conviction

4.42   Of the defendants who appeal to the higher court, approximately 30% are successful.

4.43   The Criminal Code sets out the following procedures for appeals against conviction. First, a person appealing against his or her conviction on the basis of a question of law alone may appeal as of right. Secondly, a person appealing against conviction on a question of fact or a question of mixed law and fact must obtain the leave of the Court of Appeal or a judge of that court, or obtain the certificate of the trial judge that the case is a proper one for appeal. The latter procedure is seldom used. In many provinces there is no separate leave process. The leave application and the appeal are heard together.

4.44   After the Court of Appeal, there is a further appeal to the Supreme Court of Canada, with leave, for questions of law alone. There is an appeal as of right if one of the Court of Appeal judges dissents on a question of law or if there was an acquittal at trial which is reversed by the Court of Appeal. The Supreme Court of Canada favours abolition of some appeals as of right in which the Court of Appeal orders a new trial. Leave applications to the Supreme Court of Canada are in writing only. An oral hearing may be ordered by the Court. A Notice of Appeal may be filed only after leave is granted.

4.45   When a convicted person launches an appeal against sentence the Court of Appeal has jurisdiction to increase the sentence. The practice of the Court of Appeal is not to increase the sentence unless the prosecution gives notice that it is seeking that the sentence be increased. This happens most often where there is an illegal sentence imposed. The Court of Appeal does not have jurisdiction to increase a sentence where the appeal is against a conviction.

4.46   In the Criminal Code there is provision for the summary dismissal of frivolous appeals on a question of law alone. There is also a provision concerning release while an appeal against conviction or an appeal to the Supreme Court of Canada is pending. It requires the appellant to establish, among other grounds, that the appeal or application for leave to appeal is not frivolous.

4.47   Evidence, in order to be admitted as fresh evidence at an appeal, must:-

(i)   not have been able to be adduced at trial, by exercising due diligence, provided that this general principle will not be applied as strictly in a criminal case as in a civil case;

(ii) be relevant in the sense that it bears upon a decisive or potentially decisive issue in the trial;

(iii) be credible in the sense that it is reasonably capable of belief; and

(iv) be such that if believed it could reasonably, when taken with the other evidence adduced at trial, be expected to have affected the result.

4.48   It is clear from the case law that an absence of due diligence is not an absolute bar to the introduction of fresh evidence. In *McMartin v. The Queen*[4] it was stated "in all the circumstances, if the evidence is considered to be of sufficient strength that it might reasonably affect the verdict of the jury, it should not be excluded on the ground that reasonable diligence was not exercised to obtain it at or before trial". There must be a balancing of factors in all the circumstances to ascertain whether justice requires the evidence to be excluded or not.

4.49   The Criminal Code provides that the Court of Appeal may allow an appeal against conviction where it is of the opinion that:

(i)   the verdict should be set aside on the ground that it is unreasonable or cannot be supported by the evidence;

---

[4] (1964) S.C.R. 484.

(ii) the judgment of the trial court should be set aside on the ground of a wrong decision of a question of law; or

(iii) on any ground there was a miscarriage of justice.

4.50   It is common for the Court of Appeal to order a retrial where the trial judge has made an error of law. The only time an acquittal is entered is if the verdict was unreasonable or not supported by the evidence. There do not seem to be serious problems with retrials, except that the defence is entitled to argue that the right to a trial without unreasonable delay has been breached, a safeguard which is enforced by the Charter. However, this is rare. Often the Crown do not proceed with a retrial, particularly if the accused has already served the sentence.

4.51   If, on the facts of the case, the accused's counsel was flagrantly incompetent in his or her handling of the defence, the Appeal Court may allow the appeal. However, this incompetence is not, in itself, a specific ground of appeal. It would instead fall under the ground of appeal of a miscarriage of justice.

4.52   The Court of Appeal may uphold the conviction even though there is an error of law or procedural irregularity where there is no substantial wrong or miscarriage of justice. The test on this ground is whether or not the verdict would necessarily be the same had the error not occurred.

4.53   There is a procedure for cases to be referred back to the Appeal Court by the Executive. Section 690 of the Criminal Code provides that the federal Minister of Justice may, upon an application for the mercy of the Crown on behalf of a person who has been convicted in proceedings by indictment: (a) direct, by order in writing, a new trial before any court that he or she thinks proper; (b) refer the matter at any time to the Court of Appeal for hearing and determination by that court as if it were an appeal by the convicted person; or (c) refer to the Court of Appeal at any time, for its opinion, any question on which he or she desires the assistance of that court, and the court shall furnish its opinion accordingly. At the subsequent hearing the normal evidentiary and procedural rules are generally followed.

4.54   There are no set rules for the procedure to be followed when the Minister of Justice receives an allegation of a wrongful conviction. As a matter of practice, the Ministry of Justice conducts an investigation and makes a report to the Minister with recommendations for action. When an application is incomplete, the Ministry makes a written request to the applicant for information relating to the issues raised by the applicant. In many instances no reply is received to this letter, and the departmental investigation goes no further. If a reply containing some substantiating evidence in support of the allegation is received, a departmental lawyer is designated to look into the complaint. This lawyer carries out an investigation in much the same way as a *"juge d'instruction"* would in France, gathering information and taking evidence on oath before a court reporter. The departmental lawyer does not, however, have the power to compel any person to appear and testify. Matters not before the trial court are taken into account and the Ministry expect to be given full co-operation by an applicant including the waiver of client/lawyer professional privilege for access to defending counsel whom the officials will interview. The defendant does not receive legal aid.

4.55   Following the investigation, a report is prepared for the Minister, setting out the findings, making a recommendation and giving reasons for the recommendation. Successive Ministers of Justice have granted a remedy where there is a reasonable basis to conclude that a miscarriage of justice was likely to have occurred in a case. In many cases a remedy is granted when significant new evidence is discovered that calls into question the correctness of the verdict. Previously, the departmental report to the Minister was not provided to the applicant. The practice that is now emerging is to disclose the evidentiary findings to the applicant. However, the departmental analysis and recommendations, and information that was obtained exclusively in confidence, is not disclosed to the applicant. The recommendation is almost always accepted by the Minister of Justice, although in some instances a request for further particulars has been made before a decision is made. In 1991, 30 – 40 applications were made to the Minister of Justice and two applicants obtained relief. The Minister referred one case to a provincial Court of Appeal, and granted a new trial in another case after receiving the advice of the Supreme Court of Canada.

4.56   Where it is ultimately found that there was a wrongful conviction, compensation can be awarded in appropriate cases in order to relieve the consequences of the wrongful conviction and subsequent imprisonment.

4.57   The Ministry of Justice is currently reviewing section 690 of the Criminal Code. A Royal Commission was set up after the case of *Donald Marshall Jr*. This case involved a man who spent eleven years in prison for a murder before evidence was discovered which showed that he had not committed the crime. The Commission recommended that the Minister of Justice of Canada and other provincial Attorneys General discuss whether an independent review mechanism ought to be created to facilitate reinvestigations of alleged cases of wrongful conviction. A more recent case, *Milgaard*, which involved a man who had been in prison for twenty three years resulted in intense media coverage that questioned the ability of the present system to review cases of potential miscarriages of justice. Some critics have said that the system is too closed to scrutiny and that the position of the Minister of Justice as both chief prosecutor and reviewer of cases is untenable.

4.58 There are various kinds of pardons but the main distinction lies between pardons provided for by statute and pardons arising from the exercise of the Royal Prerogative of Mercy. Pardons granted under the Royal Prerogative may be granted on compassionate grounds unrelated to any statutory criteria. The Criminal Code of Canada authorises the Governor in Council to grant either a free or conditional pardon, or a remission of fine or forfeiture. These powers do not limit or affect the exercise of the Royal Prerogative of Mercy. In addition, the Criminal Records Act provides relief for rehabilitated convicts who may apply for a pardon. The grant of this type of pardon effects a sealing of the record of conviction (but unlike a free pardon does not quash the conviction).

Appeals against acquittals

4.59 Appeals against acquittals have been available since the 1930s. In indictable proceedings, under section 676 of the Criminal Code the Attorney General may appeal against an acquittal (or the quashing of an indictment, a stay of proceedings or a refusal to exercise jurisdiction on an indictment) to the Court of Appeal on any ground of appeal that involves a question of law alone. Leave to appeal is not required. Under section 691 of the Criminal Code, the decision of the Court of Appeal in indictable proceedings can be further appealed to the Supreme Court of Canada:

(a) on any question of law on which a judge of the Court of Appeal dissents; or

(b) on any question of law, if leave to appeal is granted by the Supreme Court of Canada. Leave is granted sparingly, and used only in instances raising points of law which are of clear significance to the nation.

Training

4.60 The National Judicial Institute has a mandate to foster a high standard of judicial performance through programmes that stimulate continuing professional and personal growth, and engender a high sense of social awareness, ethical sensitivity and pride of excellence. It has offered seminars on criminal procedure and evidence to all judges which include such topics as testimony of a witness, and confessions and admissions.

4.61 Under the Judges Act, the conduct of federally appointed judges can be reviewed.

Aboriginal justice

4.62 In addition to proposing reform of section 691 of the Criminal Code the Royal Commission on the Prosecution of Donald Marshall Jr. (see paragraph 4.57 above) also provided the spark that generated several subsequent inquiries, commissions and studies which have examined the deficiencies in the relationship between the Canadian Aboriginal community and the criminal justice system. In Manitoba, a Justice Inquiry produced a comprehensive report on Aboriginal issues. In 1990, the Task Force on the Criminal Justice System was established to complete a review of the criminal justice system in Alberta as it related to Indian and Metis people. In 1991, the Government of Canada, the Saskatchewan Department of Justice and regional Aboriginal associations established justice review committees to consider recommendations relating to the delivery of criminal justice services to Saskatchewan Indian and Metis people and communities. The Indian and Metis Justice Review Committees recommended a number of practical, community-based initiatives in areas of youth justice, policing, corrections and the courts. In Quebec, a justice summit resulted in a travelling commission chaired by Judge Jean-Charles Coutou which will explore ways that the administration of justice can be modified to meet the needs of Aboriginal people more effectively. In British Columbia, the Sarich Inquiry is currently in the process of hearing evidence from Aboriginal people on issues relevant to policing services and the broader aspects of the administration of justice.

4.63 In June 1990, the Minister of Justice asked the Law Reform Commission of Canada to examine the extent to which the Criminal Code and related statutes ensured Aboriginal people had equal access to justice and were treated equitably by the legal profession. The Commission proposed a number of reforms focusing on the development of new approaches to the administration of justice.

4.64 In September 1991, the federal and Yukon governments jointly sponsored a National Conference in Whitehorse to identify priorities and to develop a practical agenda for Aboriginal justice reform. During the Whitehorse Conference, the federal Minister of Justice announced the establishment of a new initiative to improve the administration of justice as it affects Aboriginal people. The Aboriginal Justice Initiative was provided with $26.4 million over five years to develop policies and programmes which recognise greater Aboriginal responsibility for justice administration. The initiative is based on a tripartite approach involving Aboriginal people, the Government of Canada and provincial and territorial governments. The Aboriginal Justice Initiative provides support and assistance to local justice initiatives and projects developed by Aboriginal communities themselves.

4.65   In June 1991, a First Nations Policing Policy was announced with the aim of improving the level and quality of policing services in the Aboriginal communities and establishing greater involvement by Aboriginal people in the administration of policing services. In April 1992, a new Aboriginal Policing Directorate was established to be responsible for implementation of the First Nations Policing Policy, and to support and research into off-reserve Aboriginal policing issues flowing from the Aboriginal Justice Initiative.

4.66   In 1991 the Government of Canada established the Royal Commission on Aboriginal People. The Royal Commission has a broad mandate. Justice is one of the central issues at which the Commission will be looking.

Part 5
Denmark

Police investigations

5.1   The police must bring a suspect before a court within twenty four hours after the arrest has been made. In serious cases, the court can decide to uphold the arrest for a further seventy two hours.

5.2   As soon as possible after an arrest the police must inform suspects of the charge and their right to silence. Before questioning suspects, the police must inform the person again that they are not obliged to answer questions apart from giving their name, address and date of birth.

5.3   Before questioning, the police must tell the suspect of his or her right to legal advice.

5.4   In 1986 studies based on interviews amongst 147 prisoners found that around 75% of suspects knew that they had the right to have their lawyer present during the police questioning, but only 50% had been informed about this right by the police and only 20% requested that their lawyer should be present during police questioning. According to Mr Preben Wilhjelm, a former member of the Danish Parliament who carried out the study, these figures are probably not representative. It is his opinion that the right to have a lawyer present during police questioning is not used to this extent.

5.5   Persons charged with a crime have the right to choose their own lawyer and if they do not do so, a lawyer will be appointed for them in serious cases. Suspects must be informed that if they are convicted, they must pay the costs of their lawyer.

Evidence

5.6   It is a fundamental principle of evidence that a court must have firsthand evidence, which means that the parties, witnesses and expert witnesses must testify directly, before it passes judgment in the case.

5.7   This principle acquires a particular importance in relation to the issue of using police reports as part of the evidence. It is a controversial question whether evidence given by the accused or by witnesses to the police prior to court proceedings may, or should, be used during such proceedings as part of the production of evidence.

5.8   In practice, however, the general rule is that the person concerned is confronted with such evidence during the trial and there is a tendency to attach not insignificant weight to police reports.

5.9   A confession must be corroborated by other information on the matter.

5.10   Silence cannot be used as evidence of guilt.

5.11   The courts have a discretion to admit improperly or illegally obtained evidence. However, they tend in practice to be prepared to admit such evidence rather than exclude it. In deciding whether to exclude the evidence, the court will take into account the gravity of the illegally or improperly obtained evidence in relation to the nature and the gravity of the crime.

Prosecution

5.12   Investigations are carried out by the police, who as a matter of form are subject to the prosecuting authority's instruction. The prosecution has the power to instruct, direct and supervise police investigations. However, in practice, except for special financial crimes, the police investigation is generally carried out without interference from the public prosecutor. In some cases, the police may need to ask for the assistance of the court in order to carry out specific acts during the investigation. The police prepare reports regarding the individual steps of the investigation.

5.13   Although in practice prosecutors are not directly involved in the investigation, they are bound to be objective and have the power to discontinue cases started by the police and to alter the charges.

5.14   Prosecution of offences takes place through the Attorney General. The structure of the prosecution authority is hierarchical. The *"Rigsadvokaten"* (Attorney General), a civil servant, is assisted by a number of *"Statsadvokater"* (district attorneys); they generally decide whether a charge is preferred in criminal cases and carry out the office of public prosecutor in the High Court. The district attorneys are in turn superior to the chiefs of police and their assistants, who act as the representatives of the public prosecution office at the preliminary stages of the cases and often perform the office of public prosecutor during the trial before a lower court.

5.15   In principle the hierarchy of the prosecution authority is subordinate to the Minister of Justice who is entitled to make decisions regarding prosecution in individual cases. In practice this is a very rare phenomenon. Supervision is exercised by issuing regulations of a very general nature.

5.16   In certain petty cases the injured person has the right to bring his or her claim before the court.

Disclosure

5.17   Counsel for the defence have the right to acquaint themselves with the material produced by the police, even though the material has not yet been produced in court.

5.18   Counsel for the defence may, however, not give copies to the defendant, but unless otherwise ordered by the court the counsel for the defence may freely discuss the material with the defendant.

5.19   The defence have the right to see relevant material in the possession of the prosecution which the prosecution do not intend to use. A request to see all relevant material will normally be met. As mentioned above, the prosecution are bound to be objective and if counsel for the defence fears that the police or prosecution will not reveal material, counsel can ask the court to order such revelation.

5.20   The defence are under a duty to make advance disclosure to the prosecution of the evidence they intend to call at the trial. Evidence may be used at the trial, however, even though the defence have failed to comply with the rules on advance disclosure. If necessary the court will postpone the trial. There are no sanctions imposed on defendants for failing to comply with the disclosure obligations. However, if the noncompliance is due to the negligence or wilful behaviour on the part of the lawyer, the court has the right to dismiss the lawyer from the case and the lawyer may be liable to a fine. In practice, defence lawyers comply with the rules. One witness wrote: "to my knowledge, there is no precedent of a court dismissing a lawyer from the case due to noncompliance with the disclosure rules".

Expert evidence

5.21   There are no statutory rules ensuring that evidence from the scene of the crime or from suspects themselves will be collected properly. Scientific evidence is normally taken by the technical departments under the police and the reports may be produced in court. Questions to the technical department are normally put forward in a neutral way. It is therefore not possible to identify the defendant or the matter, except by reference numbers.

5.22   Experts employed by or on behalf of the state are in practice able to work also for the defence, and the defence have the right to ask the prosecution and/or experts employed by or on behalf of the state to carry out further investigations. The defence can also carry out their own investigations, although this is extremely rare. The defence can apply to the judge for such assistance to be paid for by the state. The medico-legal institute and the medico-legal council are to a great extent independent institutions and may serve the defence as well as the prosecution.

5.23   There is no system for attempting to get the prosecution and defence to agree their evidence.

5.24   The court is entitled to commission expert evidence in addition to evidence commissioned by the parties. The court will either commission the expert itself or request the prosecution to do this. In practice, this opportunity is rarely used.

Pre-trial procedures

5.25   There is no pre-trial procedure whereby the accused is obliged to submit to examination or to co-operate actively in any way in the elucidation of the case. He or she is furthermore under no obligation to meet with police for questioning. However, if the accused refuses, the police may have him or her summoned for questioning in court.

Detention pre-trial

5.26   Official figures for detention in custody are:

1986: 5,074
1987: 5,512
1988: 5,989
1989: 5,665
1990: 5,296

The witness who sent in the figures wrote: "the majority is without doubt suspects who have not yet been convicted but it is not possible to distinguish between those not yet convicted and those convicted but not sentenced".

5.27   The population of Denmark is 5.2 million.

Juries

5.28   In the lower court cases are heard by one legal judge and, apart from police prosecutions and cases where a full confession has been made, two lay judges. In the High Court, when it sits as an appeal court for cases from the lower court, three legal judges and, apart from police prosecutions, three lay judges hear the cases.

5.29   In graver cases, more particularly cases of homicide, rape, robbery and certain political crimes etc., the High Court acts as a Court of First Instance. The legal element consists of three High Court judges sitting with a jury composed of twelve jurors.

5.30   The jury deliberates alone, but may summon the presiding judge and have him or her answer any points which might arise during their consideration on which they are doubtful.

5.31   The courts have no power to seek to adjust the composition of the jury. No measures are taken to ensure that the jury reflects a racial mix. When the jury is appointed, the public prosecutor and the defendant have a right to excuse two jurors each without stating any grounds.

Trial

5.32   If a suspect confesses (i.e. pleads guilty), the case can be dealt with in a more summary fashion than if he or she does not. However, certain conditions must be fulfilled. The accused must make a full confession regarding all aspects of the statutory violation before the court. The confession must be supported by other information. The accused as well as the prosecuting authority and the court must agree to the summary procedure being applied. The summary procedure can be applied in all cases coming under the jurisdiction of the district attorney, regardless of the scope of the case and the size of the possible sanction. The effects of summary procedures are that the case is dealt with without the participation of lay judges at first instance. The prosecuting authority is the chief constable instead of the district attorney, the phrasing of the indictment is somewhat simplified, there is no actual trial and the production of evidence is normally considerably limited.

5.33   In other cases, the procedure is as follows. After the indictment has been read out in court, the prosecution is allowed to start the trial with an opening speech stating the evidence that he or she intends to call.

5.34   The judge has the power to call witnesses, but rarely does so in practice.

5.35   The indictment is in an interrogative manner, which enables the jurors to decide all issues regarding the guilt of the accused, including the issue of mitigating circumstances, if any, by answering "yes" or "no". Once the questions have been framed, the presiding judge briefly reviews the case and the evidence presented and also outlines the legal principles to be applied in answering the questions.

5.36   The summary of facts must be strictly objective. However, the judge is permitted to comment on the evidence, provided he or she makes it clear to the jury that questions of fact are ultimately for the jury to decide.

5.37   The judge in the lower court where there is no jury must state in the judgment the premises on which he or she bases or substantiates the result reached.

Previous convictions

5.38   The legal judge has the accused's previous convictions before him or her, but the lay judges and the jury do not.

5.39   Prior convictions are generally only of relevance after conviction for sentencing. They are not normally admissible in evidence during the trial as evidence of guilt unless there is a striking similarity between the facts of the cases.

Appeals

5.40   There is no right of appeal in some petty cases which result only in a fine.

Appeals from the lower court

5.41   Appeal is of right from the lower courts to the High Court. When the High Court sits as a court of appeal, it sits with three legal judges and three lay judges.

5.42   The High Court as a court of appeal can act either as a "revising appeal", in which case it reviews only procedural errors and errors in application of the Criminal Code, or a complete appeal, in which case it tries the whole case anew and assesses the evidence produced. In the latter case the prosecution and defence have the right to submit new evidence and call new witnesses for the purposes of the appeal.

5.43   The High Court as a court of appeal can either give its own judgment on the substance of the case, or it may cancel the judgment under appeal and refer the case to a retrial before the lower court. Where the issue under appeal is one of erroneous application of rules of procedure at the lower court, the Court of Appeal normally quashes the judgment and refers the case to the lower court, unless the error committed can be disregarded as having had no concrete bearing on the case. There is a tendency not to cancel decisions because of a minor flaw.

5.44   There is no statutory formula that the Court of Appeal must apply when deciding whether to quash the appeal.

5.45   It is a principle of Danish law that normally it should only be possible to have a case tried at two levels. However, there are exceptions. One is that the Minister of Justice may grant a special petition for bringing a case before the Supreme Court as a court of third instance where there is a general interest in the case or where it has far reaching consequences for the accused.

5.46   The Supreme Court cannot consider any issue of evidence. It is always limited to a revising appeal.

Appeals from High Court when it acts as a court of first instance

5.47   In cases which come before the High Court as a court of first instance with the participation of jurors, i.e. in cases of homicide, rape, robbery and certain political crimes, the decision regarding guilt is final. There can be an appeal to the Supreme Court on a matter of procedure or law but the Supreme Court cannot consider any issue of evidence.

5.48   There is no procedure for cases being referred back to either the High Court or Supreme Court by the Executive.

"Court of Last Resort"

5.49   There exists something similar to a "Court of Last Resort", called the Court of Revision, which passes judgment on petitions for the resumption of criminal cases. In such cases a Supreme Court judge, a High Court judge, a lower court judge, a counsel for the defence and a university professor sit on the bench. The reconsideration of a case may be decided by the Court not only where new relevant evidence has been produced, but also where there are special circumstances indicating that the available evidence has not been properly assessed. This provision is based upon the fact that the assessment of evidence is not subject to examination by the Supreme Court. It has, therefore, been found desirable to provide an exceptional opportunity to set aside the assessment of the evidence by the High Court which cannot otherwise be challenged. The provision has been rarely used, but is of preventive importance against any tendencies on the part of the courts to weaken the requirements of evidence in criminal cases. It provides an additional legal protection to the individual citizen against erroneous decisions.

Training

5.50 Judges are trained throughout their professional career as civil servants, whether as assistant prosecutors or assistant judges.

5.51 Police have special training at the Police College, which includes issues of false confessions, unreliable eye witness testimony, etc.

Recent changes

5.52 Following a judgment by the the European Court of Human Rights in 1989, legislation has been introduced which provides that a judge who has ruled on pre-trial custody cannot act as trial judge in the same case.

PART 6
FRANCE

Introduction

6.1 Offences under French law are divided into three categories:

(1) Minor offences (*contraventions*);

(2) Major offences (*délits*);

(3) Grave offences (*crimes*).

6.2 Minor offences are heard in the Police Court (*Tribunal de Police*). Major offences are heard in the Correctional Court (*Tribunal Correctionnel*). Grave offences are heard in the Assize Court (*Cour D'Assises*), following a preliminary hearing in a division of the Appeal Court (*Chambre d'Accusation*). A system exists for transferring some grave offences to the Correctional Court (*correctionalisation*).

6.3 The investigation process differs depending on the category of the offence. All grave offences and major offences which are discovered at the time of commission or shortly afterwards (*délits flagrants*) are investigated under a serious crime enquiry (*l'enquête flagrante*). Minor offences and major offences discovered some time after the event come under a preliminary enquiry (*l'enquête préliminaire*).

6.4 In all serious crime enquiries the prosecutor should be informed immediately. However, it is only for grave offences that the examining magistrate (*juge d'instruction*) must be involved at some stage. For other offences the magistrate is called in at the discretion of the prosecutor if he or she needs the wider powers that would be available.

Police investigations

6.5 A suspect, or witness, may be held by the police for questioning under the *garde à vue* system. The detention must be authorised by a senior officer and it must last for no more than twenty four hours. This period can be extended for a further twenty four hours on the written authority of the public prosecutor or the examining magistrate (who up to this stage need not have seen the detainee). In drug trafficking cases, this period can be extended in the same way for a further seventy two hours and in terrorist cases for a further forty eight hours.

6.6 Under the French Penal Code, during the *garde à vue* there is no right to the assistance of a lawyer or contact with the suspect's family. There is, however, a right to demand a medical examination. The police are not under any duty to inform suspects of their right to silence. Suspects are not informed of this right until the first appearance before the examining magistrate.

6.7 At the end of *garde à vue*, suspects must be brought before the prosecutor who must decide whether:

(i) to abandon the proceedings and to set the suspect free;

(ii) to summon them to appear at court at a later date;

(iii) to order, in the case of a major offence where enquiries are completed, the suspect to appear before the Correctional Court for trial the same day;

(iv) to order in the case of a grave offence, or of a major offence where enquiries are not yet completed, the suspect to be remanded in custody to appear before the examining magistrate, who will then decide upon further detention.

Evidence

6.8 There are no rules restricting the admissibility of confessions made during a *garde à vue* but not repeated in front of an examining magistrate. However, they do not have the same solemn force as an admission made before the examining magistrate. The weight to be accorded to them is for the ultimate determination of the court. The tape recording of interviews is not required.

6.9 It is a principle of French law that guilt may not be based on a confession unless that confession, however voluntarily made, is supported by corroborative evidence. There is no such requirement for identification evidence, but it is up to the judge to warn of the danger of relying on identification evidence.

6.10 There is a right to silence before the police or an examining magistrate, but silence can be commented upon at the trial and therefore could count against the accused.

6.11 The court will not admit evidence obtained unfairly or improperly.

Prosecution/pre-trial procedure

6.12 The French system is one in which investigations are conducted by the police under the authority and control either of a prosecutor or an examining magistrate, depending upon the type and gravity of the case and the stage which the investigation has reached. "Control" does not signify minute direction by a superior, but rather oversight and answerability.

6.13 The prosecutor cannot issue direct orders to the police. The prosecutor merely gives advice, directions and instructions (failure to follow which would probably lead to disciplinary action against the officer concerned). Usually the police perform the investigative function, using their own powers, subject to scrutiny after the event. Hence they enjoy a considerable degree of autonomy. There is said to be a generally good relationship between the various actors in the system.

6.14 If the case is one of *crime* or *délit flagrant* (*enquête flagrante*) the prosecutor should by law be involved at once, but usually they simply authorise the reporting police to proceed until there is good reason to confide the investigation to other hands. In serious crime enquiries (*enquête flagrante*), the prosecutors' powers are wide. If called upon, they can authorise the seizure of certain items, authorise arrest and detention under the *garde à vue* procedure, and interrogate suspects and witnesses. They supervise police work, including checking some of their records (in particular they scrutinise the police record of all persons detained in custody). They also have the power to discontinue cases started by the police and to alter the charges. Their powers are much more limited in a preliminary enquiry (*enquête preliminaire*).

6.15 In the case of *crime* for which there must be an examination by the examining magistrate the law does not specify a time at which he or she must be seised of the case. In any event, he or she must be brought in before the case can go for trial.

6.16 The examining magistrate is obliged, upon requisition, to assume responsibility for the investigation. If an examining magistrate cannot perform certain acts in person, he or she empowers the police to do so by *commission rogatoire*. The police are then allowed to act only to the extent authorised expressly by such a *commission*.

6.17 The enquiry which follows is not only into the circumstances of the offence, but also into the personality and circumstances of the offender. It inquires into innocence as well as guilt. The examining magistrate can compel witnesses for questioning. The prosecutor and defence lawyer may be present when the witness is questioned (except for the first interview), but may themselves only pose questions with the permission of the examining magistrate. Only the magistrate has the power to order searches of dwellings and to intercept communications, and he or she can order a report from an expert witness.

6.18 In cases of *crime*, when examining magistrates have finished their work, they must send the file to the Chief Prosecutor, who will then start proceedings in a division of the Appeal Court (*Chambre d'Accusation*). The Court has a duty to consider the evidence in detail and consider whether charges should be dismissed or the case sent to trial at the Assize Court. The *Chambre d'Accusation* sits with three judges. The hearings are in private.

6.19 The victim may initiate legal proceedings either by presenting the case directly to the court (*citation directe*) or by constituting himself or herself as a *partie civile* before the examining magistrate, who will investigate the case and refer it to the court.

6.20 For a detailed study of the pre-trial phase, see Professor Leigh's and Doctor Zedner's report on the pre-trial phase in France and Germany[1].

Disclosure

6.21 During the pre-trial enquiries the prosecutor (and the examining magistrate if involved) compile a file (*dossier*) of all the relevant material in the case. The defence has access to this file two working days before a hearing or questioning.

6.22 It is up to the defence to ask a judge for any other relevant material that is required from the police or other body.

6.23 The defence are under no duty to make advance disclosure to the prosecution of the nature of the defence or of the evidence to be called by them. They are free to use any strategy they like, including surprise, but all witnesses have to be designated at the start of the trial.

6.24 When an examining magistrate is appointed, however, it is in the accused's best interest for the defence to disclose any evidence which would work in their favour. The courts are reluctant to take into consideration any evidence which was not disclosed before the end of the investigation. In some cases the prosecutor may ask for a delay of the trial in order to prepare an answer.

Expert evidence

6.25 To ensure that scientific evidence is collected properly, all relevant material seized by the police will be shown to the people who have

---

[1] Royal Commission on Criminal Justice, Research Study No. 1, London, HMSO, 1992.

apparently participated in the crime (if they are present). This material will then be sealed, and a report compiled of these operations. The police can order that technical investigations take place. In a serious case, where forensic tests of some difficulty have to be undertaken, the prosecutor would involve the magistrate, who would then commission a forensic examination. The results of that examination occupy a higher footing, from an evidential point of view, than does the technical investigation commissioned by the police themselves. The magistrate must chose the expert from an official list.

6.26 A report commissioned by an examining magistrate is a report to the magistrate as judge and is paid for by the State. It is therefore a report in the case rather than a report for the prosecution or the defence. The examining magistrate can commission up to three experts and the results of their deliberations will be contained in one report unless the experts are in fundamental disagreement. The report of the expert(s) appointed by the magistrate is included in the file seen by all the parties.

6.27 The official expert's conclusions may be challenged by the parties in four ways:

(i) the parties can request that the magistrate instruct the expert to carry out particular tests, or hear any particular person who seems able to give them technical information. If the prosecutor makes such a request and it is refused, there is a right of appeal. If the defendant's request is refused, there is no such right.

(ii) when the expert completes his or her report, it must be shown to the parties and if the parties are dissatisfied with it, they have a right to ask the magistrate to require the expert to do more tests or provide further information, or appoint another expert. At this point either side can appeal against a refusal, but in practice such requests are usually granted.

(iii) at trial the expert can be examined.

(iv) the defence can bring their own expert to the trial. However, this is not very common for three reasons. First, legal aid is not available for experts. Secondly, the private expert is not allowed access to the exhibits. Thirdly, a private expert called to supported the theory of one party will be considered by the court to be biased.

Statistics for detention in custody

6.28 The population of France in the 1990 census was 56,614,493.

6.29 **Prison statistics (6 December 1991)**

Total prison population	51,169
Number convicted	29,781
Number not yet convicted	21,389

6.30 There are no prisoners waiting for sentence, as sentences are announced immediately after guilty verdicts.

Juries

6.31 Juries are only used in the Assize Court, which hears grave offences. Here nine jurors deliberate with three judges on guilt and sentence. There must be a majority of eight if the defendant is to be convicted. While they are deliberating, jurors are encouraged to ask the judges questions and express their opinions.

6.32 Jurors are drawn by lot from the electoral registers. They must be French citizens aged between 23 and 69 who are able to read and write. The defence has the right to challenge up to five citizens called by the President of the Court to be a member of the jury. The prosecution can also challenge the choice of up to four citizens. There are no other measures to achieve a particular racial balance.

Trial

6.33 The trial is under the control of the President of the Court. He starts the trial. There is no legal right for the prosecutor to start with an opening speech. Defendants are questioned first about their background and criminal record. They are then allowed to state their account of the facts. They are then questioned by the President. When the President is finished, the prosecutor can ask more questions. The defendant's lawyer can suggest questions, but cannot put questions directly to the defendant. Jurors can also ask questions with the President's permission. All the other witnesses are then called in the order chosen by the President. The witnesses are questioned by the President and then by the prosecutor and the defence lawyer. The President can call further witnesses if he or she wishes.

6.34 At the end of the trial the prosecutor makes a speech and then the defence lawyer does the same. In the Assize Court, the President then sums up for the jury on the facts, but he or she is not allowed to express any opinion on the evidence. The issues put to the jury are usually set out in the form of a number of questions.

Prior convictions

6.35 The trial judges have before them during the trial the prior convictions, together with all the facts concerning the background and personal life history of the accused.

6.36   All these facts are made known to the whole court before it reaches its judgment.

Appeals

6.37   There are two appeal courts. The Supreme Court of Appeal (*Cour de Cassation*) deals only with questions of law and procedure. The Court of Appeal (*Cour d'Appel*) will rehear the cases.

6.38   The Court of Appeal can only hear appeals from the Correctional Court or the Police Court (not from the Assize Court). There is no appeal against a finding of fact by the Assize Court. No leave is required for an appeal to the Court of Appeal, but there is a time limit of ten days to lodge the appeal. The prosecution may also appeal within two months of the trial. There is a further appeal from this court on purely legal grounds to the Supreme Court, which can refer the case back to the Court of Appeal. An appeal can also be made to the Supreme Court from the Assize Court on a point of law. Notice of the appeal must be given within five days. One of the judges of the Supreme Court will decide if the case is admissible.

6.39   In the Court of Appeal the accused cannot have his sentence increased as a result of his own appeal, but almost always the prosecutor will counter-appeal and so allow the court complete freedom on the sentence. The Supreme Court has no power to increase sentence, but can order a re-trial.

6.40   Mishandling of a case by the lawyers is not a recognised ground for appeal.

6.41   Any appeal to the Court of Appeal takes the form of a retrial. However, the Court of Appeal is not obliged to hear oral evidence and usually rules on the basis of the file, court record and submissions from the lawyers. The Supreme Court does not consider questions of fact. It considers only questions of law and procedure. The Supreme Court can either:

   (i)   refuse the appeal; or

   (ii) accept the appeal but rule that it was a mistake so small that the original judgment should be allowed to stand; or

   (iii) accept the appeal and order a retrial with different judges.

6.42   The statutory formula that the Court of Appeal applies when deciding whether to quash a verdict of the trial court is "*Par ces motifs, statuant contradictoirement, reçoit l'appel regulier en la forme, au fond, infirmant le jugement entrepris"*.

6.43   A person may not appeal more than once.

6.44   There is a system for reviewing cases when the normal appeal procedures have been exhausted. There are four grounds for review of a conviction: (1) when after a conviction for murder, the victim is discovered still to be alive; (2) when someone else is convicted of the same crime and the two convictions cannot be reconciled; (3) when a witness at the trial is convicted of perjury against the convicted person; and (4) when a new fact is discovered that might cause a doubt as to the convicted person's guilt. If a case falls under these heads then the convicted person, his or her family or heirs can write to a Commission of the Supreme Court citing one of these grounds. The Minister of Justice can also refer a case to the Commission. There is no limit to the number of times a review can be requested.

6.45   The Commission is composed of five judges from the Supreme Court, with five surrogates. It acts as a sort of examining magistrate and after consideration of the file can decide either to refer the case back to the Court of Appeal, or find no grounds for referral, or decide that further investigation by the Commission itself is needed (which may include the calling of witnesses etc.) before a decision can be reached. The discussions of the Commission are not public, but its decisions are, and are communicated to the convicted person.

6.46   If the case goes to the Court of Appeal it can overturn the conviction (with the possibility of damages), order a new trial, or decide that there are no grounds to review the sentence.

Training

6.47   The *École de la Police* and the *École Nationale de la Magistrature* teach police officers and judges to deal with problems of false confessions, bias etc. Police officers have to sit an examination and show that they have attained a minimum level of legal knowledge.

Reform

6.48   Criminal procedure in France has been very much under review. In particular, there is concern about the *garde à vue system*. The defendant's rights are not thought to be sufficiently protected. Also, the role of the *juge d'instruction* has been criticised. *Juges* are thought to have too much power. They are often young (usually between 28 and 35) and inexperienced and therefore thought to be easily influenced. The fact that the *juge* is both in charge of the investigation and responsible for making decisions regarding pre-trial detention has been a cause for concern. The figure for those held in pre-trial detention in France is allegedly high compared to other European countries.

6.49 The report of the *Commission Justice Pénale Et Droits De L'Homme* (1990) concluded that the *juge d'instruction* should be divested of his investigative powers in favour of the prosecutor but should retain power over such jurisdictional matters as detention before trial. This recommendation was not accepted by the government. However, the government has made proposals for reform which came into effect on 1st January, 1993. These include:

(i) with regard to the *garde à vue*, it is proposed that the criteria for holding a suspect in police custody should be clarified and made more specific. The police must notify the prosecutor or *juge d'instruction* as soon as the suspect is taken into custody so that the judicial authorities can exercise stricter supervision. In future, witnesses will not be held in custody except in cases involving terrorism or drugs;

(ii) as regards detention before trial, the *juge d'instruction* will no longer make such decisions alone. The case will be referred to a review commission consisting of three judges, one of whom will be the *juge d'instruction*. The decisions of this new review body will be open to appeal to a division of the Court of Appeal;

(iii) to avoid a *juge* being exposed in terrorism or organised crime cases to pressure or to threats and to accelerate the instruction process in more complex cases, the President of the High Court will be able to nominate up to three *juges* to oversee the instruction of one case. The *juges* will then operate as a team. It is also felt that this will facilitate the training of young *juges*;

(iv) in the course of the instruction, both the defence and the *partie civile* will have the right to call for certain investigatory measures, in particular the examination of witnesses and reports by experts. The *juge* will not be able to reject such a demand without a ruling giving reasons which will be open to appeal.

Part 7
Germany

Police investigations

7.1   Officially a judicial warrant is required if someone is to be arrested. However, the police can make an arrest "provisionally" without a warrant if they suspect a person of having committed a criminal offence. In both cases, the suspect must be brought before a judge without delay, at the latest the day after the arrest.

7.2   Suspects must be given an arrest warrant that informs them of what they have been charged with.

7.3   At the start of the first examination by the police, suspects must be informed that they have the right to refuse to answer any questions and to remain silent. It is illegal to hold suspects who rely on their right of silence in order to persuade them to change their minds and reply to questions.

7.4   At the start of the first examination by the police, suspects should be informed that they have the right to consult a lawyer at any stage in the proceedings and to speak with him or her privately. However, lawyers have no right to be present at the police interview (unlike interviews with the public prosecutor or judge), but they can be admitted at the discretion of the police and suspects are free to declare that they will only make a statement in the presence of their defence counsel. There is no right to counsel free of charge at this stage.

7.5   The above rights apply irrespective of the seriousness of the offence.

Evidence

7.6   The courts in Germany are not bound by "rules of evidence". There is free evaluation of evidence.

7.7   There is therefore no rule requiring the corroboration of confessions or identification evidence. The admissibility of confessions at trial does not depend on their being tape-recorded or repeated in front of a judge. However, there is a distinction between confessions made in front of a judge and those made to police officers or prosecutors: while transcripts of the former can be recited as evidence at the trial, the latter can be introduced only by hearing the interrogating officer as a witness.

7.8   Silence at the police station cannot be used as evidence of guilt.

7.9   Confessions and witnesses' statements obtained by force, deception, threats and similar illicit means are not admissible, not even with the defendant's consent. Other illegally obtained evidence is not subject to statutory rules but is admissible in the discretion of the court. The state's interest in clearing up an offence has to be weighed against the individual's interest in preserving his or her legal rights.

Prosecution/pre-trial procedures

7.10   According to the Code of Criminal Procedure (StPO), the public prosecutor conducts the investigation after the police have done what was immediately necessary to secure evidence after the commission of an offence. The prosecutor can use the assistance of the police, who are regarded as the prosecutor's "auxiliary officers". The prosecutor can request the police to conduct further inquiries and can interrogate defendants, witnesses and experts.

7.11   However, in recent years there has been a shift of operational responsibility from the prosecutor to the police. In practice, the overwhelming majority of cases are processed independently by the police and not presented to the Public Prosecutor's Office until after the investigations have been concluded. The Prosecutor's Office then merely decides whether to discontinue the proceedings or to file charges.

7.12   The prosecutor is not meant to be "partial". He or she must not compile one-sided incriminating evidence against the accused, but must also ascertain exonerating circumstances. The public prosecutor may also make use of appeal procedures in favour of the accused and apply to have the proceedings reopened with the aim of acquitting the convicted person.

7.13   During the pre-trial phase the prosecutor may interview all the witnesses, both those going to innocence and guilt. The prosecutor can insist that witnesses be examined before a judge. It is open to the defence to invite the prosecutor to interview witnesses valuable to the defence case, or to ask the prosecutor to have witnesses interviewed by the judge.

7.14   Interrogation of the defendant by the police, prosecutor or judge can take place at any time during the pre-trial phase. The defendant's lawyer has the right to be present at interviews by the prosecutor and judge, but not at police interviews. The prosecutor will request that the defendant be interrogated in front of a judge only in exceptional circumstances. The prime purpose of judicial examination of the accused is to obtain a record of a confession which can be read out in court. (See paragraph 7.7 above).

7.15 The investigation stage is terminated by the prosecutor deciding whether to prosecute or not. The right of a prosecutor to refuse to prosecute is much more limited in Germany than it is in England and Wales. If the investigation discloses sufficient evidence to justify prosecution, the prosecutor must prosecute. This duty exists to avoid inequality before the law and discrepancies in prosecution policies. However, there are some exceptions to this duty to prosecute. The prosecutor need not prosecute where the offence is trivial, the culpability of the offender is minimal, and there is no public interest in a prosecution (s.153 of StPO), nor where the public interest can be satisfied in an other way (e.g. by payment of compensation or payment to charitable organisations or community work) (s. 153a of StPO). In both cases the court must give its consent, which in practice it generally does, withholding it in only the most extreme cases. In a case where conditions are imposed under s.153a, the consent of the offender is required. This procedure is seen very much as a "deal" between the prosecutor and defence lawyer. If the defendant complies with the condition, the prosecution is terminated. The payment of the sum of money etc. is not a punishment in the technical sense. One commentator has written, "in practice more affluent offenders take advantage of this procedure to avoid full trial. Termination under s.153a is frequently used in cases of substantial economic offences. There is also a danger that an innocent accused might choose this procedure in order to avoid full trial."

7.16 As soon as the prosecutor considers that there is sufficient evidence to proceed and there is no reason to discontinue the prosecution, he or she must consider whether the case is suitable for a full trial or whether it can be disposed of by a penal order or by an expedited procedure. A full trial is always held in serious cases. An expedited procedure is provided for in simple cases before Local Courts, in which it is possible to give an immediate verdict and no pre-trial procedure is necessary. The maximum penalty that can be imposed is 1 year's imprisonment. This procedure is rarely used in practice. The penal order procedure allows the prosecutor to apply to the court for a penal order to be made against the defendant. There is no trial and there is no need to hear the accused. The court need not be convinced that the defendant committed the crime. Mere reasonable suspicion that he or she has committed the offence is enough. The sentence imposed in this procedure can be a fine, disqualification from driving for up to two years or conditional discharge. Unlike the settlements under s.153a of the StPO, the penal order is a criminal order. The defendant can appeal against a penal order. An appeal has to be filed within fourteen days after receipt of the order, otherwise the order becomes final and is treated as a conviction and sentence. The appeal, however, obliges the court to hold a trial unless the prosecutor decides to drop the case. In practice, defendants frequently do not appeal against unjust or mistaken orders either out of disinterest, intimidation or ignorance. It is said that the state prosecution office and court choose to deal with a case by the penal order procedure in order to save time and that they sentence leniently in order to forestall an appeal.

7.17 When the prosecutor decides to send a case to trial, a written indictment must be lodged, together with the files in the case, with a competent court. The prosecutor has a certain discretion as to which court to select in a particular case. The choice will depend on the character of the offence and the probable sentence. There is then an intermediate procedure whereby the court decides whether or not there should be a trial. The court examines whether further investigations are necessary. The defendant is given a chance to persuade the court not to proceed to trial. If the court decides that the case against the accused is strong, it will set the case down for trial. It has become a very routine procedure. However, it is said to be of some use in sensitive cases.

7.18 For a more detailed study of the role of the prosecutor in the pre-trial phase, see Professor Leigh's and Doctor Zedner's report on the pre-trial phase in France and Germany[1].

Disclosure

7.19 Once an investigation has been completed, defence counsel has the right to full access to the files. Before the investigation has been completed, access can be denied if this would endanger the purpose of the investigation. However, at no stage can the defence be denied access to records concerning the examination of the accused, to records of judicial acts at which defence counsel had the right to be present and to expert opinions.

7.20 In general, access to files is granted by allowing the defence counsel to remove the files to his or her office or home, although there is no legal right to do this.

7.21 The problem of the prosecution failing to disclose information which they do not intend to use is said to be less acute in Germany. This is because the prosecutor is under a legal duty to investigate not only incriminating evidence but also circumstances favourable to the accused. The prosecutor's file will therefore often contain material useful for the defence, and the defence have a right to inspect it.

7.22 There may still be evidence which the police have accumulated, but which the prosecutor does not regard as relevant for the court, e.g. results

---

[1] Royal Commission on Criminal Justice, Research Study No. 1, London, HMSO, (1992).

of pursuing leads on persons other than the defendant. In a 1983 decision, the Federal Constitutional Court held that the defence cannot insist that such information be included in the file but, they can request the prosecutor to make the additional information available to the defence. A refusal on the part of the prosecutor can be challenged in court.

7.23   Further problems may arise where the police have kept their own internal files for their own purposes which are not in the official files of a case. The defendant can apply to the court to inspect these files, but the court is not obliged to agree to the request unless there are indications that these files may produce facts which are important to the case.

7.24   The defence need not reveal their tactics nor do the prosecution have a right to inspect any defence documents. However, if the defence intend to call witnesses or experts of their own, they must inform the court and the prosecutor of their identity and address before trial. If the defence have failed to give the information early enough for the prosecution to make inquiries of the witness or expert, the prosecutor can move for an adjournment of the trial. The court decides on such a motion in its discretion.

Expert evidence

7.25   According to the Code, experts are to be appointed by the court. They are to be objective and not serve one of the parties in the proceedings. In practice, however, the prosecutor is assumed to have authority to appoint experts "provisionally". In practice courts often acquiesce in the prosecutor's prior choice of experts and continue their appointment. This has been the subject of a good deal of criticism. The defence can make suggestions to the court or to the prosecutor as to possible experts. A defence motion for the court to appoint an additional expert will be successful only if the defence can show that the original expert is in some way below standard or that the new expert suggested by the defence has superior means of research. Experts must be chosen from a list of experts who have been officially appointed as experts in a specialised field.

7.26   The defence can call their own experts but this is expensive. Experts employed by the state are not debarred from working for the defence but may "often appear less than desirable from a defence point of view."

7.27   Since the law does not expect experts to be partisan, there is no provision for facilitating agreement among experts.

Detention pre-trial

7.28   Pre-trial custody is compulsory in capital cases, such as murder and manslaughter, and in all other cases if there is strong risk of the suspect absconding or suppressing evidence if released.

Courts/juries

7.29 The German criminal justice system does not use juries.

7.30 There are three tiers of court at Local State, Regional State and Federal level. The jurisdiction of the courts depends upon the seriousness of the charge.

7.31 At Local State level, there are two types of court: the Single Judge Court and the Lay Judges Court. In the Single Judge Court, one judge sits alone and can hear minor offences where the penalty is not more than one year's imprisonment. In the Lay Judges Court, a single judge sits with two lay judges. It can sentence the defendant up to three years' imprisonment. In complex cases, on application of the prosecutor, an extra judge can be added to form a Special Lay Judges Court made up of two professional and two lay judges.

7.32 More serious cases are heard at Regional State level where there are also two types of court: the Smaller Criminal Court and the Greater Criminal Court. The Smaller Criminal Court sits with one professional and two lay judges. The Greater Criminal Court sits with three professional judges and two lay judges. The Regional Court also hears appeals from the local courts.

7.33 The Higher Regional Court deals with offences against the state and other grave offences conducted in the course of these offences such as murder or bank robbery. It sits with five professional judges. This court also deals with appeals from the Local State Courts under *Revision* procedure (see paragraph 7.52 below). As an appeal court, it sits with three professional judges.

7.34 The Federal High Court is the highest court in Germany. It hears appeals from the Regional courts. It sits with five professional judges.

7.35 Lay judges are selected every four years from a list of nominations complied by each Local Authority within the jurisdiction of the Local Courts. The list is derived from the Local Authority registers and is intended to be representative of the population between the ages of 25 and 70, omitting lawyers, clergymen, the mentally handicapped and those with criminal records. In practice, the local political parties exercise considerable influence and different authorities adopt different systems of selection.

7.36 A commission consisting of one professional judge, one state administrative officer, and ten "trustworthy" citizens elected by the Local Authority, assembles at each Local Court to select the lay judges from amongst the nominees. The most likely people to be chosen are teachers, social workers, business people etc. The consent of the lay judge is not necessary. It is an enforceable public duty to serve and the law provides for only a few reasons for a lay judge to resign.

7.37   The rota of lay judges is decided long in advance of the trial by a ballot conducted by the judge. Lay judges must sit twelve days in every year and are paid a small sum.

7.38   Neither the prosecution nor the defence can object to the selection of a lay judge unless there is a very good reason (such as personal involvement).

7.39   The lay judges sit with the professional judges and can ask questions of witnesses and make notes but they have no right to see the file.

7.40   Lay judges have an equal vote and in the courts where they are in the majority they can out-vote the professional judges. However, the influence of lay judges in the outcome of cases is thought to be small, but it is said that they usually favour the defendant.

Trial

7.41   The presiding judge examines the dossier in advance of the trial. If he or she is sitting with one or more other professional judges, one of them will be nominated to study the dossier and research any difficult points of law that are likely to occur. The other professional judges and the lay judges know nothing of a case before it is heard and the lay judges will have no access to the dossier during the trial.

7.42   Usually the prosecutor is not the same one who conducted the enquiry and he or she will not (except in serious cases) have a copy of the dossier in court.

7.43   The presiding judge has the major role in the trial. He or she conducts the trial, examines the defendant and takes the evidence. The presiding judge is responsible for the calling and examining of witnesses.

7.44   The trial begins with the examination of the defendant with respect to his or her personal circumstances. The public prosecutor then reads out the charge. There is no opening speech by the prosecutor. After being informed of the right to refuse to testify, the defendant is given an opportunity to make a statement on the charges. The defendant is then questioned by the presiding judge. The other judges, both lay and professional, the prosecutor and the defendant's lawyer may ask additional questions.

7.45   The presiding judge will then call the witnesses. He or she will do the main questioning, but the other judges, the prosecutor and the defendant's lawyer can ask additional questions. The defence and the prosecution may summon witnesses to the court, but it is up to the judge to decide whether to call them or not.

7.46   After the evidence has been taken, the prosecution and then the defence has an opportunity to make a statement. The defendant always has the right to the final word.

7.47   When the judges have retired, one of the professional judges summarises the case. The presiding judge leads the discussion and takes votes. All decisions regarding a defendant's guilt have to be decided upon a two thirds majority amongst all the judges, whereas sentence is decided by simple majority. The lay judges vote first (in ascending order of age) and then the professional judges (in order of seniority) with the presiding judge last. The purpose of these detailed rules is to preserve the independence of the decisions of the younger, more junior, or less experienced judges.

Previous convictions

7.48   The judges will have the accused's previous convictions before them during the trial. As a rule, prior convictions are only relevant in determining the scale of penalty.

Appeal

7.49   There are two types of appeal depending on whether the appeal is on law or fact. An appeal on the facts is called *Berufung*. An appeal on the law is called *Revision*.

7.50   Appeal courts do not have the power to discourage hopeless appeals by means such as adding on time to sentence. However, there are sometimes unofficial contacts between the court and the prosecution or defence through which the court might express its opinion that an appeal is not likely to succeed; but if the parties insist on the appeal, the court cannot object.

7.51   A defendant's sentence can never be increased if he appeals. There is, however, a danger that if the defendant appeals the prosecutor will do so also. A defendant's sentence can be increased on an appeal by the prosecutor.

(i) Appeals from the Local State Court

7.52   Appeals from the Local State Court are of right if they are lodged within a week of the judgment and are heard in the Regional State Court.

The appeal takes the form of a complete new trial (*Berufung*). All the witnesses will be heard again and fresh evidence may be included. The defendant can then appeal again to the Higher Regional Court only if he or she considers this second judgment to be wrong in law or the sentence to be wrong. This kind of appeal is called *Revision*.

7.53. *Berufung* is criticised because the possibilities of taking evidence diminish in time and because it is also said that judges at first instance are less thorough because they know that there is a second opportunity for the facts to be considered.

(ii) Appeals from the Regional Court

7.54 Appeals from the Regional Court are heard in the Federal High Court. There can be no appeal on the facts from the Regional Court. There can only be an appeal on a matter of law or sentence (*Revision*). The appeal is of right if filed within one week of the judgment. The appeal does not take the form of a new trial. No new evidence is heard. The court examines the dossier and record of the hearing, listens to arguments about the law from both sides and decides whether the original judge was right or not. If it concludes that he or she was wrong, it can order a retrial unless it is quite unlikely that the defendant's guilt can be established upon retrial. In the main, retrial is the rule. The case is remanded for retrial to a trial court different from the one whose judgment was reversed. One witness wrote, "This does not create serious problems in practice except that the passage of time tends to impair the availability of evidence."

7.55 The grounds on which an appeal is allowed on *Revision* are set out in the Code of Criminal Procedure. The Code lists eight instances of severe procedural defects which lead to an automatic reversal of a judgment upon appeal. These include the participation of a judge excluded by law or challenged for good cause, the illicit exclusion of the public and a substantial infringement of defence rights through a ruling of the court. In other cases a judgment will be quashed if it is based upon a violation of law. This provision has been interpreted by the courts of appeal to mean: "if there is a *possibility* that the outcome would have been different but for the violation of law."

7.56 Decisions of the Regional Court can be appealed against only once. However, if the appeal court orders a retrial, the judgment of the retrial can be appealed against.

7.57 There is no procedure for cases being referred back to the courts of appeal by the executive. However, in certain circumstances the executive can issue pardons.

7.58 In 1989, the Regional Courts passed 8,956 judgments. In 3,699 (41%) cases, appeals were made by either the defendant or the prosecution. In the same year, the Federal Court of Justice also passed 3,159 *Revision* proceedings. 578 (18.3%) of these appeals were successful and led to a reversal or alteration of the first judgment.

(iii) "Court of Last Resort"

7.59 There is no "Court of Last Resort". However, there is a special procedure (*Wiederaufnahme*) for reopening cases where a judgment cannot be appealed against by normal means.

7.60 An application for *Wiederaufnahme* must be filed with a court within the same state and of the same jurisdictional level as the one which had issued the original decision. The court competent for deciding *Wiederaufnahme* is specified for each year in advance. There is no time limit for bringing an application.

7.61 The process of examining *Wiederaufnahme* applications has three steps. First, the court determines whether the application has been made in proper form (i.e. in writing, signed by an attorney or by the clerk of the court), and whether it alleges proper grounds for *Wiederaufnahme*. The grounds for granting *Wiederaufnahme* include the fact that the judgment was affected by perjury of a witness or by forged documents, or that new evidence appears, which tends to support an acquittal of the accused. The prosecutor can also apply *Wiederaufnahme* if an acquitted defendant subsequently confesses to the crime.

7.62 Second, if the court finds the application plausible on its face, it will then evaluate the evidence proposed by the applicant and determine whether to quash the original judgment.

7.63 Third, if the original judgment is quashed, the court holds a new trial. At the new trial, the original trial and the judgment are treated as non-existent. Each party can appeal against the court's verdict from the new trial by the regular means of appeal. (If the defendant is no longer alive, and in other cases in which lack of guilt has become obvious and the public prosecutor consents, no new trial is held. The defendant is acquitted of the original charges by the decision of the court.)

7.64 Applications for *Wiederaufnahme* are not infrequent. German courts have developed fairly stringent standards for assessing the plausibility of *Wiederaufnahme* and for assessing the persuasiveness of new evidence. Official statistics on *Wiederaufnahme* proceedings are not available, but it has been estimated that approximately 150–350 court decisions per year are quashed on *Wiederaufnahme*. It is said that due to the high standards for ordering new trials, these almost always lead to the result desired by the applicant.

7.65   Long delays between the original judgment and the applications for *Wiederaufnahme* lead to problems. In a study of 1,100 *Wiederaufnahme* cases, researchers found that 39 cases in which applications for *Wiederaufnahme* were granted ten or more years after the original verdict; in some of these cases the applicant succeeded only after several attempts had failed.

Training

7.66   The legal training of prosecutors and judges is the same, as is the salary. After initial academic law studies, there is two to three years' practical professional training which precedes the final (second) State Examination for law students. This professional training is spent at court, the Public Prosecutor's Office and with a lawyer. Participation in court proceedings allows the trainee to gather experience of the practical problems of criminal proceedings which include also psychological and criminological aspects. After the final State Examination, any lawyer in theory can apply for a post of judge. Generally, however, only those candidates who have passed the examination with the best results are selected.

Part 8
The Republic of Ireland

Police investigations

8.1 The basic rule of law is that a person can be arrested only for the purpose of charging him or her in court, as soon as practicable, with the offence for which he or she has been arrested. There are two statutory exceptions to this rule:

(i) section 30, Offences Against the State Act, 1939 – A person may be arrested on reasonable suspicion of having committed an offence under the Act or which is scheduled by it for the time being (i.e. an offence under the Firearms Acts, the Explosive Substances Act, the Malicious Damage Act and the Conspiracy and Protection of Property Act). A person so arrested may be detained for up to twenty four hours which may be extended for a further twenty four hours on the direction of a Garda Chief Superintendent;

(ii) section 4, Criminal Justice Act, 1984 – A person arrested without warrant for an arrestable offence which carries a possible sentence of five or more years imprisonment may be detained for up to six hours, which may be extended for a further six hours on the direction of a Garda Superintendent if he or she deems these periods of detention are necessary for the proper investigation of the offence. If that period runs after midnight, suspects may, if they wish, be allowed up to eight undisturbed hours for rest, during which the twelve hour period ceases to run. Time during which a person arrested attends a hospital for any necessary medical examinations is excluded from the permitted detention period.

8.2 If persons detained under either of these sections have not been charged in court before the expiration of the relevant period, they must be released forthwith.

8.3 The police have a duty to inform suspects of their right to silence as soon as practicable after arrest.

8.4 The police have a statutory duty to inform suspects of their right to legal advice without delay after detention, if the case falls under either of the sections mentioned in paragraph 8 1(i) and (ii) above. This is usually on arrival at the police station. The right of persons in custody to access to legal advice is now a constitutional right as well as a legal right[1], and therefore statements obtained in violation of this or any other constitutional right must be excluded unless there are extraordinary excusing circumstances.

8.5 No distinction is drawn between serious and less serious offences, apart from the fact that a person being brought before a court as soon as is practicable after arrest (i.e. not being detained under either of the sections mentioned above) need not be informed of a right to legal advice before being charged in court.

8.6 Suspects are entitled to have notification of their detention and of the station where they are being detained sent to one other person, apart from a solicitor, named by them.

8.7 About 19% of detained persons ask for a lawyer, and 15% get a lawyer to attend at the Garda station.

8.8 Where persons are detained, the Garda may demand from them their name and address, search them, photograph them, take their fingerprints and palm prints, carry out any test designed to ascertain whether they have been in contact with any firearm and for that purpose take swabs from skin or samples of hair, and seize and retain for testing anything that they have in their possession. Any records concerning the suspect must generally be destroyed if proceedings are not instigated within six months, or on acquittal, discharge or discontinuance of the case. The person concerned can witness this destruction.

8.9 The Treatment of Persons in Custody in Garda Siochana Stations Regulations, 1987, place upon the "member in charge" of a Garda station the responsibility for seeing that, in so far as persons in custody are concerned, the rules are fully complied with. The rules necessitate visits to detained persons from time to time, making any necessary inquiries, adopting the role of custodian of the arrested person's rights, and keeping a detailed custody record. Defence solicitors generally feel that the member in charge takes his or her responsibilities seriously and ensures meaningful compliance with the Regulations.

8.10 The machinery provided by the Garda Siochana (Complaints) Act, 1986, which allows the making of complaints against members of the Garda Siochana in respect of the manner in which statements are taken, constitutes a further protection.

---

[1] *People (DPP) v. Paul Healy* (1989)

Evidence

(i) Confessions

8.11 There are no rules restricting the admissibility of confessions that have not been tape-recorded or repeated in front of a judge/magistrate. Section 27, Criminal Justice Act, 1984, states that the Minister for Justice may provide, by regulations, for the recording of the questioning of persons by the Garda at Garda stations, or elsewhere, in connection with the investigation of offences. The regulations may be made to apply generally, or to questioning at a specific place and time. However, not complying with these regulations would not, by itself, render inadmissible in evidence anything said during the questioning. A recent report into criminal procedure[2] recommended audio-visual recording of interviews with suspects. No general regulations for recording interviews have yet been made.

8.12 The Judges' Rules are not rules of law, but rules of practice drawn up for the guidance of police officers in an effort to encourage the observance of fair procedures in the taking of statements. If a statement has been obtained in circumstances not in accordance with the Rules, it is not by that fact alone rendered inadmissible if it is voluntary, but a judge retains a discretion as to whether to admit it in evidence or not. Statements obtained in breach of constitutional rights, for example the right to legal advice, must be excluded unless there are extraordinary excusing circumstances.

8.13 Corroboration is defined as independent testimony which affects the accused by connecting or tending to connect him with the crime and which is something independent of the evidence which it corroborates. It is not required by law for confession evidence. However, if a confession is challenged on the ground that it was not voluntary, the trial judge must in the absence of the jury hear and consider all available evidence as to the circumstances under which the statement came into being. He or she must come to a conclusion as to its voluntary nature or otherwise. It is for the prosecution to satisfy the trial judge beyond reasonable doubt that the statement upon which reliance is placed was made voluntarily. In the event of failure to do so, the judge has properly no discretion in the matter, and must refuse to accept the statement in evidence. The recent report into criminal procedure recommended a warning be given for any confessional evidence. The Department of Justice announced on 16 September 1992 that legislation is to be introduced which will provide that an accused person, on his or her first appearance in court, must be given an opportunity to comment on the voluntariness of any confession made.

8.14 If the judge is satisfied that the statement has been made voluntarily and consequently allows it to be put in evidence, the jury must then also

---

[2] Report of Committee to enquire into certain aspects of criminal procedure, March 1990.

hear and consider all the circumstances, and come to their own decision as to the degree of credibility to be attached to it.

(ii) Identification

8.15 Corroboration is regarded as desirable almost to the point of being essential in cases involving identification. In 1962 the Supreme Court[3] made it incumbent upon trial judges to warn jurors that, if their verdict as to guilt were to depend wholly or substantially on the correctness of a visual identification, they should remember that there had been a number of instances in the past in which responsible witnesses, whose honesty was not in question and whose opportunities for observation had been adequate, made positive identifications on a parade or otherwise, which were subsequently proved to be erroneous.

(iii) The accused's silence

8.16 Every citizen has a fundamental right, save in those cases where the terms of a statute purport to provide to the contrary, to remain silent and decline to answer questions put by police officers, without fear of adverse legal consequences.

8.17 The Criminal Justice Act, 1984, provides that the court can draw inferences from a suspect's failure to account for certain matters. Section 18 provides that where a person is arrested without warrant by the Garda, and there are any objects, substances, or marks which the Garda reasonably believe may be attributable to the participation of the person arrested in the commission of the offence, and having been asked, the person fails to account for the presence of these, then the court can draw such inferences from the failure or refusal as appear proper. Section 19 provides that the court can also draw inferences from the unexplained presence of an accused at a particular place around the time the offence was committed. Such inferences by themselves cannot constitute a prima facie case, but can amount to corroboration. The number of persons failing to comply with sections 18 and 19 was 2 and 13 respectively, for the period 1 July 1987 to the end of December 1990. The Department of Justice have said that there have been no particular problems with the operation of the sections.

(iv) Improperly obtained evidence

8.18 Evidence obtained in breach of constitutional rights must be excluded unless there are extraordinary excusing circumstances. Illegally obtained evidence (as distinct from the above) may be admitted at the discretion of the court. The discretion is based on the interests of justice. The tendency is to exclude.

---

[3] *People v. Casey (no.2)* (1962)

Prosecution

8.19 The investigative and prosecutorial functions are separate and are performed independently of one another. However, the police regularly exercise prosecutorial functions in minor cases. They do so in the name of and subject to direction by the Director of Public Prosecutions. In practice the Garda often consult the prosecutorial service for advice in the course of investigations. It is advice, not directions, which is given. Such advice is almost always accepted. Further, when an investigation file is submitted for prosecutorial directions, the prosecution service often request further investigation of specific matters. Such requests are invariably complied with.

Disclosure

8.20 In cases involving trials on indictment, the defence have the right of full access in advance of the trial to the evidence to be given by prosecution witnesses. The evidence must be served in the course of the preliminary examination of the offence, before the case is returned for trial to the court which has jurisdiction to try the charge.

8.21 The defence have the right to see relevant material in the possession of the prosecution which the prosecution does not intend to use. This is done on an informal basis. There are no specific rules dealing with non-disclosure, but if this conduct came to light it, would prejudice the prosecution case and attract the gravest censure from the court. The system appears to work well.

8.22 There is no system or procedure to guard against concealment or non-disclosure by the police or scientists. No such case has come to light and the Government feels that there is no reason to suspect that any such case exists.

8.23 The defence are obliged to reveal only alibi evidence to the prosecution. In default, the leave of the judge is required before it can be admitted.

Expert evidence

8.24 The Garda, the scientists and the pathologists are well trained in taking scientific evidence at the scene of the crime or from suspects themselves, so as to ensure that the evidence is collected properly. They are meticulous to ensure non-contamination and continuity of trace of evidence discovered at the scene of the crime.

8.25 Adequate assistance for the defence from forensic or scientific experts is primarily covered by the strict rules of total disclosure. In addition, members of the Forensic Science Laboratory will afford every possible assistance and facility to the defence on request. They regard themselves as being independent experts, not tools of the prosecution. As full-time salaried employees of the State, however, they are not permitted to accept private commissions.

8.26 There is no system or institutionalised procedure for attempting to get the prosecution and defence experts to agree on their evidence before the trial. Occasionally the experts will consult for a particular reason and such pre-trial consultations are usually valuable. Where any evidence is agreed in advance and is therefore uncontested, there is a procedure for its admission without oral presentation.

8.27 There is no system for the court to commission expert evidence. However, the court is always free to require a party (normally the prosecution) to provide further information or evidence on any relevant matter.

8.28 The defence are entitled to have their own experts examine the scientific/forensic exhibits.

Pre-trial procedures

8.29 There are no pre-trial procedures for enabling the prosecution to question the accused in front of a judge or other judicial officer.

Statistics for detention in custody

8.30 On 1 October 1991, there were 152 suspects detained in custody, who had not yet been convicted. There were also 3 people in custody who had been convicted but who were awaiting sentence. The population of Ireland is about 3,500,000.

8.31 In Ireland unconvicted persons have a right to release on bail pending their trial, unless the court considers that they are likely to interfere with witnesses or not appear at the trial. Almost all suspects, including persons accused of serious crimes such as murder, are released. Normally a person convicted on indictment would be remanded in custody for sentence, but some are released on bail.

Juries

8.32 Juries deliberate alone.

8.33 There are no steps taken to secure that the jury reflects any racial balance.

8.34 The verdict of a jury in criminal proceedings need not be unanimous in a case where there are no fewer than eleven jurors, if ten of them agree on the verdict.

Trial

8.35 Minor offences are dealt with by a District Court in which a District Justice may impose sentences not exceeding two years imprisonment.

8.36 Other cases go before a Special Criminal Court, and are conducted by three judges.

8.37 The judge has a power to call witnesses, but it is very rarely used.

8.38 The prosecutor is allowed to start the trial with an opening speech, as in England and Wales.

8.39 The judge does sum up to the jury on the facts. The judge is permitted to comment on the evidence, provided the judge makes it clear to the jury that questions of fact are ultimately for them, as in England and Wales.

Previous convictions

8.40 Trial judges do not have prior convictions of the accused before them during the trial.

8.41 The rules for the introduction of prior convictions of the accused are similar to those in England and Wales. Therefore the prosecution can introduce them in evidence during the trial: (1) to refute the accused's claim to be a person of good character; (2) in cases where there is a striking similarity between the facts of the cases; (3) where the defence cast aspersions on the character of the prosecution's witnesses; and (4) where one co-accused has given evidence against another co-accused.

Appeals

8.42 A full right of appeal from the District Court lies to the Circuit Court, where a judge enters into an entire rehearing of the case, fresh evidence (if any) being admissible as a matter of course. Subject to the right to have any point of law which may arise definitively clarified by a Superior Court and to have judicial review of the procedures, a person whose appeal from conviction in the District Court has failed can be said, on the conclusion of the Circuit Court hearing, to have exhausted the appeal procedures.

8.43 Appeals from conviction in the Special Criminal Court lie to the Court of Criminal Appeal, composed of three judges. The manner in which the appeal is dealt with by the Court of Criminal Appeal is not by way of an entire rehearing. The Court of Criminal Appeal exercises a "supervisory" function. The function of the court is not to reach for itself a conclusion on the facts, but rather to ascertain whether the conclusion of fact reached by the trial court was justified having regard to the onus of proof which the law imposes upon the prosecution. If there is evidence upon which the trial court could reasonably have reached the verdict they did, and the trial was otherwise conducted fairly and in accordance with the law, then the Court of Criminal Appeal will not disturb a finding of fact.

8.44 In the year 1988/89, 8% of defendants dealt with in the higher courts appealed against conviction. 15% of those appeals were successful.

8.45 Leave to appeal is sought from and usually refused by the trial judge. There is an absolute right to appeal against the refusal, in the course of which the merits of the case will be fully examined. The Court of Criminal Appeal is enjoined by Section 32, Courts of Justice Act, 1924, to grant leave to appeal if the trial appears to it to have been unsatisfactory or there appears "to be any other sufficient ground for appeal". It has jurisdiction to make a variety of orders including affirming or reversing a conviction, varying a sentence, ordering a retrial and (in effect) substituting a verdict of not guilty by reason of insanity, for a conviction. If the Court of Criminal Appeal finds that there are grounds upon which the conviction should be quashed, it will treat an appeal against the refusal of leave as being the full appeal and will proceed to make an appropriate order.

8.46 The Court of Criminal Appeal does not have a power to discourage hopeless appeals by adding on time to the sentence for unmeritorious appeals. The Court of Criminal Appeal does have jurisdiction to alter a sentence in either direction provided that the appeal has not been limited by the appellant to an appeal against conviction only. It can exercise such jurisdiction to vary only if it considers that the sentence imposed was inappropriate.

8.47 The Court of Criminal Appeal has power to consider fresh evidence not adduced in the trial court. The Court of Criminal Appeal generally does not consider that evidence which was available at the trial, but which was not called by the defence, can be "fresh evidence" for the purposes of an appeal. However, the general power and duty to ensure that justice is done would, for instance, treat such evidence as fresh evidence if the reason for it not having been called in the trial court was professional incompetence for which the accused could not be held responsible.

8.48 If the Court of Criminal Appeal quashes a conviction solely because of an irregularity at the trial, it would normally order a retrial if the irregularity could be corrected at a retrial without injustice to the accused. It might also do so if fresh evidence were tendered which, in its opinion, might have affected the verdict. Otherwise, a retrial would not be ordered. Retrials present no special problems apart from possible non-availability of witnesses due to the passage of time.

8.49 There is no statutory formula that the Court of Criminal Appeal has to apply when deciding whether to quash a verdict of the trial court. It has power to determine any question necessary for the purpose of doing justice in the case. This principle would also mean that appeals on the ground that the case was mishandled by the lawyers are possible, but there seems to be no precedent for this.

8.50 The determination of an appeal by the Court of Criminal Appeal is final and unappealable except where the court, the Attorney General or the Director of Public Prosecutions certifies that the decision of the Court of Criminal Appeal involves a point of law of exceptional public importance which should be decided by the Supreme Court. An appeal to the Supreme Court pursuant to such certificates is not confined to the point of law. The constitution provides that the decision of the Supreme Court "shall in all cases be final and conclusive".

8.51 There is no procedure for cases to be referred back to the Court of Criminal Appeal by the executive.

8.52 The provisions of the constitution vest in the President of Ireland the right of pardon and the power to commute or remit punishment imposed by any court exercising criminal jurisdiction. A pardon can negate guilt and blame. These powers are to be exercised on the advice of the Government.

8.53 There is no special tribunal to hear appeals in cases of alleged miscarriages of justice where the normal appeal processes have been exhausted. However, the Department of Justice announced on 16 September 1992 that legislation is to be brought forward which will provide new mechanisms for reviewing suspected miscarriages of justice after normal appeal procedures have been exhausted. Under the proposed Bill, allegations of a miscarriage of justice will normally be dealt with by the Court of Criminal Appeal. Allegations that cannot be dealt with by that court will be considered by the Minister of Justice with a view to the possible grant of a presidential pardon. This is only expected to arise when fresh evidence supporting an alleged injustice is for any reason not legally admissible or where the offence in question was dealt with summarily, so that no record of the original proceedings is available. The Department of Justice expect that, in the first instance, alleged miscarriages of justice cases will be investigated informally by the Minister of Justice. Only in appropriate cases would an enquiry into such a case be carried out by an ad hoc body which will be given statutory powers, including the right to summon witnesses, under the new Bill. The Bill will also provide for compensation where a miscarriage of justice is established.

Training

8.54　There is no special training of judges in the problems of false confessions, bias etc.

8.55　Police training stresses the necessity for objectivity and the importance of establishing the truth of the matter rather than merely securing a conviction. It is considered that all involved in the criminal justice system take those objectives very seriously.

Part 9
Israel

Introduction

9.1   The criminal system in Israel is essentially based on an accusatorial model.

9.2   Criminal law and procedure, as well as the law of evidence, are mainly statutory (the Israeli Criminal Procedure Law 1982, referred to as "the Law"), yet strongly influenced by English common law.

9.3   In March 1992, the Knesset enacted the Basic Law: Human Dignity and Freedom. The law includes, inter alia, the right to life, body and dignity and the protection of these interests; liberty of the individual, the right to privacy and personal confidentiality. The Basic Law does not contain an express entrenchment clause. Section 8, however, states as follows:

> "The rights according to this Basic Law shall not be infringed except by a statute that befits the values of the State of Israel and is directed towards a worthy purpose, and then only to an extent that does not exceed what is necessary."

Police investigations

9.4   Arrested persons must be brought to the police station immediately. If they were arrested by virtue of a warrant issued by a judge, or arrested without a warrant and not released by the police, they must be brought before a judge within forty eight hours of the arrest, so that the judge can decide whether they should remain in custody or be released on bail. However, if it is not possible to do so due to the temporary absence of the judge, or for some other adequate reason, they may be held for an additional period that must not exceed forty eight hours.

9.5   A minor over 14 but not yet 18 must be brought before a judge within twenty four hours. For special reasons this period can be extended for a further twenty four hours. A minor under 14 cannot be kept in custody without a judicial warrant for more than twelve hours.

9.6   When the arrested person is brought before a judge, the judge can issue an order for detention for the purpose of interrogation before charge, for a period not exceeding fifteen consecutive days. The total period of detention ordered by a judge must not exceed thirty days. Detention for more than thirty days is conditional upon the submission of a request made to and signed personally by the Attorney General.

9.7   If a charge is not filed within ninety days after arrest, then the suspect must be released, unless a judge of the Supreme Court extends the arrest for periods, each of which may not exceed three months. This rarely happens.

9.8   In general, the provisions delineating the duration of permissible detention are interpreted in a strict manner.

9.9   Criticism has often been levelled against the regulation of detention in Israel. Draft laws designed to change the present situation, shortening the period allowed for detention before charge, have been discussed. However, no change is yet planned.

9.10   There is no statutory regulation of an obligation to caution suspects. At the same time, the case law has adopted the English "Judges' Rules" as guidelines for the police. The rule is that suspects must not be interrogated, and their confessions must not be taken, until they have been cautioned. Non-compliance with the obligation of cautioning does not, in itself, lead to exclusion of the confession, but the absence of a warning constitutes one factor, amongst others, that the court examines in considering the admissibility of a confession, and whether it was freely and voluntarily given.

9.11   The officer in charge of the police station to which the arrested person has been brought, must inform detainees of their right to notify a lawyer of their choice of the arrest and of their place of detention. The obligation only arises upon arrival at the police station.

9.12   The arrested person has the right to consult a lawyer privately under conditions which ensure the confidentiality of the conversation. If the arrested person is being questioned by the police, and the police officer believes that an interruption of the proceedings is likely to harm the investigation or interfere with the arrest of other suspects in the same matter, then he may order that the meeting of the suspect with a lawyer be deferred for a few hours. It can be delayed for up to forty eight hours if necessary to protect state security or human life, or to prevent the commission of a felony. It can be delayed for up to fifteen days for serious crimes affecting state security such as spying, terrorist activity or certain offences in the Occupied Territories. However, the Supreme Court has decided that even in the context of these serious crimes, the decision not to allow the suspect to meet with a lawyer is subject to judicial review, which will be conducted in camera.

Evidence

(i) Confessions

9.13   There are no rules restricting the admissibility of confessions that have not been tape-recorded or repeated in front of a judge. A Private Member's Bill was tabled in the Knesset in 1991, whereby the following section would be added to the Evidence Ordinance:

> ". . . Evidence as to the confession of the accused that he committed an offence which is punishable by a minimum of ten years imprisonment will be admissible only if the confession was taped on an audiovisual magnetic tape presented by the prosecution and the court is convinced that no visual or aural editing was done on the tape; however, the court may direct that evidence concerning a confession which was not taped as aforesaid be admitted, if the court is satisfied that there were special reasons preventing this."

9.14   The Bill has now been transferred to the standing Advisory Committee on Criminal Procedure at the Ministry of Justice. The Committee intends to look into the proposal as part of a general review of confession evidence.

9.15   The Evidence Ordinance provides as follows:

> "Evidence of confession by the accused that he has committed an offence is admissible only when the prosecution has produced evidence as to the circumstances in which it was made and the court is satisfied that it was free and voluntary."

9.16   For the purpose or convicting a person upon an out of court confession, strengthening evidence is required, the "additional something". This is not a statutory provision, but a requirement formulated by the case law. Even where it has been decided that the confession is admissible, even credible and weighty, it is not sufficient for a conviction if no strengthening evidence has been found in the admissible evidence, confirming that it is correct. This requirement, as it has been formulated in case law, has created a rigid rule which limits the discretion of the court. The main reason for the rule is that, even after the confession has stood the test of voluntariness, there is still concern that the accused may be confessing to an offence which he or she did not commit.

9.17   An "additional something" means a small evidentiary supplement, less than corroboration[1]. The aim is to test the confession for veracity. This

---

[1] Defined in Israeli case law as "a source of evidence that is separate and independent from the testimony that requires corroboration".

is always a matter for the discretion of the court, which considers the circumstances under which the confession was made, and its independent weight – if it displays the indicators of truth or those of a fabrication, if it has internal logic and a detailed factual base which is reasonable, and other such considerations. A number of auxiliary tests have also been developed, such as the following:

(i) knowledge of the details – the requirement for an "additional something" will be satisfied if it can be shown that the details explicated in the confession are accurate. This refers to the details of the event which is the subject of the accusation, details which, in the normal course of events, are within the special knowledge of whoever committed the alleged crime;

(ii) opportunity – did the accused have the opportunity to do that to which he or she confessed? Having the opportunity means that it was possible for him or her to have been at the scene of the crime, at the time that it took place;

(iii) reconstruction – the ability of the accused to reconstruct the event which is the subject of the accusation has been determined by the case law to constitute an adequate "additional something".

(ii) *The accused's silence*

9.18 The silence of the suspect at the police station does not, per se, constitute evidence of guilt, nor additional evidence which amounts to corroboration. Where the prosecution proves prima facie guilt, however, circumstances may justify viewing a defendant's refusal to make a statement to the police as suspicious, and such silence may detract from the value of the defence evidence, or it may strengthen the evidence submitted by the prosecution.[2]

9.19 With respect to the silence of an accused in the courtroom, there were statutory changes in Israeli law in the 1970's. The most significant change was that a defendant's failure to testify on his or her own behalf could now serve to corroborate the prosecution's evidence, such as the testimony of a state witness. This change also manifested itself in the context of the claim of "no case to answer". If, at the close of the prosecution's case, the evidence against the accused requires corroboration, and this has not been provided, the defendant will no longer be acquitted on a claim of "no case": the defendant's failure to testify could serve as the otherwise absent corroboration.

---

[2] *Hajibi v The State of Israel* (1985) 39(i) P.D. 785.

(iii) Identification evidence

9.20 For identification evidence, when this is the sole evidence incriminating an accused person, the court must adopt appropriate cautionary measures, but there is no statutory or case law requirement for additional evidence. However, there do not seem to be any cases in which persons were convicted solely on the basis of identification evidence.

(iv) Improperly obtained evidence

9.21 There is no general statutory rule concerning the admissibility of unlawfully obtained evidence. According to the case law, evidence which has been obtained illegally is not excluded as a rule, and the concept of not admitting as evidence the "fruits of the poisoned tree" has been explicitly rejected by the Supreme Court. There are, however, three exceptions;

   (i) the Secret Monitoring Law, 1979, states that nothing recorded by way of secret monitoring in contravention of the provisions of this law shall be admissible as evidence in court. It therefore stipulates the absolute exclusion of illegal recordings;

   (ii) the Protection of Privacy Law, 1981, states that material obtained by invasion of privacy shall be inadmissible as evidence in court without the consent of the injured party, save where a court allows its use, for reasons that shall be recorded, or where the perpetrator, who is also a party to the proceedings, has a defence or exemption under this law. Therefore, the court has a discretion to admit evidence, despite a violation of privacy, if the court sets out special reasons for granting the exception. The discretion should involve a balancing of factors, such as the extent of the violation, whether the violation was deliberate, whether an admission would encourage undesirable behaviour, whether the violation was part of a policy of the agency that committed it, whether there is an urgent need for the evidence, the ease of obtaining the evidence by lawful means, and the severity of the crime. It was held in the case of *Moshe Va'aknin* that this law does not apply to offences involving a trespass upon the person (e.g. intimate searches);

   (iii) the Evidence Ordinance, section 12 (see paragraph 9.15 above).

Prosecution

9.22 The Attorney General directs the nationwide prosecutorial staff as its chief officer in the prosecutorial hierarchy, and is chief legal counsellor to the Government. The discretion of the Attorney General is subject to judicial review by the Supreme Court, sitting as the High Court of Justice.

9.23   There is a broad range of discretion in the Israeli criminal process. When the police receive a complaint or discover evidence of a misdemeanour (an offence punishable by imprisonment not exceeding three years), a senior police officer retains discretion not to open an investigative file if he or she determines that an investigation would not serve the public interest. When an investigation is conducted, and prima facie evidence of an offence is found, the police prosecutor, in the normal course of events, will charge the suspect. However, a senior police officer retains discretion to decide not to prosecute when it would not be in the public interest to do so, in spite of the fact that prima facie evidence of a crime has been found.

9.24   With respect to felonies (offences punishable by death or imprisonment for more than three years), the police are obliged to carry out an investigation, and must transfer the file to a chief district prosecutor who will decide whether to prosecute the suspect. When prima facie evidence of an offence is found in the file, the chief district prosecutor will usually decide to prosecute the suspect, but again, discretion is retained to decide not to do so when it would not be consistent with the public interest. Thus, in all cases, the criteria for prosecution are prima facie evidence and public interest, with the latter criterion allowing for the exercise of substantial discretion.

9.25   Where investigation material has been transmitted to the prosecution, and the Attorney General, or any attorney of the State Attorney's Office (and in practice any prosecutor), has found that the investigation must be continued in order to enable a decision of whether or not to prosecute to be taken, or for the purpose of the efficient conduct of the trial, the police may be ordered to continue investigating, and the police must abide by this instruction. The attorney may continue to issue such orders until satisfied that no further investigation is necessary.

9.26   In general, the work of the police is not subject to the constant guidance and control of the prosecutor, other than the control mentioned above. The police have recourse to their own legal advisers. However, there are sensitive cases of great public interest in which the police investigation is accompanied by, and guided by, the State Attorney's Department.

9.27   In addition the prosecutor can decide if, and on what conditions, a defendant may become a state witness.

Disclosure

9.28   Section 74 of the Law provides:

"Where an indictment in respect of a felony or misdemeanour has been filed, the accused and his defence counsel or a person empowered in that behalf by the defence counsel or, with the consent of the prosecutor, a person empowered in that behalf by the accused, may, at any reasonable time, inspect and copy the investigation material in the possession of the prosecutor."

9.29   For this purpose, the investigation material is deemed to include material which the police did not transmit to the prosecution.

9.30   The Law does not define "investigation material", but the Supreme Court has ruled that the term should not be interpreted rigidly and narrowly. It should include admissions and statements taken during the investigation from the accused, documents seized in the course of the investigation, and evidence which belongs to the periphery of the accusation. Evidence against the prosecution's case must also be included, as must laboratory testing processes. The guide as to what should be included should be "common sense and the aim of affording defence counsel reasonable opportunity to prepare the defence".

9.31   These rules do not apply to evidence designed to refute a contention of the accused which the prosecutor could not have foreseen, evidence designed to explain the absence of a witness, or relating to any other formal matter not material to the clarification of the charge. The right of access does not apply to material, the disclosure of which is prohibited by law.

9.32   Usually, when it appears to the defence that the prosecution is not respecting the right of the accused to view the investigation material and to copy it, the defence apply to the court handling the matter and request its intervention. However, when the court cannot or does not want to issue an order against the prosecution, the defence can apply to the High Court immediately, during the course of the hearing. The defence, however, cannot embark on a "fishing expedition", in a speculative hope that they may find in a particular file some material which can help them to erode the prosecution's case.

9.33   The court may refuse a request of the defence to inspect certain evidence, subject to a number of conditions, in cases that deal with particular crimes relating to state security (e.g. treason, espionage). In the wake of a decision of the District Court in 1990, it was stressed anew that the police must inform the prosecution of the existence of secret intelligence material, and the prosecution must transmit this information to the defence. The defence is entitled to demand the right to see and copy any relevant material, although the police and the prosecution will argue against access, relying on a certificate of confidentiality issued by the

Minister concerned with the matter. The court will consider and decide whether the need to allow access to the information, to do justice to the defendant prevails over the interest in not revealing the information.

9.34 The prosecution are not allowed to produce evidence in court or call witnesses unless the defence's right of access has been honoured. If the prosecution have breached their obligation to disclose evidence which is in favour of the accused, the court have to ascertain whether the right of the accused to a fair trial was prejudiced thereby; if the answer is in the affirmative, and the concealment was discovered at a stage at which it was no longer possible to correct the situation, the breach of the obligation is liable to lead to the acquittal of the accused.

9.35 Under Israeli law, defendants are required to make advance disclosure of their defence and their evidence, but only where alibi or expert evidence is concerned, as follows:

(i) defendants wishing to set up an alibi must do so immediately, in answer to the charge, and must indicate the place where they claim to have been. If they do not do so, they will not be entitled to bring evidence to prove this claim, except with the leave of the court. The court must explain this state of affairs to defendants and warn them of the consequences of their silence. The case law has adhered strictly to this requirement. However, the Supreme Court ruled that the word "place", does not, even by virtue of broad interpretation, include the naming of witnesses, and therefore, the refusal of defendants to give the names of alibi witnesses cannot prevent them bringing evidence on this matter. On the other hand, the Supreme Court held that there are cases in which the silence of the accused on this matter, without an acceptable reason, may constitute a consideration in assessing the credibility of the witnesses who will testify in the case;

(ii) the Law recognises the right of the prosecution to inspect certain items of evidence in the hands of the defence. Sections 82–84 of the Law require the accused to allow the prosecution to inspect and to copy a doctor's certificate which the accused intends to have heard in the trial, or to hand over to the prosecutor in writing the essence of the oral testimony which the accused intends to bring from an expert or from a doctor in the course of the trial. As distinct from the obligation of the prosecution to enable the accused to inspect the investigation material, here the prosecution must apply to the court to order the accused to allow the prosecution to inspect and to copy. In general, the court will grant the order. The prosecution is allowed to explore the "intentions" of the accused in this respect with a direct question in court. It is the court which prescribes the procedure for inspection and copying, but the date of inspection will only be after the prosecution has complied with the defence's right of inspection, and made available to the defence the investigation material. If the accused has not complied with such an order, he will not be entitled to submit the certificate, or have the evidence heard, unless the prosecution agree or the court allows it. In other words, the evidence is not disqualified, and if it is submitted with no objection from the prosecution, it can be assumed that it will not be possible to object at a later date to the admissibility of the evidence, because failure to object in time is equivalent to consent.

Expert evidence

9.36   Expert evidence must be presented in a way which will ensure its susceptibility to examination by the court and all the parties concerned. Hence, all the stages of gathering evidence, both at the scene of the crime and elsewhere, must be accurately documented; working papers of the experts must be kept and not destroyed; their deliberations for and against different hypotheses are to be set down; and all these have to be disclosed later at the trial. Non-compliance with these principles would reduce the weight that is attributed to the evidence by the court. In cases involving serious violations of these principles, the evidence will be held to be devoid of any probative value, or even excluded.

9.37   The professional unit which is in charge of both traditional police occupations (e.g. fingerprinting, ballistics) and "forensic science" (known together as "criminal identification"), is the Division of Identification and Forensic Science (D.I.F.S.). This is part of the Investigations Department of the Police, and all the members of the department are sworn officers. Legal medicine is the responsibility of the Institute for Legal Medicine, under the Ministry of Health.

9.38   In the Law there is no explicit reference to access to the files of the tests of the D.I.F.S.. The D.I.F.S. guidelines, which are strictly followed, state the general law on disclosure, and state that professional ethics oblige the lawyer to obtain the consent of the other party in order to speak to a person who is going to give evidence for the opposite party. This means that defence counsel must obtain the consent of the prosecutor if they wish to speak to the D.I.F.S. expert who is likely to be called to testify at the trial.

9.39   The criminal identification tests are documented in an examination file which is kept in the laboratory, and which is not handed over with the investigation file to the prosecutor. A summary of the examination file – in the form of expert opinions, examination reports, or any other similar documents – is included in the investigation file, with clear designations of the number of the examination file in the D.I.F.S., and of the division/laboratory which performed the work. Exclusion of relevant material from the examination file is held by the D.I.F.S. to be prohibited conduct. The system for control of the experts' examinations (including confirmation of the results by an additional expert, the approval of the head of the laboratory before exclusion, and also, normally, the approval of the head of the division), was designed to prevent prohibited exclusions. This possibility is also reduced through education (lectures, seminars, annual training courses for expert witnesses).

9.40 The handling of scientific evidence in serious crimes is in the hands of professional teams in mobile laboratories, which are part of the police's criminal investigation department, but are not part of the rest of the investigation team. The laboratory teams should adhere to professional principles, and should not be swayed by investigative considerations. For the most part they gather the evidence themselves, or it is done on their orders.

9.41 During the training of the D.I.F.S. investigators, they are taught about the advantages of physical evidence on the one hand, and the sensitivity and vulnerability of evidence as a result of inappropriate handling on the other hand, which can cause a miscarriage of justice for the accused. Great importance is attached to the need for detailed and unambiguous identification of the various exhibits, of the site where the exhibit was found, and of correct wrapping of the exhibits to prevent contamination.

9.42 There are no systems which serve to ensure that the defence has adequate assistance from forensic or scientific experts. In general the defence will independently commission private experts to collect such evidence for payment. Defence counsel who ask the D.I.F.S. for a referral to independent experts are always assisted.

9.43 The courts, from time to time, order the D.I.F.S. to allow defence experts to perform certain examinations. This is usually done in the D.I.F.S. laboratories. Sometimes, the tests are new, and sometimes they are repetitions of tests already performed by the D.I.F.S.. In general, if no special orders are issued by the judge, a test will not be carried out for the defence by the D.I.F.S..

9.44 There is no system for attempting to get the prosecution and defence experts to agree on their evidence before the trial. However, the Law contains a provision which allows the court, after the trial has begun, to summon the prosecution and the defence to a meeting in order to determine their agreement upon points of fact, issues and upon the admissibility of documents and exhibits. In this framework points of agreement between the prosecution and defence expert witnesses can be determined.

9.45 For criminal cases, there are no express provisions in the Law relating to court appointed experts. But there are provisions which authorise the court to order that witnesses be summoned on the motion of the court, and witnesses include experts (see paragraph 9.52 below). The court cannot commission its own experts, unless both parties request that the court appoint an agreed expert. There is some support for allowing the courts to be more active in initiating the appointment of experts.

Pre-trial procedures

9.46 There is no pre-trial procedure for enabling the prosecution to question the accused in front of a judge.

9.47 In the Israeli system, there are no pre-trial or committal hearings or grand jury examination of indictments. In Israel, in place of pre-indictment review procedures, there are post-indictment procedures for reviewing prosecutorial decisions. Suspects can appeal against a police or district prosecutor's decision to prosecute to the Attorney General, by filing a motion for a stay of proceedings. This motion is decided by the office of the Attorney General. In this manner, the Attorney General may override the Chief District Prosecutor. Victims are provided with protection against abuse of prosecutorial discretion by means of their right to appeal to the Attorney General to overturn a police or district prosecutor's decision not to prosecute.

Statistics for detention in custody

9.48 The population of Israel in 1991 was 4,350,000.

Number of people in custody but not yet convicted

For the year 1990	3,666 persons
For the period Jan-Sept 1991	2,886 persons
Annual estimate for the year 1991	3,850 persons

Juries

9.49 There is no trial by jury in Israel.

Trial

9.50 The ordinary courts in Israel are organised in a hierarchy of three levels. There is one Supreme Court sitting in Jerusalem, several District

Courts and many magistrates' courts. The Supreme Court has appellate jurisdiction and sits also as the High Court of Justice. The magistrates' courts are courts of first instance for most of the less serious offences; in more severe crimes, original jurisdiction lies in the District Courts, which also have appellate functions in reviewing the judgments of the magistrates' courts.

9.51   As a rule, a trial court consists of a single judge, and an appellate court has three judges. A bench of three District Court judges is required in trials of the most serious crimes (such as murder). All judges are professional judges.

9.52   Criminal procedure in Israel is adversarial, and therefore the judge has a passive role, and is not normally expected to initiate the summoning of witnesses. However, a provision of the Law states that when the parties have concluded their evidence, the court may, if it deems it necessary, summon a witness and order the submission of other evidence, whether upon the application of a party or on its own motion. If the witness has been summoned by the court, the court will give the parties an opportunity to cross-examine. However, there is no consensus in the case law as to the circumstances under which it is appropriate for the court to exercise this authority. The accepted view seems to be that the judge should not descend into the arena, and so should exercise the power very rarely.

9.53   The prosecution may, at their discretion, start the trial with an opening speech prior to presenting their evidence. In general, an opening statement is made in cases in which the evidence is complex, so that the court can follow the later arguments of the prosecution. At the same time, it is an accepted view that the prosecution must, as a rule, formulate the opening statement in moderate terms and limit it to a presentation of how the different pieces of evidence fit into the whole body of evidence.

Prior convictions

9.54   Judges do not have prior convictions of the accused in front of them during the trial.

9.55   The prosecution may not introduce evidence of other criminal acts of the defendant or previous convictions, unless the evidence is introduced for some purpose other than to suggest that, because the defendant has a negative record, it is more probable that he or she committed the crime. Non-compliance with this rule in the trial court is liable to constitute grounds for allowing an appeal and acquitting the accused.

9.56   There are some exceptions to this general rule excluding evidence of similar facts, including prior convictions:

(i) when the similar act constitutes part of the episode which is the subject of the present trial;

(ii) when the similar act is presented as evidence to rebut a defence argument;

(iii) when the similar act indicates that in other cases the accused adopted a typical technique, which is substantially similar to that attributed to the defendant in the present case.

9.57 Defendants who choose to give evidence may not be asked questions in cross-examination about their previous convictions, unless they claim to be of good character, whether in giving their own evidence or in cross-examination of the prosecution's witnesses.

9.58 However, when a number of accused persons are standing trial together, on a single charge sheet, and one accused person gives evidence against a co-accused, the latter may cross-examine the former about his or her prior convictions.

9.59 The tit-for-tat rule does not exist in Israel.

Appeals

9.60 All the components of the verdict and the sentence are appealable, both by the prosecution and the defence. A judgment imposing the death penalty is the subject of appeal proceedings even if the accused has not appealed against it.

9.61 Every litigant has the opportunity to appeal once as of right against any judgment. When a litigant wishes to appeal a decision given in the appeal against the original decision (i.e. a decision of the District Court in a case started in the Magistrates' Court), then leave is required. Leave to appeal may be given by the court which hears the matter, or it may be given by the court of appeal.

9.62 Leave for an additional appeal to the Supreme Court, on a decision given in an appeal in the District Court, will only be given if the party can show that the appeal involves an important legal question which justifies an additional appeal, or that there are extraordinary circumstances which justify an additional appeal, or when the appeal is the only means by which to avoid a particularly harsh, unjust result, e.g. if there is a risk of convicting an innocent person, or when prima facie the appeal has a genuine chance of succeeding.

9.63 The appeal court may do one of the following:

(i) it may allow the appeal, wholly or partially, and vary the decision of the trial court, or quash it and issue another decision instead, or it may remit the case, with directions, back to the trial court;

(ii) it may dismiss the appeal, and it may do so even though it accepted an argument that was made, if it considered that no miscarriage of justice was caused;

(iii) it may give any other decision that the lower court would have been competent to give.

9.64 The Supreme Court will interfere with the trial court where there is an error of law or an error of fact or where the trial court has not properly evaluated the weight of the evidence. It will not interfere with the lower court's opinion as to the credibility of witnesses.

9.65 If the defect that occurred in the lower court can be remedied, the appeal court can direct that there be a new trial. Remittance of the case back to the lower court must be accompanied by directions to that court, specifying the purpose for which the case has been remitted and containing guidelines concerning additional measures which must be taken: for example, taking extra evidence, the reappraisal of the credibility of evidence already heard. The lower court would then deliver a judgment in the light of its hearing or rehearing of the evidence.

9.66 The appeal court is authorised, if it considers it necessary in the interests of justice, to take evidence or to order the trial court to take such evidence as it may direct. However, applicants must produce evidence at the stage of appeal to convince the court why they could not produce the evidence in the course of the trial; they must also convince the court that the new evidence, if admitted, is capable of significantly changing the findings or the conclusions of the lower court.

9.67 It is settled law in Israel, that in general, new evidence is not allowed, unless applicants could not, by exercising due diligence, have produced the particular piece of evidence they are now seeking to introduce before the court which was charged with ascertaining the facts. Such applications are very seldom allowed. Nevertheless, where there is concern about a substantial miscarriage of justice, the appeal court will be prepared to hear such evidence, or it will order the trial court to complete that which is missing.

9.68 Sometimes, the court will not order that the case be remitted, and it will instead acquit the accused, if the accused suffered a great deal as a result of a mistake that was not his or her fault. This decision – to remit or acquit –

is in the discretion of the appeal court, and not subject to hard and fast rules. In practice, no real problems have arisen in connection with the exercise of this authority to acquit, even though it is not exercised frequently.

9.69 An appeal court cannot increase the sentence for unmeritorious appeals by the defence. However, both the accused and the prosecution are entitled to appeal. The prosecution may appeal against an acquittal or the leniency of the sentence. The Law stipulates that the court shall not increase a penalty imposed on the accused unless there has been an appeal against the leniency of the penalty. This is to ensure that accused persons will not be frightened of appealing. However, it has been held that the appeal courts can impose costs on an appellant who brings a vexatious appeal.

9.70 Incompetence by the defence lawyers is not, in principle, in itself ground for an appeal, but the appeal court is likely to take such a contention into consideration in deciding the question of whether the accused was the victim of a miscarriage of justice. The court is reluctant to open the way for a retrial when defendants complain about the conduct of their trial by their counsel (e.g. they refrained from producing some piece of evidence).

9.71 It is possible to apply to the Supreme Court, sitting as the High Court of Justice, as an alternative to appeal. That Court will not, however, intervene in criminal proceedings, unless the plea is lack of jurisdiction, or if there is evidence of extreme arbitrariness in a purely administrative area, or when the consequence for the accused is harsh and irreversible, e.g. a compulsory psychiatric committal order.

9.72 There is no "Court of Last Resort" in Israel. However, an institution for retrial does exist, as entrenched in the Courts Law 1984, s.31, which states:

(a) "the President of the Supreme Court may direct that the Supreme Court or a District Court designated by him for that purpose shall hold a retrial in a criminal matter which has been finally determined if it appears to him:

(i) that a court has decided that any of the evidence produced in the matter was based on a falsehood or forgery and that there is reason to believe that the absence of such evidence might have altered the outcome of the case in favour of the sentenced person; or

(ii) that new facts or new evidence have or has come to light which are or is likely, by themselves or together with the material which was originally before the court, to alter the outcome of the case in favour or the sentenced person and which could not have been in the possession of, or known to, the sentenced person at the time of his trial; or

(iii) that another person has meanwhile been convicted of the criminal act in question and that the circumstances which came to light at the trial of such other person indicated that the person originally convicted of the offence did not commit it.

(b) the sentenced person and the Attorney General have the right to request a retrial. Where the sentenced person has died, such right shall vest also in his spouse and in every one of his descendants, parents, brothers and sisters;

(c) at the retrial, the Supreme Court or District Court shall have all the powers vested in a District Court in a criminal case and vested in the Supreme Court in a criminal appeal, except the power to increase the penalty. The court may make any order it thinks fit to indemnify a sentenced person who has undergone his penalty or part thereof and whose conviction has been quashed as a result of the retrial, or may grant him any other relief; where the accused has died, the court may make an order as aforesaid in favour of another person."

9.73 The decision regarding retrial is final in the sense that it may not be appealed against, and it is not possible to reapply on the same grounds. The written request is submitted to the Attorney General through the District Attorney's office. The prosecution has ninety days to prepare its written reply. As a rule, the President will examine the written request and the responses of both parties, and give a decision without an oral hearing.

9.74 Most requests for a retrial are dismissed. In 1990, twelve requests were submitted, but all of them were dismissed. The President of the Supreme Court has repeatedly emphasised that a retrial should not be considered as an additional appeal. The applicant bears a heavy burden in attempting to convince the President of the existence of at least one of the three grounds for retrial specified.

9.75 Some people feel that a fourth ground should be added to the list in section 31(a), which would be where another person who was involved in the same matter has been acquitted, and in view of the findings or the reasons on which the acquittal was based, the conviction of the convicted person does not have a foundation. This has not yet been enacted.

9.76 In Israel there is no general procedure by which the executive branch refers cases back to the appeal court. However, a similar effect can be achieved in certain circumstances:

(i) as stated above (see paragraph 9.73), the Attorney General can ask for a retrial;

(ii) pardons. The authority to pardon criminals or to reduce their sentences is vested in the President of the State. The request for pardon is submitted to the President through the Ministry of Justice. If such a request is submitted to the President, and a question arises which, in the opinion of the Minister of Justice, merits discussion in the Supreme Court but which cannot serve as grounds for a retrial under s.31 of the Courts Law, the Minister of Justice may put the question to the Supreme Court. The Supreme Court will decide whether to entertain the question presented to it. If it decides in the affirmative, it will discuss the question as if the President of the Supreme Court ordered a retrial. Recourse to this procedure is extremely rare.

Training

9.77 In courses at the Training School for Judges, judges are required to read cases on false confessions, bias, etc., and there are lectures, discussion groups and moot courts on these points.

9.78 Police officers do not have any special courses which focus on these matters. Nonetheless, it appears that these subjects arise for discussion in the framework of the general training that is given to senior investigators and police prosecutors.

Occupied territories

9.79 In some key areas there is a distinction between what happens in Israel "proper" and in the Occupied Territories (e.g. periods of detention without access to a judge, access to lawyers, corroboration of confessions).

PART 10
ITALY

Introduction

10.1 Italy has recently overhauled its code of penal procedure. The new code (*Codice di Procedura Penale*, enacted September 1988, effective October 1989), discards many aspects of an inquisitorial system of criminal procedure in favour of numerous principles and processes of an Anglo-American adversarial procedure. In Italy the inquisitorial system had been maintained for the last sixty years by the Code Rocco, a Fascist-influenced document, and reform was felt necessary since the fall of that regime in the early 1940's. The Italians feel that the new code is a step towards a more civilised system that guarantees the democratic rights of the individual and speeds up proceedings. However, the legal infrastructure is thought by commentators to remain poor.

10.2 More recently there have been some changes to the new code. There have been some important rulings of the Constitutional Court which have relaxed the rules restricting hearsay evidence. The prosecution are now to retain their traditional inquisitorial function as far as they are granted the power of "freezing" a good portion of the incriminating evidence before the trial. Following these rulings, Parliament enacted a statute amending the new code with the view of broadening the trial judge's power to admit out of court statements (Criminal Procedure Revision Act n.356/1992).

Police investigations

Investigation

10.3 In order to separate the trial judge from the act of gathering evidence, the new code creates a distinct investigatory phase in criminal proceedings. Investigations are now expressly delegated to the prosecutor and, under the prosecutor's direction, the judicial police. It is the duty of the prosecution to control the police and to see that evidence is collected fairly. Independent police initiative has been limited in three ways: by imposing an obligation to refer matters quickly to the prosecutor, by regulating police activities in the meantime, and by limiting the admissibility of evidence taken during that period. However, under the 1992 Revision Act the judicial police can also follow their own investigations until the prosecutor takes up the case.

10.4   The new post of the preliminary investigation judge allows judicial authority to be maintained during the preliminary investigation without involving the trial judges. The preliminary investigation judge oversees the development of the investigation, and has control over the issue of search warrants and the imposition of pre-trial detention or other coercive measures against the suspect.

10.5   Police officers are expressly required to report the essential aspects of any crime (i.e. even when no-one has been detained) and any evidence they might have collected to the public prosecutor without delay, after the *notitia criminis* (news of the crime). The police report must be limited to the specific facts of the event, so as to eliminate subjective evaluations of the circumstances which might somehow later work their way into the trial judge's dossier.

10.6   When the police report to the prosecutor, the preliminary investigation officially begins and, if there is a suspect, the prosecutor records his or her name in the official register. This investigation can be conducted in complete secrecy until some type of questioning of the suspect, or search or investigation of property, is needed.

10.7   If questioning occurs (by the public prosecutor) the defence counsel is entitled to be present and the suspect receives notification of this right, and of the right to remain silent. A person who begins to make incriminating statements before being officially put under investigation must be interrupted, be cautioned that such declarations might result in an investigation against him or her, and be invited to nominate an attorney.

10.8   After notification to the public prosecutor, the police can secure the scene of the crime, investigate leads pertinent to the crime, and take suspects into temporary custody for identification. Persons caught in the act of committing the crime can be searched.

10.9   The new code requires a warrant for searches unless:
(a) an arrest warrant has already been issued; (b) the suspect is caught red-handed or is a fugitive; or (c) a danger exists of evidence being dispersed or lost. Whenever searches, openings of documents, or sequestrations are executed, a defence attorney may be present, although he or she need not always be warned ahead of time that such events will take place. This limited right is granted because these events constitute "non-repeatable acts", the reports of which are included in the trial dossier and admitted in evidence without requiring a police officer's evidence.

10.10   Police acquisitions of evidence are not always subject to these limitations. This is so because the police have retained under the new Code their former power to search places where weapons are thought to be hidden. The Constitution states that the police can restrict personal liberties without prior judicial approval "in cases of necessity and urgency". Thus searches with the maintenance of public order as their object, specifically searches for hidden weapons, are legally distinguishable from searches incidental to a criminal investigation. In practice, this distinction allows police to search domiciles for evidence of non weapon related crimes, as long as the search is ostensibly undertaken to look for weapons, since there is no requirement that evidence of other crimes found during such searches cannot be used against the suspect.

10.11   Warrants must be obtained from the preliminary investigation judge for any form of wiretapping or electronic eavesdropping, although in cases of absolute emergency the prosecutor can authorise such interceptions subject to prompt validation by the preliminary investigation judge. There must be weighty indications of an offence and the interception must be absolutely indispensable to the investigation. In no case may wiretaps be used to overhear defence attorneys' communications with their clients or assistants. Postal correspondence addressed to or from a suspect may be suspended for 48 hours, and sealed envelopes and packages must be given directly to the prosecutor, who can authorise their immediate opening in cases of urgency.

10.12   The preliminary investigation must generally be completed within six months of the inscription of the suspect's name in the court register. However, the six months can be extended to eighteen months. In complicated investigations, the preliminary investigation stage can be extended to two years, but no longer. At this point the prosecutor "exercises the penal action" by asking the preliminary investigation judge either to drop the case, allow a simplified proceeding (see paragraphs 10.36–10.38 below), or grant a preliminary hearing where the judge will decide whether charges are warranted (see paragraphs 10.17–10.18 below). Only at this time does the person under investigation officially gain the status of "the accused".

Detention

10.13   A suspect may not be kept in police detention (ie without a warrant of arrest issued by the preliminary investigation judge) for more than twenty four hours. After twenty four hours the police must place the person detained at the disposal of the public prosecutor by: (a) forwarding a written record of the grounds for the detention; and (b) taking him or her to the judicial prison (a place other than the police station for which the public prosecutor is responsible).

10.14   The police are not permitted to question a person detained. They can only interview him or her at the scene of the crime or immediately after the crime has been committed, with a view to developing investigations. In these situations and also when the suspect's counsel is not present, the judicial police are not allowed to take any record of the statements made by the suspect. If a suspect has neither been arrested nor detained, the police can seek to acquire information from him or her which might be useful for the investigation. While interviewing the suspect, the police do not have a duty to caution him or her about the right of silence. The presence of counsel for the defence is compulsory during this interview. The records of the statements taken during this interview are available at trial for the prosecutor to test the credibility of the accused.

10.15 Suspects generally now have the opportunity to confer with an attorney immediately after their arrest without having to obtain a judge's authorisation. However, when "specific and exceptional reasons" exist, the code permits the public prosecutor or the preliminary investigation judge to delay the accused's right to confer with an attorney for up to seven days. Suspects cannot consult legal advisers by telephone. Suspects who cannot afford their own attorney must be provided with one by the Government.

10.16 The new code contains significant precautions against abuses of pre-trial detention and other "cautionary measures". The preliminary investigation judge now has sole control over the extended imposition of such measures. No "cautionary measures" can be ordered unless the indications of guilt are "grave". Detention and lesser restrictions on mobility may be imposed only: (a) where the proceeding involves crimes for which penalties of more than three years' imprisonment are allowed; and (b) where there is a significant danger that the suspect will obstruct the gathering of evidence, that he or she will flee, or that he or she poses a violent threat to society. The maximum term for which a suspect may be detained is now identified for each stage of the proceedings, from initiation of the investigation to the preliminary hearing, sentencing, and an appellate verdict. A total of six years is the custody time limit for the whole process from original investigation to final appeal. This is often used to the limit. Under the new code there is provision for awarding reparations to persons detained where there were no serious indications of their guilt.

Pre-trial procedures

10.17 When preliminary hearings are held, they are in camera and require the presence of both the prosecutor and the defence attorney. The prosecutor begins setting out the results of the investigations and the evidence which justifies sending the case to trial. The accused is not required to give evidence but may do so on request, in which case he or she is subject to interrogation by the judge. The attorneys of any civil parties (e.g. the victim) and of the defendant then advance arguments, using any additional evidence they have brought to the hearing. Both the prosecutor and the defence/victim's attorneys have one chance to rebut each other's arguments. If the preliminary hearing judge is unable to decide whether or not to indict, he or she can suggest to the parties issues to be explored further, or ask them to produce witnesses and experts for questioning and another hearing must then be set within sixty days.

10.18 The preliminary hearing judge can require the prosecutor to modify the charge. The preliminary hearing judge makes no explicit evaluation of the weight of any probative elements if the decree is to send the case to trial. A dismissal at this stage is conclusive unless new evidence is introduced.

Disclosure

10.19 Before the preliminary hearing the defence have a right to relatively full discovery of the prosecution's evidence. When prosecutors request a preliminary hearing, they deposit in the court office the dossier compiled during the investigation (including evidence which might be useful to the defence), and a list of the sources of evidence acquired. Within two days the preliminary hearing judge must schedule the hearing for some date within the next thirty days. During this time the accused's attorney can view the dossier and learn the substance of the prosecution's case. This system of almost unlimited discovery gives the accused the opportunity to make a well-informed choice as to whether to seek an abbreviated trial or a plea-bargained arrangement rather than a full trial (see paragraphs 10.36–10.38 below). Should the police or the prosecution conceal relevant material, the defence counsel can enter a motion of nullity.

10.20 When defence counsel intend to call witnesses or technical consultants at the trial, they must file in the office of the clerk of the court at least seven days prior to the date set for the court session a list indicating the name and the address of the persons to be called and the facts around which direct examination will be developed. Should defence counsel fail to comply with this rule, the court ought not to admit the evidence, unless the defence can show (at the discretion of the President of the Court) that they have not been able to meet this obligation.

Statistics for detention in custody

10.21 Although accurate figures are not available, roughly one third of the prison population are remand prisoners, and another third are convicted prisoners awaiting definitive sentence.

Expert evidence

10.22 Experts are appointed by public prosecutors (or by police officers when the latter investigate on their own initiative). The preliminary investigation judge during preliminary investigations and the court during trial proceedings may appoint experts. If an independent expert is appointed, the prosecution and the defence are permitted to appoint their own technical consultants. The trial can be adjourned for sixty days if necessary. When independent expert evidence is not ordered, the public prosecutor and the defence counsel may appoint their own technical consultants, who are allowed to present their opinion and to submit written reports to the judge. It is up to the judge's discretion which expert's evidence to draw on in giving judgment. There is no system for getting the experts to agree on their evidence before trial.

10.23 The defence counsel is not permitted to use public forensic science services. All experts are registered in the court's "list of experts".

Evidence

Special evidence taking hearings

10.24 Although all the evidence is normally presented by the parties at trial, the preliminary investigation judge may also become involved in receiving evidence by presiding over a special evidence taking hearing called *incidente probatorio* (probative incident). These hearings were created by the new code to allow evidence usable at trial to be taken at the preliminary investigation stage if there is a substantial risk that such evidence will not be available or reliable at the time of trial. Such circumstances exist when the suspect or the prosecutor has specific and well-founded reasons to believe that a witness will be subject to infirmity, death, or bribes. *Incidente probatorio* are also possible when identifications or expert reports may no longer be possible at the time of trial, because of unavoidable alterations of persons, places, or things, or because particular urgency exists for any other reason. Either the defence or the prosecution may request these special hearings before the investigation period expires, and the other party must present a list of objections to the holding of such a special hearing within two days of them receiving notice of the request.

10.25 Any order by the preliminary investigation judge granting an *incidente probatorio* must outline the limits of the evidence to be received, and the prosecutor may request that the hearing be deferred if its occurrence would prejudice the investigation. The hearing is in trial form except for two aspects: its relative secrecy, and the possibility for the victim to request that the judge directs questions to the witnesses. The hearing must also limit itself to evidence concerning the people present at the hearing. It is forbidden to make any allegations about persons not party to the proceedings.

Generally

10.26 The admissibility of evidence acquired by the police without prosecutorial supervision is limited under the new code. Statements taken from an interrogation of a suspect without a defence attorney present cannot be recorded or used at any time during the judicial proceeding itself, although the police may act on such statements for the immediate continuation of the investigation. Generally, only statements to a prosecutor or judge (situations where defence counsel are present) may be used as evidence-in-chief. Admissions given voluntarily, or during a police search, are admissible only at the preliminary hearing and on cross-examination at trial when used to show the existence of a prior inconsistent statement. At trial, prior inconsistent statements can be used on cross-examination only to damage the credibility of the witness.

10.27   No suggestion is allowed by the judge or prosecutor at the trial that silence is evidence of guilt. However, some commentators say that the burden of proof is effectively on the defence, because the defendant who is told the charge is then asked, "what do you have to say to exculpate yourself?". Statements given by the defendant to the prosecutor or judge during the course of the investigation may be received into evidence if the defendant refuses to testify.

10.28   Both the breadth of admissible evidence and the manner of its presentation at the trial have been altered under the new code. Admissible evidence is now limited to those facts which relate to the charge and the determination of the sentence. However, if it is shown during the trial that the offence was really of a different nature than that described in the charge, or that another crime seems to have occurred as well, the charge can be modified or expanded during the course of the trial, and the defendant is allowed an extension to prepare the defence accordingly.

10.29   There is now a codified exclusionary rule, which expressly provides that "evidence acquired in violation of prohibitions established by law cannot be utilised". Illegally obtained evidence must be excluded. This broad exclusionary rule has effect on police searches, coerced witness evidence, confessions, telephone tapping and identification parades.

10.30   The burden of persuasion remains "the free conviction of the judge", but decisions must now be grounded only on the evidence given at trial rather than on extraneous matters.

10.31   When witnesses refer to others as the source of their factual knowledge, either party can demand that those other persons are called to testify. If the witnesses are not produced, the hearsay evidence becomes inadmissible, unless direct examination would be impossible because of death, infirmity, or unavailability of the witness.

10.32   As a matter of law, corroboration is not required for confession evidence. However, in practice courts do not convict defendants on uncorroborated confessions.

10.33 Where identification of a suspect is carried out complying with the strict procedure set out in the Criminal Code (i.e. before a preliminary investigation judge, in the presence of the suspect's defence counsel, and with a fair parade organised), corroboration is not required.

10.34 Accomplice evidence must be corroborated. The code says that statements made by a co-defendant should be evaluated with other elements of evidence that confirm their reliability.

Juries

10.35 In the most serious cases (e.g. homicide, mafia-related cases, kidnappings, terrorism) the Italian Court of Assizes has two judges who deliberate together with a panel of six lay assessors, recruited at random. All eight members of this panel have to decide points of fact and points of law. They each have a vote and decide by simple majority. Many lawyers agree that in the secrecy of the jury room, the professional judges are able to influence the lay assessors.

Trial procedures

Special Proceedings

10.36 The new code creates a number of special proceedings by which defendants can reach the final trial without having to pass through the preliminary hearing, or by which they can accept a penalty without having to go all the way to a full trial. This speeds up proceedings in a system where there is no guilty plea. The preliminary investigation judge affirms the parties' arrangements.

10.37 These proceedings give defence attorneys a greater role to play than they previously enjoyed, as they must now advise on the decision whether to avoid a full trial completely if a special proceeding seems advisable.

10.38 None of the special proceedings can begin until the prosecutor has turned over his dossier to the judge for trial, and any plea bargain arrangement requires the defendant's full appraisal of the prosecutor's case against him. There are five types of special proceedings, which, apart from the first one, are basically simplified trial procedures:

(i) **plea bargaining proceeding.** This is probably the most important of the new special proceedings. Officially called "application of the penalty on request of the parties", it is a sweeping procedure that is not limited to specific categories of crimes. By entering into such a bargain, the defendant can reduce the penalty by up to one-third of the sentence normally imposed, as long as the resulting period of detention does not exceed two years in duration. The conviction is expunged from the record after a few years if the defendant is not convicted again of a similar crime in the intervening period. The bargain can be made at any time until the trial. When the parties agree on the charge and penalty, the role of the preliminary investigation judge is limited to that of ensuring that the legal classification of the offence is correct, or that an outright dismissal of the charge is not required. Such an agreement is not appealable. Sometimes the defendant may request the "application of the penalty" without the prosecutor having agreed to the proposed bargain. If the judge believes the prosecutor's opposition is unjustified, the defendant's request will be honoured, notwithstanding the opposition. Since the defendant must be advised of the right to make such a plea even during the other simplified proceedings that may be invoked (i.e. (ii) to (v)), he may still receive a reduced sentence in such cases if the judge is anxious to bring the proceedings to an end;

(ii) *the abbreviated trial.* This proceeding is a trial on the merits before the preliminary investigation judge, with the hearing held in camera. If convicted, the defendant has the otherwise applicable sentence reduced by one third. The parties make no agreement as to the correctness of the charge, the prosecutor's consent is a requisite to the proceedings, and the judge can negate the proceeding if the evidence seems as yet incomplete. The defendant cannot appeal against a conviction if only a fine is imposed, and the prosecutor cannot appeal against acquittals on grounds other than those raised at the abbreviated trial. Since the abbreviated trial is held before the preliminary investigation judge, evidential restrictions do not apply and the proceeding is more inquisitorial in nature than a full trial;.

(iii) *the giudizio immediato.* This allows the prosecutor to bypass the preliminary hearing and go straight to the trial when the evidence plainly points to the accused's guilt. This procedure requires that the prosecutor approaches the preliminary investigation judge within ninety days of the beginning of the investigation, and that the prosecutor has interrogated the suspect prior to the request. The preliminary investigation judge must notify the defendant that he or she can still seek an abbreviated trial (ii), or offer a plea (i), failing this, the judge decides the case within five days;

(iv) *the giudizio direttissimo*. This is used for cases where the suspect has confessed to the crime, or was caught red-handed in its commission. In the hearing validating the arrest, the prosecutor can request that the suspect be brought to trial not less than three days and not more than fifteen days after hearing;

(v) *the procedimento per decreto or penal decree*. This is applied in those cases where the prosecutor believes that only a fine is justifiable, even though a penalty of imprisonment may be available by law for that class of crime. The fine is mitigated by up to one-half of its normal value in order to induce the defendant to accept this route.

Trial

10.39 The division of the Italian courts is as follows:

– *Pretura*, responsible for minor crimes (e.g. theft, fraud etc.) or any offence which results in pecuniary fines or prison sentences of up to four years.

– *Tribunale*, responsible for all types of organised crime, and more serious offences against the public administration, kidnapping, serious drug traffic offences, armed robbery.

– *Corte D'Assise*, responsible for the most serious crimes including crimes against the State.

10.40 Under the new code two dossiers exist: the prosecutor's (which contains everything learned during the investigation) and the judge's. The prosecutor's dossier is largely like the file of an Anglo-American prosecutor, generally not to be viewed or used by the trial judge. The dossier received by the trial judge from the preliminary investigation judge contains only the transcripts of any *incidente probatorio* (see paragraphs 10.24–10.25 above) that has been held and reports of any search and seizures performed by the prosecutor and the police i.e. "non repeatable acts". Trial judges are now largely confined to evaluating the evidence presented by the parties at trial.

10.41 The prosecutor begins the trial with an opening speech, presenting the facts in issue and indicating the evidence. This is followed by any civilly interested parties and the defendant. Questions of admissibility must be ruled upon immediately. Witnesses are examined and cross-examined. Leading questions are prohibited on direct examination, as are prejudicial questions and harassment of the witness by either party.

10.42 The trial has not been made completely adversarial. Judges can direct the parties to pursue those issues that they believe should be further explored, and may subpoena experts. Additionally, once the parties have examined a witness or defendant, judges can intervene with their own questions, although the parties still have the right to conclude the examination. Even more important, judges may require, at the end of the parties' presentation of evidence, the acquisition of additional evidence if it appears to them absolutely necessary. This power is frequently used in practice. This remnant of the inquisitorial process leaves judges with considerable power to overcome an inadequate presentation of the evidence by the parties.

Prior convictions

10.43 Trial judges must have before them prior convictions of the accused during the trial. They count as evidence of the accused's character, and are usable to ascertain his or her responsibility and to determine the sentence.

Appeals

10.44 There is an appeal to the *Tribunale* from the *Preture*, an appeal to the *Corte d'Appello* from the *Tribunale*, and an appeal to the *Corte d'Assise d'Appello* (Court of Appeal) for appeal from the *Corte d'Assise*. Final and ultimate appeal is to the Court of Cassation. There are three basic procedures for appeal:

(i) after sentence the defendant, his or her lawyer, or the prosecutor can appeal. There is a pre-appeal hearing where the case is examined, and if the appeal is approved, there is a new trial;

(ii) review by the *Court of Cassation*, which is the most senior judiciary body in Italy. The form of review is only for those judgments not subject to further appeal and is limited to appeals on points of law. In exceptional cases, however, the Court has the right to review the merits of a decision which leads to;

(iii) revision of a judgment (*revisione*). This is aimed at those cases where the appeal procedure has been carried out and there is no further possibility of review or where new evidence has been uncovered which throws a new light on the case. The case is put before the *Court of Cassation* who either quash the conviction or order a retrial. This can be requested by the prisoner, a close relative or even heir, the Italian Ministry of Justice or the judicial authorities themselves. Persons found to have been convicted or imprisoned unjustly are entitled to compensation, the sum in proportion to the amount of time they have spent in jail. The award can take the form of a monthly payment. If the person is deceased the heirs can claim the compensation.

10.45   Under the old penal procedure code, the large majority (almost 80%) of those convicted in the lower courts appealed to higher courts. Under the new code, with the introduction of special procedures (e.g. plea bargaining), the proportion has fallen to around 70%. The proportion of appeals that are successful is said to be small. The Italian Constitution guarantees the right of all, including the prosecution, to appeal against any judicial decision and to appeal right up the ladder to the highest court. Appeals to the supreme *Court of Cassation* on points of law are granted as a fundamental right by the Constitution. Appeals brought before the Court of Appeal, on questions of fact or law, do not require leave.

10.46   Before the new code it was obligatory to hold another full trial in the Court of Appeal, which led to a proliferation of slow appeals. As a corrective measure, the code now requires a hearing in camera whenever the appeal is limited to the weight of the evidence presented at the initial trial or the amount of the imposed penalty. A closed door session is also possible upon the request of the parties whenever they are in agreement as to the reason for appeal, or as to the proposed penalty.

10.47   Before the Court of Appeal the defendant can call any evidence, including evidence which was available at the trial, or new evidence. No appeal is allowed on the grounds that the case was mishandled by the lawyers.

10.48   If the defendant is acquitted, the acquittal is outright. The new code has eliminated the use of the declaration of *assoluzione per insufficienza di prove*, an equivocal decision which expressed the fact that some doubts remained as to the defendant's possible guilt.

10.49   The *appello incidentale* allows an appellate court to impose a heavier sentence in some circumstances. When one party requests an appeal (the principal appeal), the other party can propose an incidental appeal under which reasons may be advanced for modifying or increasing the sentence.

Training

10.50   The training of police officers includes attention to the problems of criminal investigation. In the police schools teachers pay great attention to the disciplinary responsibility of police officers before judicial authority. There are also courses run for the police by judges, some of which are compulsory.

10.51 The training of judicial personnel takes place principally during a period of roughly two years which they spend as "Judicial Auditors", sitting alongside criminal court judges. This gives them a grounding in the fundamental principles of criminal law and criminology.

Part 11
The Netherlands

Police investigations

11.1   There are two kind of pre-trial investigation: (i) the investigation by the police under the direction of the public prosecutor; and (ii) the judicial investigation by a (professional) examining magistrate. In contrast with French law, there are no offences for which judicial examination is obligatory. The public prosecutor decides whether there is to be a judicial examination or not. In practice, the public prosecutor only applies for a judicial investigation when he or she thinks that there is a need in the case for the powers of the examining magistrate. The Code of Criminal Procedure (CCP) prescribes a judicial examination as a check on the exercise of certain powers by the public prosecutor or a senior police officer, for example the power to search premises in a case of "urgent necessity". According to a recent research study, judicial investigations are held in 6% of all cases that reach the courts. In 1988, the Minister of Justice set up a Commission for the revision of the CCP. In September 1990, the Commission published a report on judicial investigation in which it proposed no changes to the structure of the pre-trial investigation.

11.2   Suspects who are brought to the police station after arrest can be held for six hours in order to be questioned by a senior police officer, or the public prosecutor, for the purpose of deciding whether they should be held in police custody. During this period they may be questioned by police officers involved in the investigation. The time between midnight and 9.00 am does not count as part of the six hours. After this initial period of six+nine hours, according to the CCP, suspects can be held in police custody on the order of a senior police officer or public prosecutor for forty eight hours. This period can then be extended by the public prosecutor for another forty eight hours. Thereafter, the suspect can be remanded in custody only by the examining magistrate. However, the decision of the European Court of Human Rights in *Brogan* has been understood in the Netherlands to mean that a period of four days is too long for a suspect to be detained in police custody before being brought before an examining magistrate[1]. As a result, the Public Prosecutor's Department issued guidelines under which the suspect has to be brought before an examining magistrate within three days of the start of police custody. In addition, the Minister of Justice has introduced a bill, which

---
[1] The European Convention is directly applicable in the Netherlands.

provides that a suspect must be brought before a magistrate within two days of being taken into police custody.

11.3   Since 1973, the CCP requires the suspect to be told before any interrogation that he is not obliged to answer questions. This applies to all instances of interrogation, either by a police officer, the public prosecutor, the magistrate or the court.

11.4   Suspects do not have the right to legal advice during the initial six+nine hours period of police detention. However, if the senior police officer or the public prosecutor decides to hold the suspect in police custody for a further forty eight hours, the suspect then has a right to legal advice. If suspects do not have a lawyer of their own, a duty solicitor will automatically be appointed for them. The duty solicitor must be informed by the police about the fact that the suspect is held in police custody and the solicitor must visit the suspect in the police station. However, the solicitor is not allowed to attend interrogations by the police officers involved in the investigation. In contrast, when interrogated by the examining magistrate in the judicial investigation, the solicitor in principle has the right to attend, unless in the opinion of the examining magistrate this should not be allowed in the interests of the investigation.

Evidence

11.5   There are no specific rules restricting the admissibility of confessions that have not been tape-recorded or repeated in front of a judge or magistrate. A confession taken during questioning by a police officer and registered in a police report can be used in evidence. It is not necessary for the court to examine the police officer at the trial about the confession. The report is admissible. Similarly, a confession before a magistrate, registered in a report of the examining magistrate, can be used in evidence.

11.6   A conviction, however, cannot be based on the statement of the suspect alone. There must be at least one witness statement in addition to this. Generally, the defendant cannot be convicted on the basis of a single witness statement, except in the case of a statement by a police officer who has been an eye-witness to the offence.

11.7   There is no rule forbidding the use of the accused's silence in evidence against him.

11.8   In principle illegally obtained evidence, either confessional or real, is excluded. There are certain exceptions to this. For example, the evidence does not have to be excluded if the illegality does not involve the accused but a third person. For example, the illegal search did not concern the premises of the accused but someone else.

11.9 Hearsay evidence is admissible. As a result, there is no general practice of calling and examining witnesses at trial.

Prosecution

11.10 According to the CCP, the police when investigating crime operate under the authority of the public prosecutor. The prosecutor, therefore, can direct and supervise the investigation. However, in practice this occurs only in serious cases. In other cases, the prosecutor simply receives the reports police officers have to submit to him.

11.11 Prosecutors have complete freedom to decide whether to prosecute or not. In general, they only prosecute if they think that it is in the public interest. If they decide not to prosecute, the defendant is informed in writing. Prosecutors can also decide "conditionally not to prosecute". This power is used in the same way as a suspended sentence might be used, to induce a suspect to perform a service or to make reparation (such as return stolen property) or to refrain from certain activities.

11.12 Prosecution can also be made conditional on the payment of a sum of money. This is called a "transaction". Prior to 1983 the prosecutor could offer to settle summary offences out of court and the police could settle certain traffic offences. Since 1983 the prosecutor, but not the police, has had the power to settle all indictable offences out of court, except those for which there is a maximum prison sentence of over six years. The maximum amount that can be imposed is the maximum fine. Defendants are free to refuse to agree to the transaction. If they do refuse, the prosecution will proceed in the normal way. If the main penalty fixed for the offence is a fine and the defendant agrees to pay the maximum fine fixed by the law and to abide by any conditions set by the prosecutor, he or she has a right to require the prosecutor to offer him or her a transaction. The transaction goes on the defendant's criminal record and can be referred to by the courts.

11.13 The Ministry of Justice publishes guidelines to achieve national standards in transactions and conditional non-prosecutions, but non-prosecution may be determined locally. In 1989, there were a total of 145,859 cases in which transactions were possible. These cases were dealt with as follows:

	%
Dismissed for policy reasons	25.6
Transaction by the prosecutor	23.7
Unconditional prison sentence	11.8

Unconditional fine	29.3
Other sanctions by judge	9.6
Total	100.0

11.14   In a leaflet published by the Ministry of Justice on the court system in the Netherlands, it is stated: "[The] Public Prosecutor is a very special kind of official, a "semi-judge". In the Netherlands, the Public Prosecutor is given a very free hand. So free, in fact, that other countries believe sometimes that we are risking our legal certainty. But we are still very happy with the way our system works."

Disclosure

11.15   In the course of the pre-trial investigations, the defence has full access to the dossier except where disclosure of certain material is deemed to be contrary to the interest of the investigation by the Public Prosecutor or, in the case of judicial investigation, by the examining magistrate. Some items must always be disclosed to the defence, for example the reports of interrogations of the accused. The accused can appeal to the district court if disclosure is refused. The CCP requires that all restrictions on access by the defence to the dossier must be lifted at the close of the judicial investigation, or if no judicial investigation has been held, as soon as the accused is notified that he or she will be summoned for trial.

11.16   In nearly all cases witnesses are examined before trial by the police and, if a judicial investigation is held, sometimes also by the examining magistrate. Their statements, as well as those by experts, are included in the dossier. When a witness is examined by the examining magistrate, but not when examined by the police, the defence lawyer has a right to be present. The defence also has the right to ask the Public Prosecutor and examining magistrate to summon witnesses for examination pre-trial. This can only be refused when the defence cannot reasonably be deemed to be prejudiced by the refusal.

11.17   The police and the prosecutor have the duty to look for exculpatory evidence as well as inculpatory evidence. In general, every thing relevant should be included in the dossier.

11.18   The defence is only required to submit the names of the witnesses for the defence to the Public Prosecutor three days before trial. If the accused raises an alibi defence for the first time at the trial, the court can order additional investigations, by itself or by the examining magistrate.

Expert evidence

11.19   Scientific evidence is gathered by specific police or scientific experts. The state scientific and forensic laboratory have issued directions for the police concerning the proper way to collect scientific evidence. The Public Prosecutor often supervises the gathering of evidence at the scene of the crime in major cases.

11.20 Experts are appointed by either an examining magistrate, a Public Prosecutor or senior police officer. Unless the interests of the investigation dictate otherwise, the accused and his or her counsel must be informed of the expert's assignment. The defence can recommend an expert and can be present at the expert examination. The defence must be informed about the outcome of the expert investigation as soon as the interests of the investigation permit. The accused can appoint a counter-expert. In certain cases the fees of the expert will be paid by the government. In the case of conflicting opinions the examining magistrate can appoint a further expert.

11.21 As a rule, experts are not called as witnesses at the trial. Their written opinion is admissible in evidence. However, during the trial the court can in theory (but rarely does) have an expert who is not present summoned to give opinion on particular aspects. The prosecutor and the defence can ask the court to do so. The case is then adjourned. The court can also order additional investigations by the examining magistrate, among other things for the purpose of obtaining an expert report. The case will be adjourned in this instance as well.

Pre-trial examination of the accused

11.22 The accused can also be examined by the examining magistrate during the judicial investigation, but not on oath. The accused is not obliged to answer any questions. In theory, the examining magistrate should ask the questions. The Public Prosecutor and counsel for the defence should submit to the examining magistrate the questions they wish to have put to the accused. In practice, however, examining magistrates allow questions to be put directly to the accused.

Statistics for detention pre-trial

11.23 The number of defendants remanded in custody prior to conviction were as follows:

	1.1.89	1.1.90	1.1.91
District court	2586	2958	3620
– Adults	–	2493	3001
– Juveniles	–	465	619

Court of Appeal	459	375	417
– Adults	–	374	414
– Juveniles	–	1	3

The Netherlands has a population of approximately 15 million.

11.24   Defendants are sentenced immediately after the verdict is given.

Juries

11.25   There are no juries in the Netherlands. There is no lay element in the Dutch criminal justice system.

Trial

11.26   Serious cases are tried by a court consisting of three professional judges. Less serious cases are dealt with by a single judge.

11.27   As has been stated above, hearsay statements are admissible in evidence. As a result there is no general practice of calling and examining witnesses at trial. Under the CCP, the defence has the right to request the prosecutor, prior to the trial, to subpoena witnesses for the defence. The prosecutor can dismiss the request if he or she deems the accused will not be prejudiced if the witness is not summoned. The defence may appeal to the court, which can dismiss the request on the same grounds. Requests made by the defence, during the trial, to have the prosecutor summon witnesses may be dismissed by the court on the basis of irrelevance or if the court thinks that it is unnecessary. However, under the case law of the European Court, it is now held that a defendant cannot be convicted on the basis of a statement from a witness the defence had no opportunity of examining during the pre-trial or trial stage. If a witness who has not been examined in the pre-trial stage is not examined at the request of the defence during the trial, the court refers the case to the examining magistrate for the purpose of examining the witness.

11.28   The trial procedure is conducted by the presiding judge who first asks the defendant his name, address, etc. The prosecutor then reads the indictment or a summary of it. Then there is the "investigation into the facts". The court inquires primarily on the basis of the written evidence included in the dossier. The witnesses, if any, and then the accused are then questioned by the presiding judge. The Public Prosecutor and the defence lawyer are allowed to ask supplementary questions. However, there is no system of cross examination and re-examination to test the veracity of witnesses. The written evidence is read aloud. After the investigation into the facts, the prosecutor and the defence make closing speeches. The defence always has the last word. The court then gives its verdict. The court must sum up in a written judgment the evidence that in its opinion supports a conviction. In cases where the defendant presents a relevant defence which is not accepted by the court, it must state the reasons for non-acceptance. The court then sentences the defendant. There is no time lapse between conviction and sentence.

11.29   Trials are as a rule short. It is rare, for example, for a murder trial to last for more than two or three days.

11.30   Dutch courts view prison as the last resort. When imprisonment is imposed, sentences are short. For example, in 1986 the average prison sentence for homicide was 26.6 months. However, there is a low rate of recidivism. Two thirds of persons convicted never come into conflict with the law again.

Previous convictions

11.31   The accused's criminal record will be in the dossier which the court will see. However, the record is relevant only when determining sentence and not guilt.

Appeals

11.32   The defendant and prosecutor can appeal as of right against judgments of the district courts, to one of the five courts of appeal. No distinction is made between appeals against sentence and conviction. Both the accused and the prosecutor can appeal against the decision of the court of appeal to the supreme court (*Hoge Raad*). However, no appeal to the supreme court is allowed against an acquittal. The grounds of this appeal are limited to violations of legal provisions and procedural errors.

11.33   The statistics on appeal cases for 1989 are as follows:

"common offences" (Criminal Code offences)

cases dealt with by the district courts: 77,104
verdicts of guilty: 71,117
cases dealt with by the courts of appeal: 6,838
decisions quashed: 5,961
cases dealt with by the supreme court: 1,188
appeal dismissed: 1,023

"economic offences"

cases dealt with by the district courts: 5,026

verdicts of guilty: 4,679
cases dealt with by the courts of appeal: 255
cases dealt with by the supreme court: 80

"fiscal offences"

cases dealt with by the district courts: 419
verdicts of guilty: 382
cases dealt with by the court of appeal: 51

11.34   The courts of appeal have no power to discourage hopeless appeals by adding on time to the sentence for unmeritorious appeals.

11.35   The accused has the right to be tried on the facts twice. The procedure on appeal is essentially that of a new trial. The courts of appeal consider the whole case again – the evidence in the dossier at the trial and any new evidence.

11.36   A person may appeal only once to the court of appeal.

11.37   There is no procedure whereby a member of the executive can refer a matter back to the appeal court.

11.38   There is a special procedure for reviewing final convictions. Under special circumstances the convicted person can obtain a rehearing, even though the judgment has become final. He or she can ask the supreme court for a review of the case (*herziening*). The grounds for granting a rehearing are limited to either: (i) there are inconsistent verdicts of guilty in different judgments or (ii) there is a new fact that was unknown to the court and that is not consistent with the judgment to such a degree that there are serious reasons to assume that if the fact had been known the court would have acquitted the accused, or would have dismissed the prosecution, or convicted the accused of a less serious offence. If the supreme court finds one of these grounds, it orders the suspension of the execution of the sentence and refers the case to one of the courts of appeal in order either to have the judgment upheld or quashed and have the accused acquitted, or have him convicted of a less serious offence. Recently the supreme court has accepted another possibility for review of a final conviction. This is when a judgment of the European Court of Human Rights casts doubt upon a judgment.

11.39   When the complaints of the convicted person do not fall within the above grounds, he or she may petition the Queen for a pardon.

Training

11.40   The judiciary and prosecution are professionals who have been educated together after their legal training at university and their careers are to some extent interchangeable. Their training after university consists of a two year period as a court-clerk, a two year period as acting prosecutor and a two year period as defence counsel. During this six year period, the candidate will receive training on the problems of false confessions, unreliable eye-witness evidence and bias.

11.41   The training of police officers will also cover these topics.

Part 12
New Zealand

Police investigations

12.1 There are no statutory provisions in effect in New Zealand equivalent to the Police and Criminal Evidence Act. The Judges' Rules formulated in England in 1912, while having no force of law, are still regarded as a guide by the New Zealand courts.

12.2 There is no specific time limit on police questioning prior to charge prescribed by statute. Section 316(5) of the Crimes Act 1961 provides that every person who is arrested on a charge of any offence shall be brought before a court, as soon as possible, to be dealt with according to the law. In *R. v. Alexander*[1], it was held that, if an arrested person is being detained for the purpose of being brought before a court, section 316(5) did not preclude questioning about the offence for which the person has been arrested or about other offences. However, the arrested person must not be detained any longer than is reasonably necessary to enable him or her to be brought before a court.

12.3 The New Zealand Bill of Rights Act 1990 is not entrenched in the same way as rights are in Canada and the United States. The courts have no jurisdiction to declare invalid or refuse to apply provisions inconsistent with the Act. Section 22 of the Act provides that everyone has the right not to be arbitrarily arrested or detained. Section 23(1)(c) states that everyone has the right to determine the validity of such arrest or detention without delay by way of habeas corpus, and to be released if the arrest or detention is not lawful. Everyone who is arrested for an offence has the right to be charged promptly or released (section 23(2)). Everyone who is arrested for an offence and is not released must be brought before a court or competent tribunal as soon as possible (section 23(3)).

12.4 Section 23(4) of the New Zealand Bill of Rights Act 1990 provides that everyone who is arrested, or detained under any enactment, has the right to refrain from making statements and to be informed of that right. Section 23(1)(b) provides that everyone who is arrested or detained under any enactment has the right to consult and instruct a lawyer without delay and to be informed of that right. No distinction is made between serious and less serious cases.

---

[1] (1989) 3 NZLR 95.

12.5 The Court of Appeal has recently delivered an important decision[2] regarding the meaning of "arrest" in terms of section 23. The majority of the Court held that de facto detention in police custody with the intention or contemplation that the suspect will or may be formally charged is arrest within the meaning of the Bill of Rights Act 1990. De facto detention is a situation in which the suspect is not free to go or possibly in which what is said or done by the police causes the suspect reasonably to believe that he is not free to go.

12.6 In the same case, the Court of Appeal said that, although the Bill of Rights Act had to be applied in a realistic way, "prima facie, however, a violation of rights should result in the ruling out of evidence obtained thereby. The prosecution should bear the onus of satisfying the Court that there is good reason for admitting the evidence despite the violation." In the case the Court of Appeal held that the judge had been wrong in considering breach of the 1990 Act as merely part of the overall picture to be considered by the Court in deciding whether it was fair to admit the evidence. The defendant had been denied the right to a consult a lawyer. The Court of Appeal held that confessions obtained in the subsequent interviews were therefore inadmissible.

12.7 Additional provisions exist for the questioning of young persons under 17 years old. The Children, Young Persons and Their Families Act 1989 provides, in addition to other rights, that the police must explain to young persons in language that they will understand that they are under no obligation to make or give any statement and that they are entitled to consult, and make any statement in the presence of a solicitor or barrister and any person nominated by the young person. The Act also provides that no oral or written statement made to any enforcement officer by the young person will be admissible in evidence unless the young person has been informed of these rights and the statement is made in the presence of a solicitor or barrister or person nominated by the young person or if the young person refuses or fails to nominate any person, any other adult (not being an enforcement officer). A Ministerial Review Team has recently reported to the Minister of Social Welfare on all aspects of the Act, including these admissibility rules. The Department of Justice is at present considering the Review Team's recommendations.

12.8 The Law Commission, in its discussion paper *Criminal Evidence: Police Questioning*, proposes that clearly defined provision be made to allow the police to question suspects after arrest and before charge and court appearance. The Commission proposes that the police should be allowed to detain an arrested suspect for an initial period which is reasonable in all the

---

[2] *R. v. Butcher* (1992) 2 NZLR 257.

circumstances, but which does not exceed four hours. A commissioned officer of police could extend the period by four hours' and, on application to a District Judge, a further extension of twenty four hours could be obtained in exceptional circumstances. The rules also allow for certain "time out" periods, such as time spent travelling to the police station or time spent contacting and communicating with a lawyer or waiting for a lawyer to arrive. The Commission also proposes that questioning should be subject to certain safeguards to ensure that improper pressure is not brought to bear on suspects. For example, the suspect should have the right to consult a lawyer, access to a friend or relative and access to an interpreter.

Evidence

(i) Confessions

12.9   There are no rules restricting the admissibility of confessions that have not been tape-recorded or repeated before a judge or magistrate. Video taping of police interviews, although occurring in some areas of New Zealand, has not yet been introduced nationwide. The police in New Zealand have moved directly to videoing, without ever having used audio tape recording.

12.10   Corroboration of a confession is not required. A confession will be inadmissible if it lacks voluntariness. Confessions induced by violence, force or "other form of compulsion" are inadmissible. Promises, threats, or other inducements (not being violence, force or other form of compulsion) do not necessarily make a confession inadmissible. A confession need not be rejected in these circumstances if the judge is satisfied that "... the means by which the confession was obtained were not in fact likely to cause an untrue admission of guilt to be made" (section 20 Evidence Act 1908). The test is whether or not an innocent person in the position of the accused and in the circumstances in which he or she is placed would be likely to confess to a crime which he or she had not committed.

12.11   A confession can (as stated above in paragraph 12.6) be ruled out if there has been a violation of the suspect's rights under the Bill of Rights Act 1990. The judge also has a discretion to exclude confession evidence on the ground of unfairness (sometimes also expressed as "unfairly obtained" or unfairness to the accused).

12.12   There are special rules governing the statements of children made to the police (see paragraph 12.7 above).

12.13   The Law Commission, in its discussion paper *Criminal Evidence: Police Questioning*, proposes two specific rules to govern the admissibility of confessions, a reliability rule and an oppression rule, which will take the place of the voluntariness rule and section 20 of the Evidence Act 1908. Under the reliability rule, if a defendant raises the issue, the prosecution would have to prove beyond reasonable doubt that the circumstances pertaining to the making of the statement were not likely to have affected its reliability. Factors the court would have to take in to account would be:

(a) any pertinent physical, mental and psychological condition of the defendant when the statement was made; and

(b) any pertinent characteristics of the defendant including any mental, intellectual or physical disability to which the defendant is subject; and

(c) the nature of any questions put to the defendant and the manner and circumstances in which they were put; and

(d) the nature of any threat, promise or representation made to the defendant or any other person.

12.14   Under the oppression rule proposed by the Law Commission, if a defendant raises the issue, a statement made by the defendant would be inadmissible unless the prosecution satisfied the court beyond reasonable doubt that the statement was not influenced by:

(a) oppressive, violent, inhuman or degrading conduct towards or treatment of the defendant or another person; or

(b) threat of conduct or treatment of that kind.

12.15   The Law Commission is also in favour of all interviews in indictable offences being video tape recorded but states that it is not practical to recommend a general requirement at present. The Commission favours a rule, similar to the one laid down by the High Court of Australia in *McKinney and Judge*[3], requiring the judge to give a suitable warning when a statement has not been videotaped.

(ii) Identification

12.16   Corroboration is not necessary for identification. However, section 344D of the Crimes Act 1961 provides that where, in proceedings before a jury, a case turns wholly or substantially on visual identification, a warning is to be given of the special need for caution. The warning should

---

[3] (1991) 65 ALJR 241. See Part 2, paragraph 2.8.

include the reason for the warning, alert the jury to the possibility that a mistaken witness may be convincing, and where there is more than one witness, refer to the possibility that all of them may be mistaken.

(iii) The Accused's Silence

(a) Before trial

12.17   The current law concerning silence before trial is in some respects less than certain. A distinction is made between silence in the face of an allegation and silence in the face of questioning. Evidence of an allegation made by the police and the defendant's subsequent silence is generally inadmissible on the ground that the probative value of the evidence is outweighed by its prejudicial effect. Where a spontaneous allegation is made by someone on equal terms with the defendant, the allegation and the defendant's silence may be admissible if the defendant's silence can be regarded as an acceptance of the allegation. Evidence of the defendant's silence in the face of questioning is admissible in all cases. Where questioning includes an allegation, it will be excluded from the evidence. The judge can comment on the accused's silence in the face of questioning only in exceptional circumstances.

12.18   Evidence that a defendant did not previously disclose a defence later relied upon at trial is admissible and this can be the object of adverse comment. In addition, the judge can comment adversely on the defendant's failure to explain his or her possession of recently stolen goods. The defendant is also obliged to give notice of an alibi in advance of the trial.

12.19   The Law Commission, in its discussion paper *Criminal Evidence: Police Questioning*, favours the enactment of a provision preventing any comment on the pre-trial exercise of the right to silence in response to official questioning. The Commission considers that evidence of silence in response to official questioning should always be excluded. This proposal would leave unchanged the position where the parties are on equal terms. It would change the law concerning comment on belated explanations. The Commission also proposes that the judge should no longer be able to comment on the accused's failure to explain his or her possession of recently stolen goods. However, no change is proposed with regard to alibi evidence.

(b) Silence at trial

12.20   At present, if the accused remains silent at trial, an adverse inference can be drawn and the judge may comment to that effect in his summing up (Crimes Act 1961, s.366). The prosecution, however, cannot comment. The circumstances in which comment should be made were recently considered by the Court of Appeal in *R. v. Andrews*[4]. The Court did not consider that comment should be automatic. It was suggested by Jeffries J that "there must be something in the trial itself that enables an unfavourable comment to be made". The Law Commission suggest that the current position is that silence in itself is not to give rise to an inference of guilt but is only to be taken into account in assessing the weight of other evidence. Examples of factors which might be relevant to a decision whether to comment after a defendant refrains from giving evidence are the making of an attack on prosecution witnesses, the suggestion that another person was the culprit, or an endeavour to tender an explanation through a psychiatrist.

12.21 The Law Commission recommends in its discussion paper that there should be no substantial change to the current position but thinks that further consideration needs to be given to defining the circumstances in which comment can be made, the nature the of the comment and the ability of the defendant to predict when comment will be made.

(iv) *Improperly Obtained Evidence*

12.22 The Judge has a general discretion to exclude evidence on the ground of unfairness. Breach of the Judges' Rules may, but will not automatically, result in exclusion on this ground. Before the discretion is exercised in favour of exclusion, some improper conduct of which the Crown should not take advantage will normally have to be shown. The Judge must weigh the public interest in conviction of the guilty against that of the protection of individuals from unlawful and unfair treatment.

12.23 As has already been stated, the Court of Appeal has held that prima facie a violation of rights contained in the Bill of Rights Act 1990 should result in the ruling out of evidence obtained thereby. The onus will be on the prosecution to satisfy the court there are good reasons for admitting the evidence despite the violation.

12.24 The Law Commission, in its discussion paper *Criminal Evidence: Police Questioning*, recommends that if a defendant raises the issue that evidence has been improperly obtained, the evidence should be inadmissible unless the prosecution satisfies the court beyond reasonable doubt that the evidence was not obtained improperly or the court considers that exclusion of the evidence would be contrary to the interests of justice. Evidence would be held to have been obtained improperly if it was obtained:

    (a) in consequence of a breach of the New Zealand Bill of Rights Act 1990; or

---

[4] Unreported, Court of Appeal, 15 April 1992, CA 366/91.

(b) in consequence of a breach of a provision of any enactment or rule of law; or

(c) in consequence of a statement made by a defendant that is inadmissible, or would be held inadmissible if it were offered in evidence by the prosecution; or

(d) unfairly.

12.25　Factors the court should consider when deciding to admit improperly obtained evidence would be:

(a) the special nature of the New Zealand Bill of Rights Act 1990 as an Act to affirm, protect and promote human rights and fundamental freedoms in New Zealand; and

(b) the nature and gravity of any impropriety; and

(c) whether any impropriety was the result of bad faith; and

(d) whether the evidence existed and would have been discovered or otherwise obtained regardless of any impropriety.

Prosecution

12.26　New Zealand does not have a Crown Prosecution Service, as have England and Wales, but each major city has a barrister and solicitor (the profession is partially fused) appointed under warrant from the Solicitor-General to conduct Crown Prosecutions in that area. They are called the Crown Solicitor. They are not paid a salary or retainer, but are paid fees on a time basis according to a set scale. They may act for private clients as well, but not in opposition to the Crown, and not for the defence in criminal matters. The Crown Solicitor's office prepares indictments and the Crown Solicitor or someone from that firm appears as counsel to prosecute in criminal jury trials and appear for the Crown in criminal appeals. The police conduct the prosecution in summary cases.

12.27　Police general instructions provide that a file must be forwarded to the Crown Solicitor in cases of murder or any other difficult, important or unusual prosecution. Investigations concerning cases of assault by a prisoner on a prison officer, and serious assault of a police officer, are also to be referred to the Crown Solicitor. In other cases, the Crown Solicitor has no role in the investigative process, although he or she could ask the police to make further inquiries after an accused has been charged.

12.28　Crown Solicitors have sole responsibility for deciding upon the counts contained in an indictment, regardless of the charges originally laid by the police. However, they have no power themselves to refuse to prosecute, but can refer a doubtful case to the Solicitor-General, who may enter a stay of proceedings.

12.29   The Law Commission is presently considering whether an independent prosecution agency should be created.

Disclosure

(i) By the prosecution

12.30   The Official Information Act 1982 requires all government departments and most government agencies to make available personal information relating to an individual. There are limited restrictions on this right. This Act, although not specifically intended for the purpose, has been recently used by defendants to obtain information from the police or other prosecuting agencies which might bear upon an alleged offence. The practice developed since the Court of Appeal held in *Commissioner of Police v Ombudsman*[5] that the right to personal information could be used for the purposes of a pending trial. This right to information applies to summary offences as well as offences triable on indictment. The information which can be obtained includes briefs of evidence, witness statements and notes of interviews. Access to information pursuant to the Official Information Act is upon request. Applications are usually made as soon as there has been a committal for trial in an indictable matter or immediately after a charge has been laid in a summary trial matter.

12.31   The Law Commission in its report "Criminal Procedure: Part One Disclosure and Committal" states that "the Act is unable to meet all the needs of defendants and is quite unable to meet any of the needs of the prosecution." In its report the Commission sets out a statutory code on disclosure to apply to both summary and indictable offences. Under the Code, the prosecution would be under an obligation to disclose all relevant information, that is information which "tends to support or to rebut or has a bearing upon any element of the prosecution case". Exceptions to this rule would be information, the disclosure of which would create a real or substantial risk of:

> prejudice to methods of investigating and detecting offences,
>
> prejudice to the investigation and detection of another alleged offence,
>
> facilitating the commission of an offence,

---

[5] (1988) 1 NZLR 385.

causing any person to be intimidated or physically endangered,

prejudice to national security, or

a breach of evidentiary privilege.

12.32 The Commission proposes that basic information covering the charge, the statutory authority for the charge, the prescribed penalty for the offence charged, a short summary of the facts and information which might be relevant to sentence should be given to the defendant as soon as practicable and in no instance later than fourteen days after the service of the summons. No election as to mode of trial and no plea of guilty should be accepted prior to the receipt by the defendant of such information. Further discovery should follow within twenty one days of a request by the defendant to that effect. At the same time, the defence should receive a list of documents or items of information in respect of which disclosure is resisted. In addition, the reasons for withholding them should be notified whether it be on grounds of lack of relevance or for some reason of public interest. Any difference as to whether information has been withheld for a proper reason would be dealt with by an interlocutory (pre-trial) application. If at the trial the prosecution proposed to bring forward undisclosed material as evidence, the court should have the power to exclude the evidence or accept it, subject to terms as to adjournment and costs.

(ii) By the defence

12.33 The defence is only required to disclose evidence of an alibi. The defendant must give notice of particulars of any alibi within fourteen days of being committed for trial. If notice is not given, evidence of an alibi may not be given without leave of the court.

12.34 At present the judge can comment adversely on the fact that the defendant raises at trial a defence not previously mentioned. The Law Commission has proposed that the law be changed to prevent such comment. (See paragraphs 12.18 and 12.19 above).

12.35 The Law Commission recommended in its report on disclosure that the defence should be obliged to disclose expert evidence it intends to use and that the obligation to disclose evidence of an alibi should be extended to summary trials. The Commission did not recommend extending disclosure on the part of the defendant to special or positive defences. It agreed with the conclusion of Criminal Law Reform Committee report on *Discovery in Criminal Trials* (1986) that "In practice, there are likely to be few cases in which the prosecution is not capable of anticipating the accused's answer to the charge" and that "On balance, the value of prescribing further disclosure on the part of the defence is probably minimal".

Expert evidence

12.36   The Police Manual sets out procedures for searching for and the collection of evidence from scenes of crime. All staff are taught the importance of preserving a scene of crime until it can be examined by more experienced staff or specialists. The police have their own scenes of crime specialists and in particular cases the help of the Department of Scientific and Industrial Research or other experts in pathology or explosives might be sought.

12.37   Defence counsel may call their own forensic or scientific experts. Legal aid will generally be allowed to cover the cost of independent experts, provided the court considers that they are relevant to the issues at trial.

12.38   Forensic scientists employed by the state endeavour to maintain a position of independence. In practice, however, the defence are more likely to use independent experts.

12.39   There is nothing to prevent voluntary exchange of experts' reports, but this is not statutorily provided for in criminal proceedings.

12.40   The Law Commission has proposed in a discussion paper, *Evidence Law: Expert Evidence and Opinion Evidence*, that the court should be able to appoint an expert if it considered that the evidence would help the court or jury to understand other evidence in the proceedings or to ascertain any fact that was of consequence to the determination of the proceeding *and* the defendant consented to the appointment and concurred in the choice of expert. The expert appointed by the court should produce a report which should be given to each party and should be available at the trial to be cross-examined by the parties. The Commission thought that the consent of the accused to the appointment of the court expert was necessary because otherwise such "a step might give the appearance that the court was adopting a prosecutorial role or overruling the accused's wishes concerning the conduct of the defence." However, the Commission doubted whether an accused would often take the risk of agreeing to an expert being appointed by the court as the expert's report might turn out unfavourable to the accused, but thought that on occasions it might be valuable, especially where the defence had inadequate resources.

12.41   As noted in the section on disclosure above, the Law Commission proposed the disclosure of expert evidence by both parties.

12.42   The Commission also pointed out that it was not always appropriate to deal with expert evidence in chief by way of question and answer. The

Commission proposed that the judge should have a discretion to permit whatever mode of presentation of evidence in chief best suited the case, including narrative presentation, written report, the use of diagrams, or charts, practical demonstration or video or computer presentation. This would not affect the right of the other party to cross-examine.

Detention in custody before trial

12.43   On 1 November 1991, there were 412 remand prisoners in New Zealand prisons. 188 were suspects who had not yet been convicted and were awaiting trial. 55 were prisoners who had been convicted and were awaiting sentence. The remaining 169 were either police remands or those waiting deposition hearings.

12.44   The population of New Zealand is approximately 3.25 million.

Juries

12.45   Juries deliberate alone.

12.46   No steps are taken to secure that the jury reflects a racial balance in cases where that seems to be appropriate.

12.47   Each party is entitled to challenge without cause 6 jurors.

12.48   The defendant can elect for trial by jury if he is liable to more than a three month prison sentence. The defendant can also apply to be tried by a judge alone for a trial for any offence other than for a trial for an offence for which the maximum penalty is imprisonment for life or imprisonment for a term of fourteen years or more. If a defendant does so apply, the case is referred to a judge, who must then order a trial without a jury unless he or she considers that in the interests of justice the accused should be tried before a judge with a jury. In practice, applications are usually made in long, complex fraud cases.

Trial

12.49   Technically the judge has the power to call witnesses, but this is rarely used in practice.

12.50   The prosecutor can make an opening speech, which may contain as much detail as he or she wishes.

12.51   It is customary for the judge to sum up to the jury on the facts of the case as well as the law. The position is the same as in England in that comment is permitted provided the judge makes it clear to the jury that questions of fact are ultimately for them.

Previous convictions

12.52   Usually the trial judge does not have the accused's prior convictions during the trial.

12.53   The conditions under which the prosecution may introduce evidence of the accused's prior convictions during the trial are generally similar to those in England.

Appeal

(i) Appeals by the defendant

12.54   In 1989/90, 757 and in 1990/1991, 901 cases were heard in the High Court. The number of appeals against conviction, conviction and sentence and sentence alone are given below. It must be noted that appeals may not necessarily be heard in the same year as the case was tried in the High Court so these two sets of figures do not necessarily refer to the same defendants.

	Appeals Heard		Decisions Allowed		Decisions Refused	
	89/90	90/91	89/90	90/91	89/90	90/91
Appeals against conviction	93	111	9	15	85	90
Appeals against conviction and sentence	69	73	8	9	54	52
Appeal against sentence	163	191	20	40	135	134
Total	325	375	37	64	274	276

12.55   Before 15 August 1991, an appeal on a question of law was of right but leave was required for an appeal on a question of fact or a mixed question of fact and law. However, in practice the Court of Appeal would usually hear the matter before determining whether or not leave would be granted. The law was then changed to make all appeals available as of right. The change was thought necessary to comply with article 14(5) of the International Convention on Civil and Political Rights which provides "Everyone convicted of a crime has a right to have his conviction and sentence reviewed in a higher tribunal according to law".

12.56   The Legal Services Act 1991 (which came into effect in February 1992) provides for the granting of legal aid, including at the appellate level. The general test is that the grant is necessary in "the interests of justice" and the applicant must not have sufficient means to obtain legal assistance.

12.57 The Court of Appeal has no power to add on time to the sentence for unmeritorious appeals.

12.58 The New Zealand Court of Appeal will make an order for admission of further evidence only in exceptional circumstances. If it is argued that the additional evidence should be received because there was a miscarriage of justice, the Court must satisfy itself that such evidence is cogent, plausible and relevant. It must be evidence which was not available at the trial.

12.59 Section 385(2) of the Crimes Act 1961 authorises the Court of Appeal, on allowing an appeal against conviction, to quash the conviction and in its discretion, direct an acquittal or new trial "or make such other order as justice requires". Whether the court exercises its discretion to order a new trial, or enters an acquittal verdict, rests on the facts of the case and the nature of the appeal. However, in the majority of cases where an appeal against conviction is allowed, a retrial is ordered and that retrial will take place before another judge and a jury. Retrials following a successful appeal are common in New Zealand.

12.60 Section 385(2) of the Crimes Act 1961 provides the grounds on which the Court of Appeal must quash a conviction. These are:

a. "That the verdict of the jury should be set aside on the ground that it is unreasonable and cannot be supported having regard to the evidence; or

b. That the judgment of the court before which the appellant was convicted should be set aside on the ground of a wrong decision on any question of law; or

c. That on any ground there was a miscarriage of justice; or

d. That the trial was a nullity."

12.61 In normal circumstances there is only one right of appeal. Where, however, the Court has ordered a retrial on that appeal and the retrial results in conviction again, there is still the same right of appeal against that second verdict, as there was after the first instance conviction. There is also the possibility of applying to the Judicial Committee of the Privy Council in England for leave to appeal to that body. However, leave is granted within very narrow limits.

12.62 Section 406 of the Crimes Act provides that the Governor General may refer a case back to the Court of Appeal whether or not the appellant has already exhausted his or her ordinary right of appeal. This power is usually exercised on the advice of the Minister of Justice. In such cases, the normal rules of evidence and procedure are applied by the Court of Appeal.

12.63   The Governor General can also exercise the prerogative of mercy. This too is usually exercised on advice of the Minister of Justice.

12.64   There is no "Court of Last Resort".

(ii) Appeals by the prosecution

12.65   In summary hearings, the prosecution can appeal by way of case stated to the High Court on a question of law. The High Court may reverse, confirm or amend the determination challenged, remit the matter to the District Court with its opinion or amend or quash the conviction or any part of the sentence as appropriate. The prosecution has a more limited right of appeal in trials on indictment. Sections 380–382 of the Crimes Act create a mechanism for the court to reserve questions of law during or after a trial on indictment for the opinion of the Court of Appeal. Either the prosecutor or the accused may apply to have a question reserved and the jury may be asked to make specific findings of fact where necessary. A decision not to reserve a question can be appealed. Irrespective of the conviction or acquittal of the accused at the trial, the Court of Appeal may confirm the ruling, direct a new trial, alter the sentence or set aside the conviction.

(iii) Appeals on interlocutory matters

12.66   Appeal rights on interlocutory matters before trials on indictment are set out in section 379A of the Crimes Act. The prosecutor or accused may, within ten days of a decision, apply for leave to appeal on a decision on venue, admissibility, alternative and joined charges to an indictment or the counts charged, separate trials for persons jointly charged or the identity of the undercover witness. The Summary Proceedings Act also provides for interlocutory appeals on bail and name suppression.

Training

12.67   There is no specific segment of any study programme offered to judges which focuses deliberately on the problems of false confessions, unreliable eye-witness evidence and bias in police officers, scientists, prosecutors and judges. Nonetheless, during the course of a judicial career, these topics will be covered through attendance at seminars and conferences.

12.68   Initial police training specifically deals with these areas. For example, in the first week of training a police recruit spends three periods

(50 minutes duration) on the question of ethics. Included in this is a video titled "Scale of Justice", which covers false and forced confessions and bias in police officers and perjury. It is said amply to illustrate the repercussions which eventuate when police do not exercise due care and prudence in these areas. These problem areas will also be dealt with throughout a police officer's training.

Future reform

12.69   Under references given to the Law Commission by the Minister of Justice in August 1989, the Commission is looking at criminal procedure, from the time an offence is suspected to have been committed until the offender is convicted, and the law of evidence. The Commission is dealing with this task in stages. Its report, *Criminal Procedure: Part One Disclosure and Committal*, and its discussion paper, *Criminal Evidence: Police Questioning*, are part of an intended series of reports.

PART 13
SPAIN

Police investigations

13.1 The Spanish Police are divided into two national forces, the General Police Force (*Policia Nacional*) and the Civil Guard (*Guardia Civil*). The *Policia* operates in larger cities and towns with a population in excess of 20,000 people. The *Guardia Civil* operates in rural areas and small towns. Both forces are more military in their approach than the British police. All police officers are part of the Judicial Police (*Policia Judicial*) and are responsible directly to the courts in that role.

13.2 Once the police have become aware of an offence, they must investigate it at once, unless it is not technically a crime or the report is manifestly untrue.

13.3 The police may not enter the home of a Spanish national or a foreigner resident in Spain without permission unless they have a warrant from a magistrate setting out clearly all the relevant details. This is not required when a defendant is caught in the act of committing a crime, or the police enter a house to arrest an occupant hiding there. Routine and indiscriminate personal searches must not be carried out. If officers suspect that an offence has been committed they are entitled to search suspects, but only after telling them their rights. Women can only be searched by female officers at the police station.

13.4 From the moment of arrest suspects have the following rights: (i) to be informed in a manner understandable to them of the reason for their arrest; (ii) to be assisted by counsel of their choice or otherwise by counsel provided by the Bar Association paid for by legal aid. The lawyer is there to see that everything is done properly, but may not be allowed to see the suspect in private; (iii) to be provided with the free assistance of a translator, if required; (iv) to remain completely silent, to refuse to answer questions, and to insist on answering only to the Examining Magistrate; (v) to inform any member of their family or other person of their choice of the arrest and the location of the custody site and to notify the consular authority; (vi) to be examined by a police doctor; (vii) not to incriminate themselves, and not to make a confession unless they want to; and (viii) to request an immediate appearance before a judge through a writ of Habeas Corpus.

13.5   A written statement of these rights must be given to the detainees, who must sign it in order to show that they have received it. The detainee will then have a police interview (*declaracion*). No personal visits are allowed before the suspect has been interviewed. Suspects have the right to refuse to give a statement to the police, and it cannot be held against them if they prefer to speak to the Examining Magistrate. If a suspect decides to make a statement to the police, a lawyer and translator (if necessary) must be present. Any informal conversations about the case with the police but without a translator and lawyer are illegal. Statements consist of a set of questions and answers. Leading questions, trick questions and attempts to obtain answers by undue influence or force are forbidden. The interview may last as long as is necessary, but there must be a reasonable number of rest and refreshment breaks. The lawyer present is not supposed to intervene in the making of the statement and his or her presence at this stage is merely to ensure that the suspect's rights are respected. However, it is not unknown for lawyers to ask questions to clarify matters.

13.6   The maximum length of time that the police may hold a suspect for questioning before the suspect is brought before the Examining Magistrate is 72 hours from the moment of arrest.

13.7   In the case of persons suspected of terrorism the police may hold them for ten days with the consent of the Examining Magistrate and the Ministry of the Interior. These persons may be held incommunicado and have no right to their own lawyer. They are therefore compelled to use the services of a lawyer appointed by the Legal Aid service from a roster of lawyers with generally little experience.

13.8   It is a criminal offence for any police officer to ill-treat, intimidate or assault a suspect during an enquiry.

13.9   Suspects can ask for Habeas Corpus if they have been mistreated, denied their rights or held longer than permitted. This can be done by sending a letter to the duty magistrate (see paragraph 13.18 below), or asking the police to send a letter on their behalf. The suspect will then be brought at once before the duty magistrate, who has the power to set the suspect free, to transfer him or her to another police force, or to start an enquiry into what happened. If mistreated, the suspect can also complain to the Examining Magistrate, or the Public Defender.

Evidence

13.10   Article 17(3) of the Spanish Constitution 1978 guarantees the assistance of counsel to a person arrested during police and judicial procedures. This has been interpreted by the courts to mean that the presence of counsel (of the suspect's choice or legal aid counsel) is necessary to give legal validity to any statements given by the suspect while under police arrest, or to the results of an identification parade. A distinction has been drawn, however, between the acts performed by the police and those performed by an Examining Magistrate. Examining Magistrates should respect the suspect's right to counsel, but not all acts performed during their investigation of the crime require, for their validity, the presence of counsel unless the law specifically requires it. Should defendants insist that they do not want counsel, but counsel's presence is required for the validity of the act, the legal aid counsel would be called anyway and would attend the interview.

13.11   If the defendant gives a statement to the police (when a lawyer is present), it will be written down and later, when the suspect appears before the Examining Magistrate, he or she will be asked to confirm its truth. Only then will the statement be admissible in court.

13.12   The confession of the accused either at the police station and/or before the Examining Magistrate does not authorise the Examining Magistrate to conclude the investigation, which should be continued until further evidence corroborates the confession. A confession obtained by a promise of immunity or leniency is not seen as voluntary and is therefore inadmissible in evidence.

13.13   A defendant cannot be compelled to make a statement at any stage in the proceedings, but a refusal to do so can be seen by the trial court as evidence of guilt.

13.14   As regards illegally or improperly obtained evidence, the court has a wide discretion to evaluate such evidence solely according to its conscience. However, evidence obtained in violation of basic human rights cannot be admitted.

13.15   An identity parade must be conducted with at least two other people, and in the presence of the suspect's lawyer. If suspects feel that the parade is unfair, their lawyers should not sign the record, and suspects can explain their grievance to the Examining Magistrate later.

13.16   There is no hearsay rule and the court must weigh up the value of the evidence in every case.

13.17   A witness can refer to documentary or other real evidence where it has previously been authorised by the court.

Prosecution

13.18   For serious offences tried in the Provincial Criminal Court there will be a pre-trial stage called *instruccion* (instruction). This is carried out by the Instruction Courts (*Juzgados de Instruccion*), under an Examining Magistrate (*Juez de Instruccion*). There is a duty magistrate available in the Instruction Court twenty four hours a day to deal with new cases.

13.19   The instruction stage involves the Examining Magistrate collecting all the evidence about the case. As soon as the Examining Magistrate receives notification of the commission of a crime, instruction proceedings must be started. The Examining Magistrate has a duty to hear the suspect's side of the story, generally within twenty four hours from the time the case is received. Suspects are entitled to have their lawyers present when they make any statement. The suspect is asked to give a truthful statement, but it is not on oath. The statement is then signed by all the parties present. The suspect's lawyer (but not the suspect) can be present when other witnesses are interviewed by the Examining Magistrate.

13.20   Examining Magistrates collect all the information together in a file. They can visit the site of the alleged offence and obtain detailed plans or photographs. They can take possession of objects which they think may be evidence, call an identity parade, appoint experts, and obtain a copy of the suspect's criminal record. Other witnesses can be summoned by the Examining Magistrate and they can be fined if they do not attend. Evidence of witnesses is taken on oath. The statements will be recorded and signed by all present. The Magistrate has the power to bring two or more witnesses together for a confrontation where their evidence is contradictory.

13.21   All the parties (complainant, defendant and prosecutor) can examine the file and propose further enquiries. The Magistrate must follow up these enquiries unless he considers them useless or prejudicial. If such a proposal is refused, then the matter can be appealed against to the Provincial Criminal Court, or even raised at the trial. The Examining Magistrate also has the power to decide that the proceedings be kept partially or completely secret from the defendant or the complainant for any period up to one month. This period cannot include the last ten days before the close of the instruction stage when supplementary enquiries can be suggested by the parties, and they are entitled to be present when they are carried out.

13.22   In theory the instruction stage must last no longer than one month, and if the work is not finished by then, the Examining Magistrate must make weekly reports to the Provincial Criminal Court explaining the reasons for the delay. In practice however, this stage can continue for as long as a year (and sometimes more). There is generally very close cooperation between the Magistrate and the Prosecutor.

13.23   When they have finished their investigations, the Examining Magistrates will send the file to the Provincial Criminal Court. The case is then given to the judge who will try the case and who has been chosen as rapporteur. The file is then sent to the prosecutor, and after that the complainant, and they have between three–ten days each to decide whether or not they agree that the instruction has been completed properly. They have the right to recommend that the instruction stage is re-opened, the case is dismissed, or it is set down for trial. The defendant has no such right. These recommendations, together with the file, are returned to the rapporteur, who, within a further three days, must advise the court what action to take. The court can: (1) have the case dismissed if it decides that no offence has been committed; (2) if it finds that the facts disclose only a minor offence, send the case down to one of the lower courts; (3) if further evidence is needed, send the case back to the Examining Magistrate; (4) otherwise set the case down for trial and return the file to the prosecutor. Any party dissatisfied with the decision has the right of appeal to the Supreme Court of Justice.

13.24 If defendants think that the Examining Magistrate has made a mistake or is being unfair, they can make a complaint to the Examining Magistrate or, with the agreement of his lawyer, appeal to the Provincial Criminal Court.

Disclosure

13.25 From the stage at which the Examining Magistrate starts the investigation the defence has full access to all the evidence in the file, unless the proceedings are kept secret (see paragraph 13.21).

13.26 The right of the parties to see relevant material is limited to that material which is submitted to the Examining Magistrate and to the court. There is no right to see relevant material which is in the sole possession of the prosecution and which the prosecution do not intend to use.

13.27 Spanish criminal procedure requires the preparation of pre-trial pleadings (*calificaciones*) by all parties in order to narrow down the issues for the trial. This process is known as "*calificacion del delito*". The first person to prepare and to present a *calificacion* is the prosecutor, who is allowed five days in which to complete it. The prosecutor is followed by the defendant and the complainant who each have a similar period to examine the file and the preceding *calificaciones* and to draft their own. They include a list of the matters that the party intends to prove at the trial, and also a list of the witnesses they want to call. The file then goes back to the court, which will decide which offers of proof it will allow at the trial and which witnesses it will permit. If the court refuses to call one party's witness, all the party can do is appeal to the Supreme Court of Justice. A party cannot prevent a witness being included. None of the parties is allowed to call evidence at the trial or to suggest any conclusion which they have not first mentioned in their *calificacion*, unless it relates to the credibility of a witness or any unforeseeable matter.

Expert evidence

13.28 The Examining Magistrate may appoint experts to advise on technical matters, and may order medical or psychiatric reports on a suspect or any other person. Experts (usually at least two) are always appointed from amongst persons holding qualifications approved by the government. All parties have the right to challenge the competence or impartiality of expert witnesses. The prosecution and the defence both have the right to appoint their own experts. The points under enquiry will be set out clearly by the Magistrate and the experts will be expected to file written reports within a certain time. They must then attend before the Magistrate for questioning in the same way as other witnesses. If two experts cannot agree, another will be appointed.

13.29 The defence can use the services of the Forensic Clinic free of charge.

Pre-trial procedures

13.30 The prosecution can pose questions to the accused before the Examining Magistrate during the course of the investigation, but only when the accused is assisted by counsel and informed of his or her rights.

Statistics for detention in custody

13.31 The Spanish population is close to 40 million people.

13.32 The prison population is in the region of 30,000 and over 40% are awaiting trial. People can be in prison awaiting trial for up to four years.

Juries

13.33 Article 125 of the Spanish Constitution of 1978 specifically recognised the fundamental right of citizens to participate in the administration of justice as members of a jury. However, a jury system has never been introduced despite pressure from many quarters. The main reason given by the government for this is that the implementation of a jury system would lead to greater delays in the administration of justice. The real reason, in the opinion of the majority of Spanish jurists, is that the government would lose control of the judiciary.

Trial procedures

13.34 There are two types of offences in the Spanish criminal code: serious offences (*delitos*), and minor offences (*faltas*).

13.35   Minor offences can be dealt with in the following courts: (1) Justices Court (*Juzgado de Paz*); (2) First Instance Court (*Juzgado de Primera Instancia*); (3) Instruction Court (*Juzgado de Instruccion*). A single professional judge sits in these courts.

13.36   Serious offences are tried in the Provincial Criminal Court (*Audiencia Provincial*). Trials in the Provincial Criminal Courts are conducted by three professional judges sitting alone.

13.37   The National Criminal Court (*Audiencia Nacional*) deals with cases which relate to more than one province, treason, extradition, crimes committed by Spaniards abroad, terrorism, piracy, hijacking of aircraft and complex or serious smuggling, exchange control or drugs cases. Proceedings are exactly the same as those in the Provincial Criminal Court, but, because there are fewer cases, the Court tends to be quicker and more efficient.

13.38   In most of the higher courts in Spain representation is compulsory. Legal aid lawyers are generally young people working their way up, and there are no major problems providing the service. In Spain the advocate deals with the client directly, while the solicitor handles the paperwork and the court timetable. A solicitor must always be appointed by the advocate and the selection is usually entirely in his discretion.

13.39   The President of the Provincial Criminal Court is in full control of the trial and opens the proceedings, and calls and questions the defendant, the other witnesses and the experts. It is the President's duty to ask the defendant what he has to say to the Court, and to close the trial before considering sentence. The President also has a duty to prevent unfair questioning or attempts to entrap a witness.

13.40   The Criminal Procedure Code guarantees the right of the defendants and their lawyers to be present at the trial unless they make a disturbance. Lawyers representing the victim can also attend the hearings and put questions; they sit with the prosecutor, provided the victim has been accepted by the Court as a party.

13.41   Defendants are asked to plead only in cases where they face a sentence of up to 6 years in prison. If there is a claim for damages against them, they will be asked if they accept this. If they plead guilty, their lawyer will be asked if they consent to the matter proceeding on this basis. If the lawyer refuses to consent, then the trial will go ahead despite the defendant's wishes. Even if both the defendant and the lawyer agree, the court still has a duty to satisfy itself from the file that the conviction is adequately proved before proceeding to sentence. Where the defendant denies the offence or remains silent, or his or her lawyer asks for a trial, the Court will proceed to hear the case. Similarly, where the defendants admit guilt, but deny civil liability or question the quantum of damages, the Court will order the trial to proceed. In the case of offences carrying more than 6 years imprisonment the case will proceed to trial automatically. No plea will be sought.

13.42   Neither the prosecution nor the defence are allowed to start the trial with an opening statement. The trial starts in private with the court clerk reading the provisional pleadings of the prosecution and defence in that order. Then the public are called in.

13.43   All trials in the Provincial Criminal Court are held in public and are open to the press, unless it is necessary to protect victims or their families, or the case involves issues of public morality or public order.

13.44   All witnesses are summoned to the hearing by a judicial warrant issued by the Court. If witnesses fail to attend they face criminal proceedings and the case can be put off until another summons is sent. A witness who refuses to give evidence can be fined heavily. Witnesses are called into Court by the President. Witnesses are examined by the lawyer who has asked for them to be called. The other parties to the case have the chance to question them later. The accused can be called to give evidence by the prosecution or the defence. If what a witness says and what the accused says contradict each other, the President may call for a confrontation between them.

13.45   After the evidence has been heard, all the parties have the right to modify any parts of the submissions which they made before the trial. If the prosecution decides that the evidence heard during the trial requires them to lay additional or different charges, all the parties are entitled to file fresh submissions and an adjournment will probably be necessary.

13.46   The judges retire to consider the verdict. They must give an answer within five days. They will make up their minds on all the issues at once, including guilt, civil liability (if any) and sentence (if the defendant is convicted).

13.47   For trials of minor offences only, the case is heard in one of the other trial courts. The procedure is the same as in the Provincial Criminal Court, but there will be no instruction stage and no written submissions beforehand.

13.48   An objection can be raised to any judge trying a case if there are sufficient grounds (e.g. blood ties, involvement). An objection must be in writing, signed by the maker and setting out the reasons why the judge is to be challenged. The Court may call for the objector to come to court to prove his or her objections in person before the appropriate judge.

Previous convictions

13.49   Judges have the accused's prior convictions before them during the trial, but they are generally only relevant in sentencing.

Appeals

13.50   There is an appeal from any of the lower courts to the instruction court for a completely new trial, if it is alleged that the original court decided the facts of the case wrongly. This can be applied for orally at the trial, or by sending a written notice to the court within twenty four hours. If the case was originally heard in the instruction court, there can be a completely new trial in the Provincial Criminal Court if it is alleged that the lower court decided the facts of the case wrongly. Appeals can take several months (or years), and the time spent in prison may not count towards the sentence.

13.51   The gross mishandling of a case by the lawyer appointed by the state (Legal Aid Service) could in very exceptional circumstances lead to an appeal because of the fundamental right to a defence, which is specifically stated in Article 24 of the Spanish Constitution.

13.52   There is no appeal from the Provincial Criminal Court on the grounds that the Court decided the facts of the case wrongly. The only appeal from this Court is when: (1) the court has misapplied the law; or (2) the court has made an error in procedure. All parties to the proceedings have the right to appeal, including the prosecution.

13.53   Leave to appeal from the Provincial Criminal Court must be granted by the trial court before the appeal to the Supreme Court can proceed. To obtain leave, a petition signed by the solicitor and advocate must be filed with the trial court within five days of the notification of the original judgment. In practice this time limit may be extended. The petition will request a certified copy of the judgment and set out the grounds for the appeal. The court has three days to consider the petition and, if it agrees that a ground for appeal exists, it will send the file within a further three days to the Supreme Court. The file will contain the certified copy of the judgment. If the trial court refuses leave to appeal, then the appellant has two days to lodge a complaint. The trial court will then proceed as if leave to appeal had been provisionally granted and remit the whole question of leave to the Supreme Court for decision.

13.54 All parties will then have the opportunity in turn to file submissions in support (or otherwise) of the complaint. The rapporteur appointed in the case by the Supreme Court will study the files and the submissions and report to the full court, which will decide the matter without a hearing. If leave to continue is again refused, there is no further remedy and costs will be awarded against the appellant. If it is accepted then the trial court will be ordered to grant the necessary leave to appeal and summon the parties.

13.55 Once leave has been granted, all parties must file submissions setting out the legal arguments upon which they rely. The appellant's failure to file his or her submissions in time will result in the dismissal of the appeal with costs. The rapporteur appointed by the Supreme Court will then have ten days in which to prepare a summary of the case and the arguments. The full Court must then decide if they will admit or deny admission of the petition to the Court. A petition can only by denied by a unanimous decision of the five judges allotted to the case. Sometimes the Court will decide to admit the petition without a hearing, but again this requires a unanimous judgment.

13.56 The more usual procedure is for the Court to admit the matter to a hearing before the full court. This will be in public and all parties are expected to attend. Oral submissions are made by the advocates and no evidence is called. The judgment is reached and delivered in the same way as in the Provincial Criminal Court. Costs can be awarded against any party except the prosecution. The options open to the Court are:

(1) to reject the petition with costs;

(2) to admit the petition on the grounds of a procedural error by the trial court and remit the case back to the same court with a direction for the mistake to be remedied and for the proceedings to continue from the point at which the error was made;

(3) to admit the petition on the grounds of an error in law and to give a new judgment itself. It is not permitted for this court to increase the appellant's sentence, although fines can be imposed for frivolous appeals.

13.57 Evidence available at the trial and not called cannot be considered fresh evidence for the purpose of an appeal. However, if new evidence is discovered which proves the prisoner's innocence, revision proceedings can be entered. The petition for revision can be filed with the Ministry of Justice at any time. It can be filed by members of the prisoner's close family and even after his death in order to clear the prisoner's name. The prosecutor can also act on his or her own initiative. If the Ministry of Justice decides that there is a case to be argued, it will instruct the prosecutor to bring the petition before the Supreme Court for a decision. There will either be a new trial or the Supreme Court may decide to cancel the conviction. There can also be compensation for wrongful conviction. The discovery of new evidence cannot affect an existing acquittal. This procedure is not available for minor offences.

13.58   At any time after a sentence is confirmed (no more appeals pending), the prisoner can petition for a pardon. The petition has to go to the sentencing court, the prison authorities and the Council of Ministers for their comments, and thus takes a long time (at least three months). In practice there is no chance of success during the first year of the sentence, but if an application is unsuccessful, the prisoner can re-apply every year. The granting of a pardon is entirely discretionary and will only be made if all the comments on the file are generally favourable.

13.59   The proportion of defendants appealing against conviction is close to 65%. Not more than 10% of these appeals are successful.

13.60   A defendant can appeal once to the Appeal Court, but can also appeal to the Spanish Constitutional Court which is a separate body from the ordinary judicial system and may overturn any judgment. This Court consists only of jurists.

Training

13.61   Advocates and solicitors must possess a degree from a Spanish university and be of good character with no criminal convictions. There is no further training and, although young advocates usually undergo a practical course at a private law school, this is not obligatory. Advocates must enrol in their local Bar Association. Solicitors must join the local Solicitors Association and deposit a sum by way of security. Each Association is controlled by a "*Junta de Gobierno*", which exercises discipline subject to a right of appeal to a national body.

13.62   If defendants think that their lawyer is overcharging, they can complain to the local Bar Association by way of a challenge. They should also notify the lawyer that they dispute the bill and the lawyer must refer the matter to the court. Cases of misconduct can also be dealt with in this way and, if serious, could give rise to criminal proceedings against the lawyer. Complaints are, however, rarely successful.

13.63   Candidates for the judiciary sit a competitive examination, after their degree, for entry to the Judicial College, where they follow a one year course. If they complete this course successfully, they are appointed either as prosecutors or judges after a short orientation procedure.

PART 14
SWEDEN

Police investigations

14.1   Suspects who have not been charged may be questioned for a maximum period of six hours. In cases of considerable importance a further period of six hours is permitted.

14.2   When a person has been apprehended, the prosecutor must be notified. After interviewing the suspect, the prosecutor must decide immediately whether the suspect should be charged or set at liberty. An application for a detention order must be submitted on the day of the charge, or the day after, or in certain circumstances, the day after that. The court must reply to the prosecutor's request that the suspect be remanded in custody on the same day that the request is made or the day after, or in certain circumstances, the day after that.

14.3   The whole process, from arrest to the decision to remand in custody, must not take more than four days.

14.4   There is no formal duty to inform suspects of their right to silence, although this is usually done in practice.

14.5   When the preliminary investigation has proceeded to the point at which a person is reasonably suspected of the offence, that person must be informed of the suspicion. At the same time, suspects must also be informed of their right to a legal adviser. No distinction is made regarding the seriousness of the crime.

14.6   When suspects are under arrest or in detention a public defence counsel must be appointed for them, if they so request. A public defence counsel must also be appointed on request for a person who is suspected of an offence for which the maximum penalty is six months or more. In other cases, a public defence counsel must be appointed if the suspect is in need of one, if having regard to the investigation of the offence, there is reason to believe that a sanction other than a fine or conditional sentence will be imposed, or if special reasons exist having regard to the suspect's personal circumstances or the matter at issue.

14.7   If a suspect has proposed as a public defence counsel someone competent to serve as such, the person proposed must be appointed unless this would cause considerably increased cost or special reasons indicate that the appointment should not be made.

Evidence

14.8   The Swedish system regarding the admissibility of evidence is radically different from the English system. As there is no jury system, there is not thought to be the same need to exclude evidence from the court's considerations. In principle, all evidence is admissible, but evidence obtained in circumstances prejudicial to the accused or as a result of a breach of ordinary procedure would be evaluated with much greater caution.

14.9   A police officer or any other official who has obtained evidence illegally can be disciplined or convicted of criminal offences. This has occurred. Private individuals who obtain evidence illegally also can be convicted of criminal offences.

14.10   Inferences from the accused's silence at the police station can be drawn, but generally speaking the court places greater weight on the evidence given in the court room than evidence obtained as a result of police interrogation.

14.11   It is impossible to plead guilty under Swedish law. A confession may be sufficient evidence for a conviction, but is not necessarily so. A confession is treated as all other pieces of evidence and the court must "test" it in terms of credibility and comprehensiveness. In practice, in dealing with serious crimes, the court will not regard a confession as sufficient by itself. A prosecutor must prove the crime beyond reasonable doubt, and cannot afford to go to court without presenting evidence which corroborates the confession.

Prosecution

14.12   The Swedish prosecution system is organised into 13 regions, each headed by a regional prosecutor who is responsible for the handling of serious cases. Each region is divided into several local prosecution districts, each headed by a chief prosecutor (district attorney). The national government official responsible for all prosecutions is the Prosecutor General.

14.13   The prosecutor is, in principle, responsible for the entire investigation. He or she can (and often does) give both particular and general directions to the police. In simple cases, the prosecutor tends to leave the investigation to the police. The prosecutor, however, always decides whether or not a prosecution will be instituted.

14.14   The "principle of objectivity" applies to how the investigation of the prosecutor is conducted. The prosecutor's duty is not simply to collect evidence for the prosecution, but to collect evidence for the benefit of the accused. The Swedish prosecutor acts very much like a *juge d'instruction* during the early stage of the proceedings. It is a criminal offence for a prosecutor to suppress evidence. Prosecutors and police are well trained in the need to respect the rights of the accused.

14.15   Where young offenders are concerned, the prosecutor has the right in certain cases to waive criminal proceedings and instead allow the local Social Welfare Committee to take responsibility for the rehabilitation of the young person.

Disclosure

14.16   The defence has a continuous right to be informed of all the evidence in so far as it is possible without detriment to the investigation.

14.17   The defence counsel may attend any examination if this can occur without detriment to the investigation. As soon as a prosecution has been decided upon, the suspect or his defence counsel has a right to be given the final report which summarises and lists the evidence.

14.18   Defendants have a duty to disclose the evidence they wish to offer at the main hearing and to indicate what they intend to prove by each specified item. They must do so after receipt of the formal indictment. Documentary evidence should also be submitted to the court. The court must notify the prosecutor of any statement submitted. If the defence adduce evidence at the trial that has not been disclosed in advance, the trial will be postponed. The defence may then be liable to pay the prosecution's costs. Section 6 of the code of procedure states:

> "If a party's failure to appear or to comply with a court direction, or presentation of a claim or defence that he or she should have known to be without merit, or carelessness or oversight in other respects has occasioned adjournment of the proceedings or has otherwise caused expenses for the adverse party, that party must reimburse the adverse party for such expenses regardless of how the costs are to be distributed."

In addition, failure to comply with the disclosure requirement may constitute gross misbehaviour which could lead to an advocate being dismissed from the Bar Association. In practice, the defence comply with the rules.

Expert evidence

14.19   The police officers who collect scientific evidence have special training. A record must be kept of every seizure, and the manner in which it was effected, describing accurately the seized object.

14.20 The "principle of objectivity" referred to earlier which applies to the prosecution's investigation means in the context of expert evidence that the defence can demand that the prosecutor make further inquiries, forensic science tests etc. If the prosecution refuses (which happens only very rarely) the defence can go to the court which then decides whether the inquiry, forensic science test etc. should be made. The principle of objectivity means that the people responsible for conducting forensic scientific tests are acting as much for the defence as they are for the prosecution.

14.21 If there is disagreement over how forensic science or other evidence should be interpreted, the defence may, at its own expense, hire its own experts to make further tests and testify before the court as to their findings. There is no system for attempting to get the prosecution and defence witnesses to agree their evidence before the trial.

14.22 The court can commission an expert of its own but this is relatively rare.

Pre-trial procedure

14.23 There is no pre-trial procedure for enabling the prosecution to question the accused in front of a judge or other judicial officer.

Detention in custody

14.24 During 1989, the average figure for the prison population was 872 persons. On 1 October 1991, the prison population was 1,191. The population of Sweden is 8.5 million. No figures have been given for detention pre-trial.

The court system/juries

14.25 Sweden has a three-tier hierarchy of courts: the district courts, the intermediate courts of appeal and the Supreme Court.

14.26 In the Swedish judicial system, district courts play the dominant role. In principle, there are no limitations to their jurisdiction as regards the subject areas of the cases, and the judges serving in such courts are, broadly speaking, in a position of parity with the court of appeal judges in respect of salary.

14.27 There is no jury system in criminal trials (except in very rare cases of alleged breaches of the Freedom of the Press Act).

14.28 In the district court, in more serious cases, one qualified judge sits with three lay judges. Lay judges are elected for three years by local representative councils from a roster of eligible local citizens. Most of them are re-elected for consecutive terms, and since each lay judge is on duty for around ten days in a year, they develop experience over a period of time.

14.29   When lay judges are elected, the aim is to give the collective of lay judges an all-round representative composition with regard to age, sex and profession. There are no special arrangements regarding race. One of the factors which has to be taken into account in choosing lay judges is the importance of achieving an equal degree of representation of the political parties in the municipalities within the court's jurisdiction. One witness wrote "so there is no problem of political bias here".

14.30   The lay judges deliberate with the judge on points of law and the sanctions to be imposed.

14.31   In cases where the lay assessors do not sit, the bench of the district court generally consists of three legally trained judges or, in less serious cases, one such judge.

Trial

14.32   The court has the power to call witnesses on its own motion but does not do so very often.

14.33   The court has access to the accused's prior convictions. If the offence is such that a sanction other than a fine can be expected or if special cause otherwise warrants, reference can be made during the hearing to the penalties to which the accused person has previously been sentenced.

14.34   After the prosecutor has stated the charge, the defendant is requested to indicate his or her position. Thereafter, the prosecutor introduces the case. Then, before the witnesses are heard, the injured person and the accused person are heard.

14.35   During the court's deliberations the legally qualified judge will explain the subject matter of the case and applicable legal rules to the lay judges, but never in open court. During voting the lay judges state their opinion last.

Appeal

14.36   Sweden has six Courts of Appeal. Appeal cases are heard by four, in some cases three, legally trained judges or by three legally trained judges and two lay judges.

14.37   Between 5% and 10% of defendants appeal against conviction. One witness stated "this figure can been seen as high bearing in mind the fact that the prosecutor uses his or her discretion to the advantage of the accused and so will not bring charges in dubious cases". In 1989, 28% of appeals by defendants were successful.

14.38   Leave is not required for an appeal.

14.39   In an appeal lodged by the defendant, or by the prosecutor for the benefit of the defendant, the Court of Appeal may not sentence the defendant to a criminal sanction which is more severe than the one imposed by the lower court.

14.40   The Court of Appeal can decide to look at evidence which was not called before the district court. The trial before the Court of Appeal is a wholly new trial. As appeal may be made as of right there is no need, for example, to show that there is fresh evidence which may have influenced the district court in reaching a different decision.

14.41   There is no statutory formula the Court of Appeal must apply when deciding to quash a verdict of the trial court.

14.42   A person may not appeal more than once to the Court of Appeal. However, appeals against decisions of the Court of Appeal can be made to the Supreme Court. Leave is required for an appeal to the Supreme Court. Leave is given only if it is important for the enforcement of the law. On the whole it is only cases which are of interest from the point of view of possible precedents that are tried before the Supreme Court. The Supreme Court consists of five justices.

14.43   There is no procedure for cases to be referred back to the Court of Appeal by the Executive.

14.44   There is no special "Court of Last Resort". However, there are procedures for the reopening of cases where, for example, evidence has not been produced, false evidence has been produced, or new facts have emerged. The number of successful applications for reopenings varies between 5 and 10 per annum.

Training

14.45   Legally qualified judges come from all social classes (although there is a preponderance from professional, middle-class backgrounds).

14.46   As far as training is concerned, the judiciary is a career judiciary. Judges are not recruited from the ranks of advocates. All judges serve for a lengthy period in a Court of Appeal. Many experienced judges end their careers as permanent district court judges, so there is usually a high level of expertise available at district court level.

14.47   The prosecutor is a specialist career prosecutor.

14.48   The entrance qualification for police officers is the same as the requirements for university entrance. The training period for police officers is three and a half years. All higher police ranks have a full law degree (four and a half years study at university). There is accelerated police training for lawyers who wish to become police officers.

PART 15
UNITED STATES OF AMERICA

Introduction

15.1 Each of the fifty states in the United States (US) is regarded as a separate sovereign state and each has plenary authority to enact laws touching upon a wide variety of subjects, including criminal law and procedure. The federal government in Washington D.C. is superimposed upon the state governments. The powers of the federal government are limited to the subject matters assigned to it by the Constitution of the United States, but, as to those subject matters, its powers are supreme. Thus federal laws override inconsistent state laws. Federal law includes the principles contained in the Constitution of the United States which apply in all state and federal courts and are the supreme law of the land.

15.2 It was impracticable for the Commission to attempt a study of all the individual states' systems. This review is therefore limited in the main to: (a) constitutional principles which have general applicability in both federal and state courts; and (b) the rules of criminal procedure and evidence applicable in all federal courts. The federal system has become the most important system. It is the only one which has jurisdiction nationwide, and many of the states have adopted provisions of substantive federal criminal law and the Federal Rules of Criminal Procedure as their own.

Police investigation

15.3 The function of law enforcement and peace keeping is primarily vested with the local city/municipal police departments. However, the situation is often complicated by the presence of numerous policing agencies whose jurisdiction and authority cross local boundaries, such as state police whose jurisdiction runs throughout a particular state, and the federal enforcement agencies. The US has no national police force, but the federal government has many agencies that investigate violations of federal criminal law, including the Federal Bureau of Investigation (the "FBI"), and many smaller agencies that specialise in certain areas of law enforcement, such as narcotics investigations, explosives and firearms investigations, or tax offences.

15.4 For a suspect to be arrested there must be a finding of probable cause. The Supreme Court has held that the Fourth Amendment of the

United States Constitution requires a judicial determination of probable cause before any significant restraint on a defendant's liberty may occur following arrest[1]. In May 1991, the Supreme Court[2] upheld a scheme that permitted detention for forty eight hours pending a determination of probable cause, although it held that in some cases waiting forty eight hours would violate the defendant's rights if the prosecutor could have brought him or her before the judge earlier. Detention for a period more than forty eight hours was, the court held, to be deemed presumptively excessive and might only be justified by extraordinary circumstances or a bona fide emergency. Some have questioned whether there are any real sanctions if this period is exceeded, because a dismissal on account of a breach of this rule is usually without prejudice to a re-arrest for the same offence. However, if a prosecutor regularly infringed this rule it would be professional misconduct and a court is likely to dismiss with prejudice. In the federal system, Rule 5 of the Federal Rules of Criminal Procedure requires the arresting officer to bring the accused before the nearest available federal magistrate without unnecessary delay, which is generally less than the constitutional permissible time period. For these standards to be complied with, the federal prosecutors and the judges of the criminal courts in many large cities work twenty four hours a day, although in most jurisdictions they are on call, and not utilised during after-work hours except in extreme emergencies.

15.5 A distinction is not drawn between questioning inside and outside the police station. Instead, US constitutional law draws a distinction between questioning by the police of a suspect who is in custody, as opposed to when he or she is not in custody. A suspect may be in custody, even though not physically present in a police station. The Fifth Amendment privilege protects an individual from being compelled by the government to be a witness against himself or herself. In *Miranda v Arizona*[3], the Supreme Court held that before questioning persons in custody, law enforcement officials should inform suspects that they have the right to remain silent, that their statements may be used against them at the trial, that they have the right to the presence of an attorney, and that if they cannot afford an attorney one will be appointed for them. If a suspect is not in custody the law does not require these warnings. Custody for the purposes of the *Miranda* warning involves the deprivation of the suspect's freedom of action in any significant way. Whether a suspect is in custody depends upon the perception of a reasonable person in the suspect's position. The courts must consider the totality of the circumstances involved in determining when a person is in custody. If the suspect is in

---

[1] *Gerstine v Pugh* 420 US 103 (1973).
[2] *County of Riverside v McLaughlin* 11 S.Ct. 1661, 1670 (1991).
[3] 384 US 436, 460–61 (1966).

custody, the warnings must be given in order for any confession to be admissible at the trial.

15.6   The police officer may not delay a defendant's access to a lawyer in a serious case. The Sixth Amendment to the United States Constitution provides that in all criminal prosecutions the accused has the right to have the assistance of counsel. The Sixth Amendment right to counsel encompasses all federal and state criminal prosecutions that would result in imprisonment. If a suspect retains a lawyer, the suspect can telephone him or her and the lawyer can attend at any time. An indigent suspect has a right to have a lawyer appointed. The appointment occurs at court at the initial appearance, and not before. Therefore, a lawyer would not be appointed to attend at the police station during post arrest questioning, and there is no scheme for ensuring such attendance by appointed counsel (although a suspect who has retained counsel may have counsel present at the police station). Most suspects exercise their right to counsel.

15.7   There are systems for discipline and prosecution in cases of police misconduct or corruption, although it is acknowledged that prosecution after the event is a blunt instrument. Some areas have an independent civilian board, or a board consisting of civilian and police personnel, that reviews allegations of police misconduct. Every law enforcement agency also has its own internal watchdog.

Evidence

Confessions

15.8   Admissions and confessions are admissible regardless of whether they have been tape-recorded or repeated in front of a judge or magistrate. Video recording of statements to the police is carried out in some areas of the US.

15.9   In order to sustain a conviction a confession must be corroborated. A defendant may not be convicted solely on the basis of his or her own admission. However, the corroborating evidence standing alone need not be sufficient to sustain the conviction. It must only be sufficient to establish the reliability of the confession. The extent of corroboration that is necessary depends on the nature of the case. For example, tangible crimes involving injury to persons or property may, under certain circumstances, be corroborated by proof that the act was committed, i.e. no independent link needs to be established between the injury and the defendant's admission that he or she is responsible for the injury. However, in cases where the crime involves no tangible object, e.g. tax evasion, the corroborative evidence must implicate the one making the confession[4].

---

[4] *Smith v United States* 348 US 147, 154–56 (1954).

15.10 The defence can test the admissibility of confessional evidence by making a pre-trial motion to suppress the evidence. The court will hear and determine this motion outside the presence of the jury. If the facts are not in dispute, the court can decide the motion as a matter of law. More often, the court will hold an evidentiary hearing, taking testimony from available witnesses.

15.11 There are many grounds on which the defence may seek suppression. As stated above, one is whether the defendant was informed, before the confession, of the *Miranda* right to silence and counsel, and validly waived it. As to whether the confession is allowed or not, the ultimate test is whether it was made voluntarily or was, on the other hand, the product of coercion. Coercion may consist of physical force, psychological coercion, dishonesty or trickery by the police. The court will examine the totality of the circumstances i.e. the length of detention, whether or not a lawyer was in attendance, or the number of times a suspect was questioned before he or she confessed.

15.12 If the court grants the motion to suppress the evidence, the government may appeal as of right. If the evidence is allowed, the confession is admissible at trial, but the defendant may then introduce at trial any relevant evidence concerning the circumstances of the confession, including evidence as to coercion, such evidence going to the weight to be given to the confession by the jury. Before jury deliberations, the court will instruct the jury that it should decide whether the confession was voluntary, considering all the circumstances surrounding the giving of the confession, including the existence of corroboration or the lack thereof, and that the jury should give such weight to the confession as the jury feels it deserves under all the circumstances. Some courts add that the jury should examine a defendant's statements with great care. If the jury convicts, the defence can raise on appeal whether the trial judge erred in admitting the evidence or instructing the jury.

Identification

15.13 In general, the federal system does not require corroboration of eye witness identification testimony. The rules and procedures regarding identification evidence depend in part on whether or not the eyewitness who would testify at trial has made a prior, out-of-court identification of the defendant. If the eyewitness has not, then he or she may give evidence at trial identifying the defendant as the perpetrator of the crime charged. Federal law requires, in most circumstances, particularly where the identification evidence is not corroborated by other evidence, the judge then to give a detailed instruction which inter alia indicates the circumstances which may call into question a witness's eye-witness identification.

15.14 If the witness has made a prior, out-of-court identification of the defendant, for example at a lineup, the rules are more elaborate. The defendant may move to suppress evidence of the prior identification on the ground that the procedures used by the police were unduly suggestive. If the evidence is allowed, the witness may identify the defendant in court and may testify that he or she identified the witness on a prior occasion, such as at a lineup. The trial judge would then give the same instructions set forth above, adding that the jury should consider whether the in-court identification was tainted by a suggestive out-of-court identification.

The accused's silence

15.16 An accused's silence at the police station or during the trial cannot be used as evidence against him or her and no comment by the judge or prosecutor can be made to that effect.

Improperly obtained evidence

15.17 Evidence seized in violation of the Constitution of the United States is generally not admissible in a criminal prosecution. The exclusionary rule requires the suppression of evidence obtained directly or indirectly through government violations of the Constitution. In order, however, for a defendant to attempt to exclude such evidence he or she must have "legal standing". A defendant has legal standing only if his or her constitutional rights have been violated. For example, a defendant cannot challenge evidence seized from an unlawful search of another person's apartment.

15.18 There are, however, some exceptions to the exclusionary rule. The Supreme Court has identified four specific situations in which exclusion is not required: (1) when the police act in good faith and rely on a facially valid search warrant or a statute permitting a search without a warrant; (2) when the connection between the illegal conduct and the acquisition of the challenged evidence is so attenuated that it dissipates the taint of the unlawful act; (3) when the evidence was obtained independently of the illegality; (4) when the evidence would have been inevitably discovered by lawful means.

15.19 The exclusionary rule prohibits the admissibility of the evidence unless it falls within one of the exceptions to it. The courts have no discretion to admit illegally obtained evidence.

Prosecution and defence

15.20 The police do not charge the suspect. Instead, in the federal court, the prosecution prepares a draft indictment and then appears ex parte before a federal grand jury to present evidence in support of that indictment. The grand jury then decides whether or not to return an indictment charging a defendant with a crime. No judge is present at the proceedings before the grand jury. They are secret and may be disclosed only in connection with later judicial proceedings or in other narrowly defined circumstances. The evidence presented to the grand jury will normally consist of documents subpoenaed to the grand jury, and evidence from witnesses, who can be subpoenaed to appear before the grand jury. Witnesses before the grand jury may refuse to answer questions, asserting their right against self-incrimination. Such witnesses cannot be compelled to answer unless the prosecutor first grants them immunity, in which event their answers cannot be used against them at any time. The subpoena power runs nationwide. The rules of evidence do not apply to grand jury proceedings, except for rules of privilege. A witness is not permitted to have counsel in the grand jury room, although the witness's counsel may remain outside the grand jury room and the witness may leave the room to confer with his or her counsel whenever the witness desires to do so. The grand jurors themselves can ask questions of the witnesses and often do so.

15.21   In the federal system and in most states, a defendant cannot challenge an indictment on the ground that the evidence before the grand jury was insufficient to permit a finding of probable cause. However, some states permit this. In virtually all US jurisdictions a defendant may challenge an indictment on the ground that the prosecutor engaged in misconduct before the grand jury, such as knowingly using perjured evidence. The misconduct must be flagrant, however, and challenges on this ground are rarely successful.

15.22   In the federal system, all felony offences (those being offences that carry a potential imprisonment term of more than one year) are required to be brought by way of grand jury indictment. With regard to misdemeanours, the prosecutor levels the charge by filing an information. Some states no longer have grand juries for any offences, in which case the prosecutor levels the charge by filing the indictment. However, even in these states, it is generally the prosecutor and not the police who prepares the charges to be filed against the defendant. Consequently prosecuting officials have an important role in conducting criminal investigations because those officials can refuse to charge an offence if they believe that there is insufficient evidence to convict a defendant beyond a reasonable doubt. These officials can then require the police to produce additional evidence, before charging a person with a criminal offence.

15.23   Historically, state and federal police officers and agents investigated a crime, and then presented the completed investigation to a prosecutor for court proceedings. Sometimes this still occurs, especially in less serious crimes where investigators need and receive little substantive supervision on the performance of the investigation. However, it is more often the case, especially in serious or complex crimes, that a member of the prosecutor's office participates, directs and supervises all or part of the investigation. Sometimes the police go to a prosecutor for advice (e.g. to ascertain whether they have probable cause to make an arrest).

15.24   The trend is towards the prosecutors having a greater and earlier involvement in the investigation, because of the increasing complexity of the applicable law. Moreover, the crucial point in investigations in the US is that the police cannot compel evidence from anyone, without first bringing a prosecutor into the investigation. The police can persuade, cajole and seek voluntary co-operation from a witness. But if the police want to compel evidence then they have to get a subpoena or some other compulsory process, and this can only be obtained by a prosecution attorney who can then subpoena the witness to appear before the grand jury. The grand jury can be used as an investigative tool for the prosecution even before anyone is arrested. Subpoenas are also needed for telephone records, bank records and the like. A court order, obtained on the prosecutor's application, is necessary for wiretapping or a search warrant. This means that there is a large amount of lawyer involvement in the investigation.

15.25   In complex cases the prosecution and police work together as a team. The investigative authorities generally take the initiative with respect to tactical decisions, e.g. which telephone or location should be the subject of electronic surveillance, while the prosecution officials make the strategic decisions.

15.26   It is suggested that a prosecutor is more likely than a senior agent to ensure that agents stay within the boundaries of the law because the prosecutor is an officer of the court and has a greater respect for the rule of law. Furthermore, a prosecutor can face professional discipline for misconduct in conducting or supervising an investigation. Finally, the prosecutor is less likely to condone or tolerate police misconduct because the prosecutor will have to stand up in court and justify the agents' conduct.

15.27   Federal prosecutors have the totality of authority over all the proceedings in the case, known as "case ownership", subject to supervision by senior prosecutors in the prosecutor's office. They have to handle a large volume of cases and therefore must be skilled in taking a disorganised case and preparing it for the trial in which they will appear.

Public Defender Schemes

15.28   In 1963 the Supreme Court, in the leading case of *Gideon v Wainwright*[5], held that anyone accused of a felony had a right to be

---

[5] *Gideon v Wainwright*, 372 US 335, 342 (1963).

defended by counsel in court (this rule is now embodied in Rule 44 of the Federal Rules of Criminal Procedure). If this right were to be effective, there obviously needed to be a means of paying for representation for indigent defendants. Therefore Congress enacted the Criminal Justice Act 1964. Under this Act, each separate district makes its own plans for furnishing indigent defendants with legal representation. Now every district has such a plan. The statute also makes provision for money, which counsel can request from a judge, to be provided for investigations. This request is ex parte. Three hundred hours is the maximum amount of investigative time that can be paid for, unless more is authorised at the discretion of the judge.

15.29 In New York there are two components of federal public defender schemes. First there are Legal Aid Society lawyers, whose sole job is to defend indigent people. The Legal Aid Society is a private organisation relying on charitable contributions and payment from Government funds pursuant to the Act for the defence of particular cases. Secondly there is a panel of private attorneys, who supplement the Legal Aid Society lawyers whenever there are multiple defendants. The Legal Aid Society lawyers are regarded like lawyers from any law firm, in the sense that they can only defend one client in any case. Both types of lawyers make applications for remuneration. This is limited to $75 per hour for time spent in court or out of court. The maximum remuneration for a case is $3500. The judge can authorise payment in excess of this in long or complex cases.

15.30 Most states' public defender schemes follow this structure, except that in some states the public defence lawyers are employees of the government. There have been disputes by public defence lawyers to gain parity of remuneration with prosecutors, which has now been achieved in most places.

15.31 Private lawyers undertake legal aid work for many different reasons: it is work in the public interest, it keeps the lawyer in touch with prosecutors and judges, and it is good experience. The Legal Aid Society lawyers tend to be younger, aggressive, working their way up and gaining valuable experience. They are generally of a good standard and on a par with the prosecutors, however with fewer resources. For most lawyers it is a stage in their career development but some, especially outside the main cities, work for the Legal Aid Society for all of their careers. This is often because there is a much greater difference in the big cities between the remuneration levels of public and private lawyers.

15.32 Generally speaking, during the past twenty years the public defender system has seen a vast expansion in the US and opposition to it by private practitioners has diminished. It is said to be well accepted and well established. However, some observers say that the US organisations are characterised by low morale and lack of self-esteem. Research by Professors McConville and Mirsky highlights some dangers in an institutional defender system[6]. They suggest that in the US such systems operate in a way which gives priority to their contractual obligations with their local government employers, over the interests of their clients. In New York increased pressures of work lead to public defenders coming to an arrangement with prosecutors to dispose of cases through guilty pleas, to help courts reduce backlogs and get their lists in order. They state that:

> "The rights of poor people charged with crime have a life only in the rhetoric of the system. The state, through the appointment of counsel, controls not only the form the prosecution takes but also the defence available to a poor person charged with a crime... The system sustains only those lawyers who comply with its goals by providing cost-efficient, expeditious disposition, and alienates those who view the defence function in adversarial terms".

15.33   By contrast, a recent study of nine localities by the National Centre for State Courts found that on average court-appointed lawyers succeeded in reducing sentences or won acquittals just about as often as private lawyers.

Disclosure

Constitutional requirements

15.34   The Supreme Court has held that criminal defendants have no general constitutional right to discovery in criminal proceedings. However, to prevent deprivation of a defendant's liberty without due process of law, the Court has laid down rules which require the disclosure of particular types of evidence. For example, in *Brady v Maryland*[7] the Supreme Court held that the Government's failure to disclose material evidence favourable to a defendant who specifically requested that evidence violated the defendant's due process rights. The *Brady* decision by the Supreme Court, however, does not require the disclosure of all evidence requested by the defendant. The Government need not disclose neutral, irrelevant, speculative or inculpatory evidence; evidence available to the defence from other sources; evidence the defendant already possesses; or evidence that the prosecutor does not possess or over which the prosecutor could not reasonably be imputed to have knowledge or control. Moreover, the

---

[6] Research between 1984–1988 in New York City, Professor M McConville and Professor C Mirsky, volume xv, New York University's *Review of Law and Social Changes*, pp. 581–964.
[7] 373 US 83 (1963).

prosecutor is not required to make prosecution files available to the defendant for an open-ended investigation for possible exculpatory material.

15.35   However, the defendant is entitled on request to the disclosure of information that might be used to impeach the credibility or believability of a Government witness. The Supreme Court of the United States has ruled that the failure to disclose such evidence violates the defendant's constitutional rights. This ruling requires, inter alia, that the Government disclose any promises of immunity or leniency offered to a Government witness in exchange for testimony.

15.36   The Government's failure to disclose evidence requires a reversal of the conviction only if the undisclosed evidence is material to guilt or punishment. The Supreme Court has defined materiality as "a reasonable probability that had the evidence been disclosed to the defence, the result of the proceeding would have been different".

Discovery under the Federal Rules of Criminal Procedure

15.37   In addition to the constitutional duty to disclose exculpatory evidence under *Brady v Maryland*, the Government is required by either rule or statute in federal prosecutions to disclose other information. Rule 16 of the Federal Rules of Criminal Procedure requires the government upon the request of the defendant to disclose: (1) a copy of any written statement (or the substance of any oral statement) made by the defendant; (2) a copy of the defendant's prior criminal record; (3) documents and tangible objects within the actual possession, custody or control of the Government that are either material to the preparation of the defendant's case, intended for use by the Government as evidence in chief at the trial, or which belonged to or were obtained from the defendant; and (4) reports of scientific or medical tests. In addition, all prior "statements" of Government witnesses are required to be disclosed prior to the initiation of the cross-examination by the defence. In order for a document containing information about the testimony of a witness to be considered a "statement" it: (1) must be a written, signed statement of the witness; or (2) a substantially verbatim recital of an oral statement made by the witness that is recorded contemporaneously with the making of the oral statement; or (3) a statement, however taken or recorded, made by a witness to a grand jury. The Government is not under a duty to disclose these statements until after the witness has testified in chief. The defendant then is entitled to a reasonable period of time to review the prior statements before commencing the cross-examination. In practice, it is common for federal prosecutors to disclose the statements some reasonable time prior to the trial.

15.38   Under the federal rules of procedure, with regard to certain categories of evidence, a reciprocal discovery obligation is imposed on the defence. It arises if a defendant makes a request for documents and tangible objects within the actual possession, custody or control of the Government that are either material to the preparation of the defendant's case, intended for use by the Government as evidence in chief at the trial, or which belonged to or were obtained from the defendant. Once the prosecution has produced to the defence, the prosecution is then permitted to inspect and copy books, papers, documents, photographs, tangible objects, or copies or portions thereof which are within the possession, custody or control of the defendant and which the defendant intends to introduce at the trial during the defendant's case in chief. Similarly, if the defence request to see the medical and scientific tests carried out by the Government, the defence must disclose the medical and scientific reports which it intends to introduce as evidence. If the defence fail to comply with such requests they may be prohibited from introducing that evidence at trial. However, it said that the courts have been reluctant to enforce these requirements strictly.

15.39   In addition, the prosecution is entitled to obtain a prior "statement" of a witness (other than the defendant) following that witness' evidence during the defendant's case in chief. The definition of "statement" is the same as for prosecution witnesses (see paragraph 15.37 above).

15.40   The defence are also under an obligation to disclose certain positive defences upon the request of the government. Rule 12 of the Federal Rules of Criminal Procedure require the defence to disclose the existence of any alibi defence, defence of insanity or defence based upon public authority. The sanction for failure to give the required notice is the exclusion of witnesses supporting the defence, other than the defendant himself. Some states require other positive defences to be disclosed such as self-defence, entrapment, duress or intoxication.

State procedures for disclosure

15.41   In some states, for example Maryland, disclosure is governed by agreement between the prosecution and the defence. A standard form document is submitted by the prosecutor's office which states that the prosecution and defence will disclose certain evidence, the discovery of which they will normally have to request. Disclosure under this agreement is often more liberal than that provided for under the rules of criminal procedure. Defence counsel read the agreement and then sign it if it is in their client's interests.

15.42   Some prosecutor, both state and federal, often engage in almost "open file" discovery, releasing long before trial statements of witnesses and even police reports to allow defence counsel to assess the evidence and engage in informed plea discussions.

Scientific evidence

15.43   Most federal investigative agencies have established strict evidence collection techniques, in which each item of evidence collected at the scene of the crime is marked by the officer collecting it with a tag bearing his initials and the date on which it was collected. A document is then prepared which indexes all the items collected. Thereafter, each individual who handles the object is required to note that fact on an additional form which is attached to each object and which is called the "chain of custody sheet". Generally, the items of evidence are kept in either cabinets or in safes. Access to the storage area is limited.

15.44   There is no "central" forensic science service or facility. However, the FBI operates a large and very sophisticated crime laboratory facility. FBI agents around the country have access to this facility. In addition the FBI will almost always assist other law enforcement agencies, federal and state, with particular scientific procedures and expert testimony. Federal agencies other than the FBI also have forensic services, usually in their areas of specialisation (e.g. the Drug Enforcement Administration). Every state has a crime laboratory facility of some sort and most county and city police departments, depending on their size and need, have some forensic capability as well.

15.45   A defendant does not have a right of access to government laboratories or forensic services. It would be doubtful if any defence attorney would exercise such a right even if it existed. In cases of non-indigent defendants, it is the responsibility of the defendant to obtain the necessary forensic or expert testimony. In the case of indigent defendants, federal statutory law has established a procedure to provide for expert witnesses to be compensated by the government. This provision reads as follows:

> "Counsel for a person who is financially unable to obtain investigative, expert or other services necessary for adequate representation may request them in an ex parte application [to the trial court]. Upon finding after the appropriate inquiry in an ex parte proceeding that services are necessary and that the person is financially unable to obtain them, the court, or the United States magistrate, if the services are required in connection with a matter over which he had jurisdiction, shall authorise counsel to obtain the services."

15.46   Under Federal Rule of Evidence 706, if the court determines that a "neutral expert" is necessary for a just resolution of the case, the court may, either on its own motion or on the motion of any party, appoint and call an expert witness of its own selection. The court, however, is not required to appoint such an expert witness. Expert witnesses so appointed by the court are paid for by the government. Many people believe that court appointed experts will overwhelm the jury and that the jury will place too much weight on their evidence. This could be highly prejudicial to one of the parties. For this reason, the procedure is rarely used in criminal cases.

15.47   There is no established procedure in a criminal case to obtain agreement between the prosecution and the defence with respect to expert evidence. However, most judges actively encourage the prosecution and the defence to agree expert evidence where possible.

15.48   In a recent case[8] DNA scientific evidence was admitted by a trial judge, and the resulting conviction affirmed on appeal. The Court of Appeal stated that the test for admissibility was whether the "probativeness, materiality, and reliability of the evidence outweighs its tendency to mislead, prejudice, and confuse the jury", and applying their test, held that the DNA evidence had been properly admitted. In general, in the US, the courts are not unanimous in admitting DNA evidence, and the matter is not yet settled, but the weight of authority is in favour of admitting such evidence.

Pre-trial procedures

15.49   There is no pre-trial procedure for requiring a suspect or an accused to answer the prosecution's questions in front of a judge or judicial officer. However, the government frequently gives the subject of a grand jury investigation the opportunity to testify before a grand jury. If potential defendants elect to testify before the grand jury, Department of Justice policy requires that they be informed of their constitutional right to remain silent, their right to be represented by counsel, and the fact that they are the subject of the grand jury investigation. In practice, potential defendants seldom appear before grand juries. On occasion, though, a defendant will elect to testify in the hope that he or she can persuade the grand jury not to return an indictment against him or her.

15.50   There is also a procedure whereby the defendant and government can meet and the government can offer the defendant informal and limited immunity, called a proffer agreement, to the effect that anything said during that meeting cannot be used against the defendant. This procedure is sometimes used in an effort to persuade the prosecutor not to seek an indictment. More often, however, it is used when the possibility of a plea bargain is being investigated.

---

[8] *United States v Jakobetz* (1992).

15.51 A judge or magistrate handles pre-trial proceedings. Magistrates are lawyers. They are appointed by the executive for periods of three to five years. Some go on to become judges. After an indictment is returned, the defendant is brought before a magistrate, usually within two weeks for a conference, also called omnibus proceedings. These proceedings deal with a wide range of matters including, for example, arraignment, bail or any requests for disclosure. After the omnibus proceedings, the magistrate sets up a schedule for any motions or further conferences and orders hearings if appropriate. Defendants can, if they wish, raise any matter of concern to them during these motions/hearings.

15.52 The defence may make motions for various reliefs. They may move to dismiss the indictment on the grounds that the conduct charged in the indictment, even if proven, would not constitute a crime. Such motions are rarely granted.

15.53 More common are motions to suppress evidence, to exclude certain arguments at the trial, or to sever the trial of one defendant from the main trial on a multi-defendant indictment. If the motion is successful, then it is for the government to decide whether it is still in a position to prosecute successfully.

15.54 Matters otherwise not resolved are left for further pre-trial conferences set before a magistrate. Both the court and the parties can request that a pre-trial conference take place. At the pre-trial conference, the magistrate expects to see a final list of witnesses from each party (in some jurisdictions), a set of proposed jury instructions from each party, as well as any formal agreements entered into between the parties. The magistrate expects that the parties have, pursuant to their obligations, exchanged discovery materials. The magistrate expects that each party is well enough prepared for trial to announce the anticipated length of its case. If either party is not so prepared or from appearances and responses, has not made a realistic evaluation of the strength of its case, the magistrate will strongly encourage further plea negotiations.

Juries

15.55 Jury practice varies from state to state, although the federal system is typical.

15.56 There are two aspects of the system used to ensure that the jury reflects a racial balance. Firstly, the method of compiling the pool of possible jurors. Secondly, the way of selecting the actual jury for a particular case.

15.57 The pool of jurors has historically been composed of people on the voter registration rolls. The goal is a fair cross-section of the community, and recently it has been felt that use of other lists in addition to the voter rolls would help to achieve this. Therefore the trend has been to add people from lists such as the motor vehicle registration lists or real estate lists into the pool of potential jurors. This is intended to enlarge the pool bringing in representatives of ethnic minority, social and other groups. Jurors to be summoned to the courthouse for service are then selected by drawing a number at random and then taking the person who corresponds to that number on the list. The person one hundred after the initial number is also taken, and the process repeated until the jury is selected (e.g. 17, 117, 217…). This helps to avoid getting jurors all from the same area.

15.58 The foregoing procedure will yield several dozen or, indeed, several hundred prospective jurors to be summoned to the courthouse for service as jurors for a particular time period, often a week or two weeks (but see discussion in paragraph 15.63 below). A judge who is ready to select a jury in a particular case may then summon thirty or forty prospective jurors to his or her courtroom. The judge will then ask these thirty or forty prospective jurors a series of questions designed to elicit information about each juror's fitness to serve, in general and in light of the particulars of the case (in some states, the lawyers ask these questions of the prospective jurors). Prospective jurors can be challenged by the prosecution or the defence on two grounds: challenge for cause, where there is some reason why the juror should not serve e.g. he or she knows the accused, knows the victim, was a victim in a similar case, lacks a sufficient intelligence to understand the case, or lacks a sufficient knowledge of English; or peremptory challenge, which can be for any reason or for no reason at all.

15.59 A Supreme Court decision, *Batson v Kentucky*[9] held that it was unconstitutional for peremptory challenges made by the prosecutor to be made on the basis of race. In *Georgia v McCollum*[10], the Supreme Court extended the *Batson* rule, holding that defendants may not discriminate on grounds of race when exercising peremptory challenges to trial jurors. In a separate opinion, one Justice noted that the court's decisions have moved away from protecting the defendant's rights to protecting the rights of jurors to serve on juries. In a recent case in New York's highest State Court, the Court of Appeals, three judges recommended that peremptory challenge be abolished because it appeared to be "disguising" discrimination.

15.60 Under the Federal Rules of Criminal Procedure, there is a limit of ten peremptory challenges for the defence and six peremptory challenges for the prosecution. The defence can only make ten such challenges regardless of the number of defendants, although the judge has a wide

---
[9] 476 US 79 (1986).
[10] 60 LW 4577.

discretion to enlarge these numbers and often does so, particularly in large cases. A limitless number of challenges can be made for cause. Jury selection often goes on for days, especially in large cases. The judge has a wide discretion to exclude any juror.

15.61 It is felt that having this system of challenges increases public confidence in the jury system, by excluding the extremes, and giving the parties an opportunity to participate in jury selection.

15.62 There are twelve people in a federal jury, but some states use less than twelve, and the parties may stipulate for a jury of less than twelve. The Supreme Court has allowed this, but under the Supreme Court's decisions there must be at least six jurors. An alternative jury system is common, whereby there are up to six alternate jurors who are called and who replace any jurors who become unable to act up to the moment a jury retires. Even without a stipulation, if after the jury begins deliberations a juror is excused for just cause, a valid verdict may be returned by eleven jurors.

15.63 Increasingly jurors are being called for only one day of service. If on that one day the person called gets involved in a trial, he or she is bound to that trial for its duration. However, if he or she is not selected or if the trial lasts only one day, the juror can go after that. The system is proving popular. It has the advantage that there is less time spent by prospective jurors waiting to be called for particular cases and less time spent on bargaining over excusals. But it involves much more work for the summoning officer.

15.64 The decision on technical, specialised matters is left to jurors despite their usual lack of training in the subject matter. The prosecution and defence are permitted to introduce expert evidence, to assist the jury in understanding the issues in the case. However, it remains the jury's function to decide the facts. The trial judge generally instructs the jury that expert scientific testimony should be weighed in light of all the evidence in the case, and that the weight, if any, to be accorded such evidence is up to the jury as the sole arbiter of the facts. The jury will be instructed to consider the expert's qualifications, education and experience, the soundness of the reasons given for his or her conclusions and his or her reasons for testifying. The jury will also be instructed that it should not accept the testimony merely because the witness is an expert, nor should it permit an expert's conclusions to substitute for the jury's own reason, judgement and common sense. Where experts conflict, the court instructs the jury to resolve the conflict in the same way it would resolve other evidentiary conflicts, and by considering the factors outlined above.

15.65 Juries deliberate alone, without the judge. However, they are permitted to – and frequently do – ask the judge questions or request clarifications of instructions. As a requirement of the Constitution, all jury verdicts in criminal trials must be unanimous. It is not unusual for juries to be unable to reach a unanimous decision, necessitating retrial, or occasionally dismissal of charges.

15.66   The defendant can opt for trial by judge alone instead of with a jury. In the federal court, however, both the prosecution and the court must agree to the waiver. In a minority of states, for example New York, the prosecution have no say in the matter, but a defendant's waiver must be approved by the court. An even smaller minority of states give the defendant the right to waive without the prosecution's and the court's consent. Trial by judge alone is usually opted for when the crime is very heinous, or the defence hinges on an interpretation of law rather than a resolution of fact.

Trial procedures

15.67   Although individual courts are free to decide on their own systems for setting trial dates, the "individual case assignment" system is most commonly used and is generally considered to be the most efficient.

15.68   If a plea of not guilty is entered at the arraignment, the case is assigned by lot to a judge. There is no attempt to assign a particular case to a particular judge, although in some places, an administrative judge has the power to re-assign the case to a different judge. Having been assigned a case the judge presides from that point right through to its conclusion. If a guilty plea is entered, the judge who hears that plea will usually retain the case on his docket for sentencing.

15.69   Judges decide when the case will be heard and, based on input from the lawyers, make a prediction as to how long the trial will last. In doing this they consider the other cases they have awaiting trial. If they already have a lengthy case and they are assigned another, they can ask for the case to be re-assigned. The judge holds a series of conferences with the lawyers in the case to obtain their opinion on when the case might be ready for trial, how long the case might last and to resolve any preliminary issues (see paragraphs 15.51–15.54 above). Where possible the judge normally tries to accommodate the defence lawyers' prior commitments in order to give defendants the lawyer of their choice. The judge is often less willing to do this for prosecution lawyers as they are regarded as relatively interchangeable representatives of the state.

15.70   In setting the trial date the judge must take into account two overriding principles. The first of these is that a defendant has a constitutional right (Sixth Amendment), and in some jurisdictions a statutory right, to a speedy trial. A federal statute (The Speedy Trial Act 1974) requires that a federal criminal trial begins within seventy days of the defendant's indictment. However, the trial judge may, and usually does exclude from the 70 day calculation periods of time during which motions are pending, medical tests are being conducted or for any delay which is found to be "in the interests of justice". If the right to a speedy trial is denied then the case must automatically be dismissed.

15.71   The second overriding principle is that the judge must give priority to criminal cases over civil cases. Most criminal cases are therefore given a fixed date. The listing problem of what happens when there is a late guilty plea is overcome by the contrasting position that civil cases are usually not given a fixed date. The lawyers in civil cases are told by the judge to be ready for a certain period, on any day of which their case might be called. If there is then a late guilty plea in a criminal case, the judge would fill in the gap in the timetable by calling one of his or her civil cases. Predictions as to how long cases are likely to last are usually bad. However, the judge would monitor this during the trial, and make adjustments in the trial dates of the other cases accordingly.

15.72   The individual case assignment system is considered efficient. There is accountability because each judge is responsible for ensuring that his or her cases move on speedily. To some extent it leads to shorter trials, as the judge already knows what the case is about before the trial begins. The system is more effective in shortening the time between indictment and trial, because at any pre-trial hearings a new judge does not have to start from scratch finding out about the case.

15.73   The other system for setting dates for trial is considered inefficient. Under this system rather than a judge being assigned a case from the beginning, judges rotate through the different stages of the trial process. For example, a judge is assigned to hearing pre-trial motions for a week. During that week he or she hears only motions. Then the next week he or she might be assigned to trials. It is considered inefficient for the same case to be continually re read by a number of different judges. There is also no incentive for judges not to adjourn cases since they are only temporarily responsible for the case during only one of its stages in the process.

15.74   As noted above (see paragraphs 15.52–15.53), many issues such as the admissibility of evidence can be settled in advance of the trial by pre-trial motions. This has the effect of shortening trials. At pre-trial conferences (see paragraphs 15.51–15.54), rules relating to the conduct of the trial can be agreed on, such as which defence counsel will lead. In trials where there are numerous documents and records to be introduced, the trial court can refer to a magistrate or master for a pre-trial hearing to get the parties to try and agree the records.

15.75 There are also federal rules of evidence which are aimed at shortening trials where possible without sacrifice to truth and fairness. Rule 403 of the American Federal Rules of Evidence states: "Although relevant, evidence may be excluded if its probative value is substantially outweighed by the danger of unfair prejudice, confusion of the issue, or misleading the jury, or by considerations of undue delay, waste of time, or needless presentation of cumulative evidence". This is reinforced by Rule 102, requiring the trial judge, while securing fairness, "to eliminate unjustifiable expense and delay to the end that the truth may be ascertained and the proceedings justly determined". These rules are applied in practice. For example, the trial court can and does within its discretion limit the number of character witnesses, if their testimony is merely cumulative. The trial court has a wide latitude in determining the relevance and admissibility of evidence. This is particularly important in the areas of proper impeachment of witnesses and proper rebuttal testimony. The judge can also curtail repetitive cross-examination, and will not allow counsel for one defendant to repeat questions already asked by another defendant's counsel. Bench conferences are possible on "housekeeping matters", although many judges prefer not to hold them.

15.76 In the US, the attorneys would be expected to reduce complicated cases to something more simple, to help shorten the length of proceedings. The Justice Department limits the number of counts that can be put to a maximum of 15. However, permission is frequently sought by prosecutors, and granted by the Justice Department, for indictments to contain more than 15 counts.

15.77 Generally there are no time limits on the total amount of time that parties have to put their cases in criminal trials. However, the attorneys are asked at the beginning of the trial for an estimate of the length of time they will need. Opening speeches may be limited in time. The court allows the prosecutor the time needed succinctly to identify each defendant, identify the charges in the indictment, and then outline the evidence that the government will introduce to prove the charges. The outline of the evidence is not supposed to be an argument but the line between narrative and argument is a fine one. Defence counsel has the right but is not required to make an opening statement setting forth what the evidence will show.

15.78 Closing arguments may also be strictly limited. With input from counsel the court will determine how many minutes will be allotted for these. There is not necessarily parity in the amount of time allotted per side. For example, in a three defendant case, each defence counsel may be given forty-five minutes, while the prosecution may only be allowed one and a half hours to argue its side. This is thought reasonable as many points of evidence will overlap among the defendants. The prosecution will often divide its time by a two thirds, one third formula — that is, the prosecutor may argue for one hour of its allotted time in its opening portion of closing argument, reserving no more than the remaining half hour for rebuttal. Once the court sets a time limit, these arguments are strictly timed and are not permitted to exceed the time allotted. In deciding the time limits the judge has ample discretion, and it would be a very unlikely cause of a reversal of the verdict on appeal.

15.79 The federal prosecutor can, should, and almost always does meet the witnesses prior to trial. This is in order to prepare the witnesses for giving evidence.

15.80 Judges have ample discretion to cut off any cross-examination which they feel is improper. If it continues judges can stop the cross-examination, and if the questioner repeatedly offends it would be a disciplinary matter. Curtailment of cross-examination can be urged on appeal as a ground for reversal. However, the discretion of judges in this regard is very broad, and they will not be reversed except for clear abuse of discretion. Thus, reversals on this ground are rare.

15.81 In the federal courts, judges may, on their own motion or the suggestion of a party, call witnesses, and all parties are entitled to cross-examine the witness thus called by the court. However, this power is rarely used in practice. In addition, the court has the authority to interrogate witnesses, whether called by itself or by a party (see paragraph 15.46 above for the court's power to call expert witnesses).

15.82 The prosecution and defence each draft the instructions they think the judge should give to the jury. These are then discussed and argued about during a special conference, involving counsel, held before the closing speeches. Judges choose the instruction that seems most applicable to the case, and in doing so, may use one submitted by counsel or one that they draft themselves.

15.83 Federal trial court judges have the authority to comment on the evidence. The classic statement of these powers is by Chief Justice Hughes in *Quercia v United States*[11]:

> "In a trial by jury in a federal court, the judge is not a mere moderator, but is the governor of the trial for the purposes of assuring its proper conduct of determining questions of law ... In charging the jury the trial judge is not limited to instructions of an

---

[11] 289 US 466 (1933).

abstract sort. It is within his power, whenever he thinks it necessary, to assist the jury in arriving at a just conclusion by explaining and commenting on the evidence, by drawing their attention to the parts of it which he thinks important, and he may express his opinion upon the facts, provided he makes it clear to the jury that all matters of fact are submitted to their determination ...

> This privilege of the judge to comment on the facts has its inherent limitations. His discretion is not arbitrary and uncontrolled, but judicial to be exercised in conformity with the standards governing the judicial office. In commenting upon testimony, he may not assume the role of a witness. He may analyze and dissect the evidence, but he must not either distort it or add to it. His privilege of comment in order to give appropriate assistance to the jury is too important to be left without safeguards against abuse."

15.84 In practice, however, many federal judges avoid making any comment whatsoever on the evidence. Instead, many federal judges limit their charge to the jury solely to the law, without making any indication with respect to their opinion regarding the actual evidence admitted at the trial. A judge's charge to the jury can be the subject of an appeal. A body of case law exists governing what comments have been held to be proper and improper. This is one reason why judges are reluctant to summarise the evidence. In practice, most trial judges go to great lengths to tell the jury that the judge has no view as to the resolution of any question of fact, scientific or otherwise, or the result that should be reached. Each side has an opportunity to enter on the record objections to the judge's instructions, thus preserving the issue for later appeal.

15.85 Under Rule 33 of the Federal Rules of Procedure, after conviction, the defendant may, by motion, ask the trial court to grant a new trial on the ground that a new trial is required "in the interests of justice". This motion must be made within seven days after the verdict. The court has a broad discretion to grant a new trial. For example, the court may grant a new trial because it has now concluded that it should not have admitted certain evidence previously ruled admissible, or now concludes that certain events at trial were unduly prejudicial. The trial court can also grant a new trial on the ground that the verdict was against the weight of the evidence. It is sometimes said that the trial judge sits as a thirteenth juror for this purpose. However, new trials are in practice granted rarely on this ground. The Court of Appeal has stated that trial courts "must defer to the jury's resolution of the weight of the evidence and the credibility of the witnesses". However, where testimony is patently incredible or defies physical realities, it may be rejected by the court despite the jury's evaluation.

Plea bargaining and the federal sentencing guidelines

15.86 The great majority of criminal cases in the US are disposed of by plea of guilty rather than by trial. Only 5–10% of cases eventually result in trial. The guilty plea is very often a negotiated plea, that is, a defendant agrees to plead guilty to a criminal charge in exchange for the government agreeing to give some consideration to the defendant. Plea bargaining is very controversial. To some, it erodes the cornerstones of the adversary system: the presumption of innocence and the right to trial. To others, it allows the guilty to escape with a light penalty. To still others, it is a modern-day necessity if the courts are to dispose of their large caseloads.

15.87 Two types of plea bargaining have to be distinguished:

(1) where the defendant co-operates with the government; and

(2) where the defendant does not.

15.88 Where there is co-operation the defendant is usually offered some deal. The concept is to wrap up his or her potential criminal exposure with a single plea to an appropriate offence. The sentence will then be lower because of the co-operation. There may be an agreement on the sentence that the co-operating defendant will receive. If not, the sentencing judge will be asked to take the defendant's co-operation into account as a mitigating factor.

15.89 Where the defendant does not co-operate with the Government there are basically two types of plea bargain. First there is "count bargaining". Here an agreement is reached that the defendant pleads guilty to a certain count or counts in satisfaction of his or her whole criminal exposure, but there is no agreement on sentence, which remains at the discretion of the judge. This is felt to be the least objectionable form of plea bargaining as it avoids costs, time, and risks for the prosecutor and the defendant, but does not by agreement necessarily lead to a lesser sentence.

15.90 Secondly, there is "sentencing bargaining". This is felt to be more objectionable, but in busy courts a practical necessity. The prosecutor talks to the defence attorney. They then reach an agreement about the sentence that is to be imposed for a guilty plea to a certain charge. This agreement is subject to judicial approval. The problem is deemed to be that the charge is often disposed of without any reference to the actual conduct of the defendant, or his or her prior offences, or the punishment appropriate if that conduct was proved.

15.91 The foregoing is a general description of plea bargaining as that process has developed in federal and state courts in the US. In federal courts, plea bargaining now is influenced by the federal sentencing guidelines which make specific provision for plea bargaining.

15.92 The background to the guidelines was an intention to reduce the disparities of sentences handed out to similar defendants by different judges. The Sentencing Reform Act 1984 therefore established the United States Sentencing Commission and delegated to it authority to promulgate sentencing guidelines for the federal courts. The guidelines technically became law for crimes committed after November 1, 1987. Their constitutionality was challenged but upheld in *Mistretta v United States* [1989]. They were implemented nationally in January 1989.

15.93 The guidelines contain what are referred to as two primary dimensions – offence seriousness and criminal history. Offence levels range from level 1 (least serious) to level 43 (most serious). Once the offence level has been determined the court then determines the defendant's criminal history. There are six possible criminal history categories. The applicable guideline range is located in a table at the intersection of the defendant's offence level and criminal history category.

15.94 The court has discretion to select a sentence within the guideline range. The court may impose a sentence outside the range established by the applicable guideline, if the court finds that there exists an aggravating or mitigating circumstance of a kind, or to a degree not adequately taken into consideration by the Sentencing Commission in formulating the guidelines.

15.95 With respect to co-operating defendants, the guidelines authorise the prosecutor to make a motion under s.5k(1.1) stating that the defendant has made a good faith effort to provide substantial assistance in the investigation or prosecution of another person who has committed an offence, in which case the court can depart from the guidelines.

15.96 The court is required to defer a decision in acceptance of any recommendation or agreement until it has considered a presentence report. S.6b(1.2) articulates the Commission standards for acceptance of agreements. S.6b(1.4) governs the use of stipulations of "facts relevant to sentencing". These stipulations should set forth the relevant facts of the actual offence conduct and offender characteristics and also the reasons why the sentencing range resulting from the agreement is appropriate. They should also identify any facts which remain in dispute.

15.97 The Sentencing Commission was aware of the need to control prosecution discretion to select charges and so to destroy the sentence guidelines. It therefore adopted a strategy which includes the requirement that a federal prosecutor should "initially charge the most serious, readily provable offence or offences consistent with the defendant's conduct ... the basic policy is that charges are not to be bargained away or dropped, unless the prosecutor has a good faith doubt as to the Government's ability to prove a charge for legal or evidentiary reasons". (Early research into the operation of the guidelines suggests, unsurprisingly, that negotiated pleas do not, as required, always reflect the "total offence behaviour" which could be proved by the prosecution. About one fourth of prosecutors interviewed indicated that they sometimes will not charge all known criminal behaviour of the offender who co-operates with the authorities in the investigation of other offenders or if the guideline sentence seems inappropriate.)

15.98 The sentencing guidelines are said to be unpopular with many judges, who resent the intrusion into their sentencing discretion. The system has proved popular with prosecutors and, although opposed by many defence counsel, it has resulted in more predictability as to the sentence that will be imposed after a plea bargain.

15.99 Judges are said to suggest that discretion has not been eliminated but has been shifted from judges to prosecutors, who can affect the sentencing result by deciding whether or not to charge all the criminal conduct possible. Indeed, there is now a great deal of bargaining between defence counsel and prosecutors over the charges and the facts which will be part of the calculation under the guidelines.

Prior convictions

15.100 The trial judge is normally aware of the defendant's prior convictions as the result of a bail hearing.

15.101 There are two separate aspects of the admissibility at trial of evidence of prior convictions or "prior bad acts". First, evidence which can be introduced in cross-examination of the defendant and second, evidence which can be introduced as part of the prosecution case.

15.102 As regards evidence which can be introduced in cross-examination of the defendant, the Federal Rules of Evidence provide that if the defendant testifies, the defendant's credibility may be impeached by the introduction of evidence that the defendant was convicted of a prior felony, provided that the court determines that the probative value of admitting the evidence of the felony offence outweighs its prejudicial effect to the accused. In addition, evidence of a felony conviction is generally not admissible if a period of more than ten years has elapsed since the date of the conviction or of the release of the defendant from imprisonment imposed for that conviction, whichever is the later date. However, should the court determine that the probative value of the conviction in the specific facts and circumstances surrounding the case substantially outweigh the prejudicial effect of the conviction, the court may waive the ten year rule and admit evidence of the prior conviction.

15.103   Under Federal Rule of Evidence 404(a) prior convictions are admissible to refute a defendant's claim to be either of truthful character or a law-abiding citizen.

15.104   As regards evidence which can be introduced as part of the prosecution case, Rule 404(b) provides that evidence of other crimes, wrongs or acts is not admissible to prove the character of a person or in order to show action in conformity therewith. Such evidence is therefore to prove bad character on the theory that "he did it before, he did it again". However, such evidence is admissible for other purposes, such as proof of motive, opportunity, intent, plan, knowledge, identity, or absence of mistake or accident. For example, in a murder case, the prosecution contends that the defendant killed the victim because the victim cheated the defendant in a prior narcotics transaction. Proof of the prior narcotics transaction would be admissible not to show that the defendant is a narcotics dealer as well as a murderer, but rather to show the motive for the murder. Similarly, in a prosecution for possession of counterfeit $50 notes with intent to pass them as genuine, if the defence contends that the counterfeit notes were accepted by mistake and without any intent to pass them further, evidence that the defendant had possessed counterfeit notes on a prior occasion would be admissible to rebut the defence, because prior possession makes it less likely that the current occasion involved mistake and more likely that the defendant knew that the notes were counterfeit and intended to pass them further. Finally, in a narcotics prosecution, the government has proven that the defendants spend sums of money in excess of their known legitimate income. The defence contends that it has nothing to do with narcotics and that the excess sums come from gambling winnings. The government can then prove that the defendant was convicted of a narcotics offence on a prior occasion because this shows knowing and intentional involvement with narcotics and rebuts the claim that the defendant is merely a gambler.

15.105   The evidence of prior wrongful acts is admissible even if there has been no conviction. In the absence of a conviction, the admissibility of the evidence of the prior wrongful act is determined by the following four-step inquiry announced by the Supreme Court in *Huddleston v United States*[12]: first, the evidence must be offered for a proper purpose; second, the

---

[12] 485 US 681 (1988).

evidence must be relevant; third, the probative value of the evidence must outweigh any potential for unfair prejudice to the defendant; and fourth, the jury must be instructed as to the limited purposes for which the evidence may be considered.

15.106 The prosecutor must give the defence advance notice that it intends to use evidence of prior convictions or wrongful acts. If the prosecution fails to provide such notice and fails to establish good cause as to why it did not provide such notice such evidence is not admissible. At the trial, the prosecutor will call witnesses to testify that the prior acts have taken place. If the prior act resulted in a conviction, a certified copy of the judgment of conviction is admissible.

15.107 There is no "tit for tat" rule. The prosecution is not allowed to introduce evidence showing the defendant's bad character merely because the defence impeaches the character of a prosecution witness.

Appeals

15.108 In the US federal courts for the twelve month period ending 30 June 1991, there were 9,198 criminal appeals decided: of those appeals 460 resulted in reversal, in whole or in part, of a conviction. This produced a reversal rate of 7.4%.

15.109 In the federal system the defendant is entitled to appeal against conviction as of right once to an appellate court composed of three judges. Thereafter, a defendant may petition for a writ of certiorari for the United States Supreme Court to review his or her case. Regardless of whether a defendant files a petition for a writ of certiorari, a defendant who has been convicted and exhausted his or her rights of direct appeal may file a motion for a collateral review of the case in the appropriate federal trial court. Such a motion is generically called a petition for a writ of habeas corpus. There are many technical legal rules regarding the type of claims that may be raised in such a collateral attack.

15.110 In the state system, a defendant is generally entitled to appeal as of right once to an appellate court, generally composed of a panel of three judges. Thereafter, some states allow discretionary review by the highest court in the state, usually the State Supreme Court. In some cases, most notably death penalty cases, certain appeals are mandatory, in the sense that the court has no discretion to decline to review the case. Some states, however, have only one appellate court. Thereafter, if the defendant is raising a federal constitutional issue, as opposed to merely a state law issue, the defendant may file a petition for writ of certiorari in the Supreme Court of the United States. Appeals from the highest court of a state to the United States Supreme Court lie at the discretion of the latter.

15.111 As in the federal system, regardless of whether the defendant files a petition for writ of certiorari, in most states the defendant is allowed to petition for collateral review of the conviction in the state court. Such motions are generally created by statute and are known generically as state petitions for writ of habeas corpus. There are numerous technical rules regarding the type of issues that may be raised in such collateral state proceedings. If the defendant has exhausted all state procedural remedies that are available, he or she may file a federal petition for a writ of habeas corpus alleging that in securing the conviction the state government violated certain rights guaranteed by the federal constitution. If fresh evidence comes to the prisoner's attention later, he or she is generally free to commence a second collateral attack, without regard to time limits. These collateral attacks are controversial, as they flood federal courts and run counter to the general policy of finality of judgments.

15.112 The appeal courts, state and federal, have no power to discourage hopeless appeals by adding time on the sentence for unmeritorious appeals.

15.113 Issues raised on direct appeals fall into the following three general categories: (1) claims that there was insufficient evidence to support the verdict of the jury; (2) allegations that the trial court committed a legal error before sentencing; and (3) allegations that the trial court committed a legal error with respect to the sentencing of the defendant.

15.114 With respect to claims regarding the insufficiency of the evidence, the appeal courts are deferential to the jury's determination. Specifically, the legal standard for reviewing the sufficiency of the evidence is whether a reasonable mind could fairly find the defendant guilty beyond a reasonable doubt when viewing the evidence in the light most favourable to the government.

15.115 Appeals relating to sufficiency of evidence are one of the few situations in which the appeal court can reverse the judgment of the trial court and dismiss the charges. In almost all other cases (e.g. procedural error at trial), reversal will yield a remand to the trial court for a retrial. Therefore, retrials are common in practice and do not present any serious problems. Appeal courts often invoke the "harmless error" rule, under which a judgment of conviction will not be reversed, even though error was committed in the court below, if the error did not affect substantial rights or materially contribute to the conviction.

15.116 A motion for a new trial on the ground of newly discovered evidence must be made within two years of judgment. The test for granting this is stated differently from jurisdiction to jurisdiction, but generally is quite strict. To win a new trial on this ground, the defendant must show that the evidence in question: (1) was unknown to him or her at the original trial; (2) could not, in the exercise of diligence, have been discovered in time for the original trial; and (3) would probably produce an acquittal at a retrial. Generally, cumulative evidence and evidence that impeaches the credibility of a witness does not satisfy these tests.

15.117   Ineffective assistance from counsel can be used as a ground for a direct appeal and for a "collateral attack". In general few convictions are reversed on this ground. In order to obtain a reversal of a conviction and a new trial based on the ground of ineffective assistance of counsel, the defendant must prove: (1) that counsel's performance fell below an objective standard of reasonableness; and (2) that a reasonable probability exists that, but for counsel's unprofessional errors, the result of the proceeding would have been different. Under the test in (1), there is "a strong presumption" that counsel's strategy and tactics fall "within the wide range of reasonable professional standards".

15.118   There is no procedure whereby a member of the executive can refer a case to a court. Individuals may seek to have their sentence or conviction overturned by a Presidential pardon or in the state system by the Governor of the state.

15.119   The Government has limited rights of appeal because of the doctrine of double jeopardy (Fifth Amendment). The government may appeal from a pre-trial order dismissing an indictment, from a pre-trial order suppressing evidence, from a post-trial order granting a new trial or judgment of acquittal after a verdict, and from an order regarding bail. In federal courts, the government has recently won the right to appeal against the sentence imposed by the trial judge. Finally, if the defendant prevails on appeal, the government may appeal to a higher court, subject to other rules of appellate procedure including the discretion of the higher court.

15.120   Most of the argument for appeals in the US is done on paper and not orally in the court. Briefs – that is written arguments – presenting the central arguments are submitted prior to the oral argument, and these form the most important part of the appeal. Oral argument is usually limited to about 15–20 minutes for each side, and rarely more than 30 minutes.

Training and sanctions

15.121   Bar Associations, seminars, and judicial conferences regularly address issues of false confessions, unreliable eye-witness evidence, bias etc. There is a movement to allow expert evidence on these failings if the facts of the case support the issue at trial.

ANNEX 1
INFORMATION ABOUT CRIMINAL JUSTICE PROCEDURES

In your jurisdiction

1. What, if such exist, are the rules governing the length of time that the police may hold a suspect for questioning prior to charge?[1] At what point must a suspect who has not been charged be brought before a court (or magistrate/judge)?[2]

2. At what stage, if at all, do the police have a duty to inform a suspect of his right (1) to silence[3] and (2) to legal advice?[4] (In particular, must this information be communicated outside the police station or only on arrival at the police station?) Is any distinction drawn in regard to the right to consult a lawyer between serious and less serious cases?[5]

3. Are there any studies providing figures on the take-up by suspects of the right to consult a lawyer in the police station?[6] (If so, can you supply references?)

4. Are there any rules restricting the admissibility of confessions that have not been tape recorded or repeated in front of a judge/magistrate?[7]

5. How do the rules of evidence treat silence by the accused at the police station?[8]

---

[1] In England [for "England", read England and Wales], it is twenty four hours for non-serious cases and thirty six hours in serious cases – plus another sixty hours with the permission of magistrates' court. In Scotland it is six hours in all cases.
[2] In England it is after thirty six hours.
[3] In England, the caution must be administered when the police officer has grounds to suspect the person, regardless of whether that it is outside or at the police station.
[4] In England, the suspect need not be told until he is at the police station of his right to legal advice, and that it is free.
[5] In England, a police officer may in certain circumstances delay access to a lawyer in serious cases.
[6] In England, it seems that around 25 per cent of suspects ask for a lawyer and about 20 per cent get legal advice – about half over the telephone.
[7] In England, admissions and confessions are admissible in evidence regardless of whether they have been tape-recorded or repeated in front of an independent person.
[8] In England, neither the judge nor the prosecution may suggest at the trial that silence is evidence of guilt.

6. Is there a rule requiring the corroboration of confession or identification evidence?[9] If yes, how is corroboration defined?

7. What are the powers and duties of the prosecution service vis-a-vis the police? In particular, do prosecutors have a role in directing or supervising police investigations?[10] If so, is it known how this appears to work?

8. Do the defence have the right of full access in advance of the trial to the evidence to be given by prosecution witnesses?[11] If so, at what stage is such access given and how?

9. Do the defence have the right to see relevant material in the possession of the prosecution which the prosecution do not intend to use?[12] If so, how does the system work? What, if anything, is done to deal with the danger that such material may in practice not be revealed by the police or by forensic scientists to the prosecution lawyers or by the prosecution lawyers to the defence?

10. What, if any, rules, procedures or other means are used to ensure that in the gravest cases scientific evidence taken at the scene of the crime or from suspects themselves will be collected properly?

11. What methods or systems exist to ensure that the defence have adequate assistance from forensic or scientific experts? Insofar as such experts are employed by or on behalf of the state are they in practice able to work also for the defence?

12. Is there any system for attempting to get the prosecution and defence experts to agree on their evidence before the trial? If so, how does this work?

---

[9] In England, there is no such requirement, though a judge has to warn the jury of the danger of relying on identification evidence. In Scotland, confessions must be corroborated.

[10] In England, the police charge the suspect. The Crown Prosecution Service has the power to discontinue cases started by the police and to alter the charges. It has no power to direct the police investigation – although it can ask the police to pursue further inquiries. In Scotland, the procurator fiscal has much greater power in that he can direct the police investigation. Such power, it seems however, is not used very frequently.

[11] In England, where the case is to be tried at the higher level (the Crown Court), the prosecution are required to give the defence in advance of "committal" by the magistrates, the details of the statements of witnesses the prosecution intends to call. If further evidence becomes available later it has to be handed to the defence then. The general principle is that no surprise prosecution evidence should be produced.

[12] In England, under the rules laid down by the Attorney General, the prosecution are under a duty to make available to the defence "unused material" i.e. material that may be relevant to the defence that the prosecution do not intend to use. (There are some exceptions.)

13. Is there any system for the court to commission expert evidence either instead of, or in addition to, expert evidence commissioned by the parties?[13] If yes, how does this work?

14. Are the defence under any duty to make advance disclosure to the prosecution of the nature of the defence or of the evidence to be called by the defence and, if so, in regard to what evidence or material and at what stage?[14] How is failure to comply with these rules treated?

15. Is there any pre-trial procedure for enabling the prosecution to question the accused in front of a judge or other judicial officer?[15]

16. Please could you state recent official figures for detention in custody of:

   a. suspects who have not yet been convicted; and

   b. persons who have been convicted but who are waiting for sentence?

Please could you also state the total population of your country.

17. If your system uses juries, do juries deliberate alone?[16] If not, with whom do they deliberate (i.e. the judge)?

18. Does the judge in criminal cases have, and if so does he use, the power to call witnesses?[17]

19. Is the prosecutor allowed to start the trial with an opening speech in which he states, often in detail, the evidence that he intends to call[18] – or is he required simply to call his first witness?[19]

20. Does the trial judge have before him prior convictions of the accused during the trial?[20]

21. Under the English rules, the prosecution can introduce in evidence during the trial the prior convictions of the accused – (1) to refute the

---

[13] In England there is none.
[14] In England, in advance of the trial, the defence need reveal only an alibi defence and the details of testimony of an expert witness on which the defence intend to rely.
[15] In England there is not.
[16] In England this is always the case.
[17] In England, the judge technically has the power to do so but in practice never does.
[18] This is the case in England.
[19] This is the case in Scotland.
[20] In England, this is common.

accused's claim to be a person of good character; (2) in cases where there is a striking similarity between the facts of the cases; (3) where the defence cast aspersions on the character of the prosecution's witnesses (the "tit for tat" rule); and (4) where one co-accused has given evidence against another co-accused. Are all these four rules followed in your jurisdiction? Are there any other situations in which prior convictions can be introduced in evidence by the prosecution?

22. Is it customary for the judge to sum up for the jury on the facts? If so, is the judge also permitted to comment on the evidence in such a way as to indicate to the jury what he thinks?[21]

23. What steps, if any, are taken to secure that the jury reflects a racial balance in cases where that seems to be appropriate?[22]

24. Is prosecution evidence that has been obtained illegally or improperly admissible in the discretion of the courts?[23] If yes, what are the principles applied by the courts as to the exercise of this discretion?

25. What facilities exist for the defence in regard to scientific/forensic evidence?[24]

Appeals

26. What proportion of defendants dealt with in the higher criminal courts (e.g. not for the equivalent of summary offences) appeal against conviction? What proportion of such appeals are successful?

27. Are such appeals as of right or is leave required?[25]

28. Does the Appeal Court have a power to discourage hopeless appeals by adding on time to the sentence for unmeritorious appeals?[26]

29. Does the Appeal Court consider that evidence which was available at the trial but which was not called by the defence can be "fresh evidence" for the purposes of an appeal?[27]

---

[21] Comment is permitted in England provided the judge makes it clear to the jury that questions of fact are ultimately for them.
[22] The Court of Appeal has recently ruled that English courts have no power to seek to adjust the composition of the jury in such cases. (*R v Ford* (1989) 3 All E.R. 445.)
[23] In England it is – s.78 of the Police and Criminal Evidence Act 1984.
[24] In England, the defence usually employs its own experts. The defence are permitted to use the public forensic science services but this is not done very often.
[25] In England, leave is required unless the appeal is on a pure point of law.
[26] In England, this power exists but is very rarely used. (The maximum time that can be added on is ninety days.)
[27] In England, such evidence would not normally be regarded as "fresh".

30. Does the Appeal Court allow appeals on the ground that the case was mishandled by the lawyers?[28]

31. Where the Court of Appeal considers an appeal against conviction on the ground that the decision of the trial court was wrong, is it common to order retrials?[29] If so, does it seem to give rise to serious problems?

32. What is the statutory formula that the Appeal Court has to apply when deciding whether to quash a verdict of the trial court?[30]

33. Are there rules restricting the number of appeals?[31]

34. Is there a procedure for cases to be referred back to the Appeal Court by the executive?[32]

35. If so, when cases are so referred, does the Appeal Court apply its normal rules of evidence and procedure or are special rules applied?[33]

36. Is there any special tribunal (a "Court of Last Resort") consisting perhaps of a mixture of judges and lay assessors, to hear appeals in cases of alleged miscarriages of justice where the normal appeal processes have been exhausted?[34]

Training

37. To what, if any, extent does the training of judges and police officers include attention to the problems of false confessions, unreliable eye witness evidence, bias in police officers, scientists, prosecutors and judges? How are such difficult topics tackled?

---

[28] This is not a ground of appeal recognised by the English Court of Appeal.
[29] In England it is exceedingly rare. Until 1988 the Court of Appeal had power to order a retrial only on the ground of fresh evidence but it virtually never did so. It either quashed the conviction and the accused went free or it upheld the conviction. Now under the Criminal Justice Act 1988 it has the power to order a retrial whenever it considers this to be in the interests of justice. But it is still exceedingly rare for a retrial to be ordered: in 1989 there was no such case.
[30] In England, it is whether the verdict is "unsafe or unsatisfactory".
[31] In England, a person may not appeal more than once.
[32] In England, the Home Secretary has the power to refer a case back to the Court of Appeal.
[33] The English Court of Appeal treats a reference from the Home Secretary as a normal appeal subject to all the ordinary rules of appeals.
[34] There is no such body in England.

ANNEX 2

We are grateful to the following individuals and organisations who either provided information on the criminal justice systems in other jurisdictions or assisted in the distribution of the Royal Commission's other jurisdictions questionnaire:

General

Commonwealth Secretariat.
British Institute of International and Comparative Law.
International Bar Association.
The Foreign and Commonwealth Office.
Justice.
The Society for the Reform of the Criminal Law.

Australia

Ian Glasgow, Attorney-General's Department.
Law Reform Commission of Australia.

New South Wales

Professor Mark Aronson, The University of New South Wales.
David Blunt, Project Officer for the New South Wales Joint Parliamentary Committee on the Independent Committee against Corruption.
N.R. Cowdrey Q.C., Edmund Barton Chambers, Sydney.
David Dixon, University of Hull.
B.R. Home, Deputy Registrar, Supreme Court of New South Wales.
Malcolm Kerr MP, Chairman of the New South Wales Joint Parliamentary Committee on the Independent Committee against Corruption.
G.R. James Q.C., Chairman, NSW CLA, Forbes Chambers, Sydney.
The Honourable Mr Justice Michael Kirby, Supreme Court of New South Wales.
R.W. McClelland, Registrar, District Court Registry, New South Wales.
The New South Wales Law Reform Commission.
Peter Nagle MP, New South Wales Joint Parliamentary Committee on the Independent Committee against Corruption.
S.J. Odgers, Editor, Criminal Law Journal, Forbes Chambers, Sydney.
G.F.K. Santow, Freehill, Hollingdale & Page Solicitors, Sydney.

Northern Territory

Simon Nish, Department of Law.

Queensland

Sir Max Bingham Q.C., Chairman of the Criminal Justice Commission.
Doctor Keith Bryett, Griffith University.
The Honourable Mr Justice Mackenzie, Supreme Court of Queensland.
R.N. Millar Q.C., Director of Prosecutions.
Robertson O'Gorman Solicitors, Brisbane.
Bruce A. Window, Director of Technical Services, Queensland Police Service.

South Australia

M.R. Goode.
The Honourable Justice Zelling, Supreme Court of New South Wales.

Victoria

Doctor Andrew Goldsmith, Monash University.
Richard Read, Prosecutor for the Queen, Melbourne.
B.K.C. Thomson Q.C., Owen Dixon Chambers, Melbourne.
The Honourable Mr Justice Vincent, Supreme Court of Victoria.

Western Australia

B. Bull A.P.M., Commissioner of Police.
Chief Justice Malcolm, Supreme Court of Western Australia.

Austria

Doctor Rudolf Machacek, Vienna.
Doctor Sebastian Mairhofer, Zamponi, Weixelbaum & Partner, Linz.

Belgium

British Embassy, Brussels.
Professor L. Dupont, Katholieke Universiteit, Leuven.
Professor C. Fijnaut, Katholieke Universiteit, Leuven.
L. Schuid, Advocate, Brussels.
Pascal Vanderveeren, Advocate, Brussels.
Professor R. Verstraeten, Katholieke Universiteit, Leuven.

Botswana

Edward W. Fashole-Luke II, Pilane, Luke and Associates, Gaborone.

Bulgaria

Svetoslav Apostolov, Plovdiv.

Canada

Doctor Aaron Chaplan, Director, Statistics Section, Department of Justice, Canada.
Brian Barrington-Foote Q.C., Deputy Minister of Justice and Deputy Attorney General, Saskatchewan.
Elizabeth Bennett, Crown Counsel, Ministry of Attorney General, Columbia.
Kim Campbell Q.C., Minister of Justice and Attorney General of Canada.
Andre Charbonneau, First Secretary, Canadian High Commission.
Gilles Letourneau, President, Law Reform Commission of Canada.
Bruce A. MacFarlane Q.C., Assistant Deputy Attorney General, Canada.
Gordon MacKay, Canadian Centre for Justice Statistics.
R.G. Mosley Q.C., Chief Policy Counsel, Criminal and Social Policy Sector, Department of Justice, Canada.
John C. Pearson, Director of Public Prosecutions, Novia Scotia.
John Tait, Deputy Minister of Justice and Deputy Attorney General of Canada.
Eric L. Teed, Teed, Teed, & McPhee, Saint John, New Brunswick.
John F. Townsend, Assistant Director, Statistics Section, Ministry of Justice, Canada.

Denmark

Thomas Federspiel, Gorrissen & Federspiel, Copenhagen.
N.E. Norsker, Norsker & Jacoby, Copenhagen.

Finland

Matti Joutsen, The Helsinki Institute For Crime Prevention and Control.

France

Professor Antoine Bullier, University of Paris.
Jean-Pierre Bloch, Ministry of Justice.
Anne Carblanc, Ministry of Justice.
Barbara Deleuze.
British Embassy, Paris.
R.L. Jones.
Eric Lombard, Ministry of Justice.
Jenny Monahan.
Francois Serres, S.C.P. Ornano, Societe D'Advocats, Paris.

Germany

British Embassy, Bonn.
Judge Martin Dyer, Council of Her Majesty's Circuit Judges.
Professor Johannes Feest, University of Bremen.
Doctor Hilger, Federal Ministry of Justice.
Peter Michael Muller, Chairman Criminal Law Committee, International Bar Association.
Professor Thomas Weigend, University of Cologne.

Greece

Doctor Ilias Anagnostopoulos, Anagnostopoulos & Fifis, Athens.

Hong Kong

S.M.I. Stoker, Law Reform Commission.
Michael Tam, Independent Commission against Corruption.

Republic of Ireland

Eamonn M. Barnes, The Director of Public Prosecutions.
British Embassy, Dublin.
Robert Browne, Department of Justice.

Israel

British Embassy, Tel Aviv.
Doctor Eliahu Harnon, The Hebrew University of Jerusalem.
The Ministry of Justice.

Italy

Professor Ennio Amodio, Milan University.
British Embassy, Rome.
Professor Luigi Favino, Rome.

Kenya

John Olago Aluoch, Olago-Aluoch & Co., Kisumu.

Kuwait

Wadih Phillipe Khalaf, Alothman & Khalaf, Safat.

Malta

V.A. DeGaetano, Deputy Attorney General.

The Netherlands

Peter Alldridge, Cardiff Law School.
British Embassy, The Hague.
Stewart Field, Cardiff Law School.
Mr Rolf de Groot, Department of Justice, The Hague.
Mr Hofstee, Department of Justice, The Hague.
Nico Jorg, Cardiff Law School.
Doctor Hans Lensing, Katholieke Universiteit, Nijmegen.
Doctor Dato w. Steenhuis, Prosecutor-General, Leeuwarden.
Liesbeth van der Veen, Office of the Prosecutor-General, Leeuwarden.

New Zealand

Sir Kenneth Keith, New Zealand Law Commission.
M. P. Smith, Department of Justice.
K.G. Stone, Crown Solicitor, Luke Cunningham & Clere, Wellington.
New Zealand Law Society.
Nicola White, Senior Legal Research Officer, New Zealand Law Commission.

Norway

Finn Lynghjem, District Judge, Aalesund.

Singapore

Yang Ing Loong, Attorney General's Chambers.
Tan Boon Teik, Attorney General.

South Africa

Ann Skelton, Lawyers For Human Rights, Cumberwood.

Spain

Doctor Gustavo Lopez-Munoz Y Larraz, Madrid.

Sri Lanka

Neil Dias, Advocate, Columbo.

Switzerland

British Embassy, Berne.
Anne Imobersteg, Federal Office of Justice.

Sweden

British Embassy, Stockholm.

Doctor Iain Cameron, Uppsala University.
Lecturer Lena Holmqvist, Uppsala University.
Professor Nils Jareborg, Uppsala University.
Elisabeth Lager, Ministry of Justice.

United States

J.K. Bredar, Project Director, Vera Institute of Justice, New York.
British Embassy, Washington.
Professor William K. Carrol, The John Marshall Law School, Illinois.
Kenneth Caruso, Shearman & Sterling, New York.
Roger Karr, The Federal Judicial Centre, Washington.
Douglas B. Farquhar, United States Attorney, District of Maryland.
The United States Government.
Sheryle L. Jeans, Assistant United States Attorney, Western District of Missouri.
Professor J. Jeans.
Sarah Lyon, Vera Institute of Justice, New York.
William K. Slate, The Justice Research Institute, Philadelphia.
Joseph E. Stevens, District Judge, Western District of Missouri.
Harold A. Wasserman, Counsellor at Law, New York.

West Indies

Professor A.R. Carnegie, The University of the West Indies.

Zaire

M.G.B. Chigaga, Deputy High Commissioner for the Republic of Zaire.

Zimbabwe

C.K. Nyati, Ministry of Justice.